Citizens, Context, and Choice

Volumes of a Collaborative Research Program Among
Election Study Teams from Around the World

Series editors: Hans-Dieter Klingemann and Ian McAllister

The Comparative Study of Electoral Systems (CSES) is a collaborative program of research among election study teams from around the world. Participating countries include a common module of survey questions in their post-election studies. The resulting data are deposited along with voting, demographic, district, and macro variables. The studies are then merged into a single, free, public dataset for use in comparative study and cross-level analysis.

The set of volumes in this series is based on these CSES modules, and the volumes address the key theoretical issues and empirical debates in the study of elections and representative democracy. Some of the volumes will be organized around the theoretical issues raised by a particular module, while others will be thematic in their focus. Taken together, these volumes will provide a rigorous and ongoing contribution to understanding the expansion and consolidation of democracy in the twenty-first century.

Further information on CSES activities can be obtained from:

CSES Secretariat
Center for Political Studies
Institute for Social Research
The University of Michigan
426 Thompson Street
Ann Arbor, Michigan 481042321
USA

CSES web site: http//:www.cses.org

Citizens, Context, and Choice

How Context Shapes Citizens' Electoral Choices

Edited by
Russell J. Dalton and Christopher J. Anderson

OXFORD
UNIVERSITY PRESS

OXFORD
UNIVERSITY PRESS

Great Clarendon Street, Oxford ox2 6DP

Oxford University Press is a department of the University of Oxford.
It furthers the University's objective of excellence in research, scholarship,
and education by publishing worldwide in

Oxford New York

Auckland Cape Town Dar es Salaam Hong Kong Karachi
Kuala Lumpur Madrid Melbourne Mexico City Nairobi
New Delhi Shanghai Taipei Toronto

With offices in

Argentina Austria Brazil Chile Czech Republic France Greece
Guatemala Hungary Italy Japan Poland Portugal Singapore
South Korea Switzerland Thailand Turkey Ukraine Vietnam

Oxford is a registered trade mark of Oxford University Press
in the UK and in certain other countries

Published in the United States
by Oxford University Press Inc., New York

British Library Cataloguing in Publication Data
Data available

Library of Congress Cataloging in Publication Data
Data available

Typeset by SPI Publisher Services, Pondicherry, India
Printed in Great Britain
on acid-free paper by
MPG Books Group, Bodmin and King's Lynn

ISBN 978–0–19–959923–3

1 3 5 7 9 10 8 6 4 2

To Hans-Dieter Klingemann.
A mentor, colleague, and friend –
and as thanks from us all
for your many contributions to the field.

Series Editors' Preface

Few topics generate as much interest among observers and practitioners of politics as the quality of the democratic process. The relentless expansion of democracy during the twentieth century, which accelerated rapidly after the collapse of communism in 1990, has meant that a majority of the world's countries are now electoral democracies. But not all democracies can be considered equal; they differ widely in terms of institutional arrangements and practices and in the levels of public support that they attract. It is the public's support for democracy that the Comparative Study of Electoral Systems (CSES) project is designed to investigate. This volume series presents the key findings from this major research project that commenced in 1994.

The first CSES volume, edited by Hans-Dieter Klingemann, has documented much of the historical groundwork, the basic principles of data collection, and provided sample chapters showing many of the analytical possibilities of this unique data set. This volume is based on the first module of survey questions in the CSES, completed in 2001, which examines the performance of democracy, the extent of social cleavages, and attitudes to political parties, political institutions, and the democratic process generally.

As with the first volume, this second volume, edited by Russell J. Dalton and Christopher J. Anderson, addresses the fundamental question of whether the institutional structure of elections affects the nature of the public's choices. However, unlike the first volume, this second volume systematically addresses two major questions. The first question looks at explanations of turnout, and how institutions structure the likelihood of voting. The second question discusses determinants of individual electoral behavior and examines the role of institutions in shaping what kinds of political information voters acquire.

These are key questions for extending our understanding of individual citizen behavior. Most studies of voting have been based on single country studies, often covering a single election. By comparing a wide range of countries, for the first time the CSES project enables the institutional environment to be brought into the equation, enhancing our understanding of the complex relationship between individual choice and institutional context. Indeed, as Dalton and Anderson point out, such analyses were impossible until the CSES was established.

The current volume is based on the second module of the CSES, completed in 2006, which examines accountability and representation. A third volume, edited by Jacques Thomassen, to follow soon, is set to inquire into the nature of political representation and accountability and will also use the second CSES module. Future planned volumes in the series, using the second and third modules as well as the combined data series stretching over two decades, will examine among other topics electoral choices and institutions, globalization, and gender and political behavior.

All of the CSES data are freely available and can be downloaded from our website (http://www.cses.org).

Hans-Dieter Klingemann
Ian McAllister
Series Editors

Preface

One of the fundamental questions in comparative electoral studies is whether the institutional structure of elections affects the nature of the public's choices – whether to participate, which party to select, and the relative weight of different factors influencing voter choice. Scholars have long debated the impact of factors such as majoritarian versus proportional electoral systems, ballot formats, or the number of parties on the public's voting behavior. If democracy is to be representative, do certain institutional structures facilitate representation? If democracy requires accountability, do certain structures increase or decrease accountability? Which aspects of the institutional context have the greatest effect on voter choice? And what are the mechanisms by which contextual factors affect individual electoral behavior? In short, does a nation's institutional structure significantly influence how democracy works through the electoral process? These are the theoretical questions we address in this volume.

There is a rich literature theorizing on how the institutional context shapes electoral behavior, but previous research has not been able to bridge two distinct research traditions. First, several aggregate-level comparative studies describe the institutional features of elections and examine aggregate national patterns, such as how votes are translated into seats, or how contextual factors affect levels of turnout. Second, an even more voluminous literature analyzes the sources of individual electoral behavior, but often without examining context because this research is based on a single nation (where context was relatively constant) or a small set of established democracies.

This volume represents the merger of these two research traditions to study how institutional context potentially affects individual electoral behavior. This is possible only because of the development of the Comparative Study of Electoral Systems (CSES) project. The CSES project recognized that researchers needed comparable election study data on individual voters from a large and diverse set of democracies in order to examine the impact of electoral systems on the choices citizens make. By broadening our analyses to the large and diverse set of democracies represented in the CSES, this collection offers the most definitive study of party and electoral system consequences that has yet been assembled. Our empirical analyses are possible only because of the CSES – and the research presented here represents the raison d'être of the CSES.

As it turns out, many of our findings run counter to previous theorizing and empirical findings. We find that context matters, but in complex and often contingent ways. For instance, the nature of the electoral system in the form of proportional representation of single-member district systems or the effective number of parties often matters less than the ideological choices offered by parties. And rather than directly affecting outcomes, contextual effects mostly work by strengthening or weakening the individual-level correlates of political behavior. We also demonstrate a tension between contexts that encourage clear voting choice and representation versus a closer match between voter preferences and the elected government.

In part, our reliance on the CSES led us to dedicate this volume to Hans-Dieter Klingemann. Hans-Dieter was one of the four scholars who drafted the original research plan for CSES (along with John Curtice, Steven Rosenstone, and Jacques Thomassen). He also hosted several early planning meeting for the CSES at the Wissenschaftszentrum Berlin, and edited the initial CSES volume, *The Comparative Study of Electoral Systems* (Oxford University Press, 2009). This CSES network now numbers dozens and dozens of scholars in the various national election studies. We are indebted to all these election study investigators (see www.cses.org for the full list) and in dedicating this volume to Hans-Dieter, we also want to thank all those scholars who contributed to the CSES project over the years. In addition, we want to recognize Hans-Dieter's personal contributions to the study of citizens in the democratic process. His career spans the emergence of empirical electoral research in Germany and Europe, from the landmark 1961 German Election Study to a long series of German and cross-national electoral and party research projects. He helped to develop a range of projects that dramatically advanced empirical electoral research, and has always been generous in sharing these data, his advice, and experience. This volume's dedication is a collective thank you for what Hans-Dieter has contributed to our field, and expresses our personal thanks for his continuing friendship and support.

As editors, we also want to thank all the authors in this volume for their contributions. We assembled an international team of top scholars to address the topics of this volume, and each produced a major contribution to the literature and tolerated our editorial advice. The Mario Einaudi Center for International Studies and the Cornell Institute for European Studies (CIES) at Cornell University and the Center for the Study of Democracy (CSD) at the University of California, Irvine provided financial and institutional support for this volume. CIES also hosted a research conference where contributors presented their initial findings and we developed our analyses. Our thanks go to Sydney van Morgan, Cindy Greco, and Liane O'Brien for their help in pulling the conference together; Yuliya Tverdova, Sílvia Mendes, Grigore Pop-Eleches, Ryan Shirah, Ben Thomas, and Israel Waismel-Manor assisted with data preparation and analysis; Natalie Cook assisted in the preparation of the manuscript. The Oxford University Press reviewers and Rein Taagepera provided very helpful advice on improving our analyses and interpretation. Willy Jou developed the index for this volume. As editors of the CSES series at Oxford University Press, Ian McAllister and Hans-Dieter Klingemann provided valuable advice in developing this project. Dominic Byatt and the wonderful team at Oxford University Press provided the support that we thankfully appreciated.

In the end, our findings indicate that there are substantial commonalities in electoral behavior across nations, but that institutional context also matters in predictable ways. The impact of institutional context is rich and complex. Many of the contextual factors stressed in earlier scholarship actually have a limited effect on individual electoral choice, but other contextual variables have significant effects. Moreover, there is no single, simple answer to the question of how and how much institutions matter. Contextual influences that have beneficial effects in one area may have less-desirable effects in other areas. However, by tracing out these complex relationships, this study advances our understanding of how nations might design electoral institutions to improve the democratic process. The CSES is an important international research vehicle for extending our understanding of the commonalities and differences among democratic publics and thus an indispensable tool for understanding how citizens make electoral democracy work.

Russell Dalton
Irvine, California
Christopher J. Anderson
Ithaca, New York

Contents

Contents

List of Figures

List of Figures

List of Tables

Author Biographies

Christopher J. Anderson teaches at Cornell University where he is Professor of Government and Director of the Cornell Institute for European Studies. His research focuses on contextual models of politics and the link between inequality and popular consent in democracies. He has written on the popularity of governments, the legitimacy of domestic and supranational political institutions, and the link between welfare states and citizen behavior. His most recent books are *Losers' Consent: Elections and Democratic Legitimacy* (Oxford University Press; with André Blais, Shaun Bowler, Todd Donovan, and Ola Listhaug), and *Democracy, Inequality, and Representation: A Comparative Perspective* (Russell Sage Foundation; with Pablo Beramendi).

Susan A. Banducci is Associate Professor of Political Science and Department Chair at the University of Exeter. Her research interests are in the areas of political behavior, media, and political communication in the context of European elections and public opinion. Current research projects include the EU-funded PIREDEU [2009 European Parliamentary Elections] and the ESRC-funded Perceptions of Power. She also coordinates the Marie Curie ITN in Electoral Democracy ELECDEM. Banducci is a member of the Centre for Elections, Media and Parties and the Centre for European Governance. She participated in the 5th Framework project on turnout and political communication in systems of multilevel governance and in the 6th Framework project examining civic engagement in the EU. She recently completed work on a project on gender and political engagement funded by the Dutch Science Foundation (NWO). She has published articles in the *British Journal of Political Science*, *Electoral Studies*, the *European Journal of Political Research*, the *Journal of Politics*, *Comparative Political Studies*, *Party Politics*, and other international journals.

Robin E. Best is Assistant Professor of Comparative Politics and Research Methodology at Leiden University (the Netherlands). Her main research interests include the politics of advanced industrialized democracies, political parties and party systems, electoral politics, electoral systems, and democratic representation. Her work on party system size, party vote shares, and minor party candidacies can be found in *Political Analysis*, *Electoral Studies*, and *Party Politics*.

André Blais is Professor in the Department of Political Science at the Université de Montréal. He is a Fellow of the Royal Society of Canada, and a Research Fellow with the Centre for the Study of Democratic Citizenship, the Centre interuniversitaire de recherche en économie quantitative (CIREQ), and the Center for Interuniversity Research Analysis on Organizations (CIRANO). He is past President of the Canadian Political Science Association. His research interests are elections, electoral systems, turnout, public opinion, and methodology.

Russell J. Dalton is Professor of Political Science at the University of California, Irvine and was the Founding Director of the Center for the Study of Democracy at UC Irvine. He has received a Fulbright Professorship at the University of Mannheim, a Barbra Streisand Center fellowship, German Marshall Research Fellowship, and a POSCO Fellowship at the East/West Center. His recent publications include *The Good Citizen* (2009) and *Democratic Challenges, Democratic Choices* (2004); he is the coeditor of *Party Politics in East Asia* (2008), *The Oxford Handbook of Political Behavior* (2007), *Citizens, Democracy and Markets around the Pacific Rim* (2006), *Democracy Transformed?* (2003), and *Parties without Partisans* (2001). His scholarly interests include comparative political behavior, political parties, social movements, and empirical democratic theory.

Timothy Hellwig is Assistant Professor of Political Science at Indiana University. His work on comparative voting behavior, political accountability, and the electoral consequences of globalization appears in several journals and book chapters, including the *British Journal of Political Science*, *Comparative Political Studies*, and the *Journal of Politics*. His current research focuses on responsibility attributions, on party strategies, and on the relationship between economic globalization and political representation in established democracies.

Jeffrey A. Karp is Associate Professor of Political Science at the University of Exeter. He specializes in research on public opinion and elections, and political behavior. His research appears in many of the leading and specialized journals in political science including the *British Journal of Political Science*, *Comparative Political Studies*, *Electoral Studies*, the *European Journal of Political Research*, the *Journal of Politics*, *Party Politics*, and *Political Psychology*. He has also edited or coauthored three books on New Zealand elections and contributed to a number of book chapters in edited volumes. He has held positions at universities in the United States, New Zealand, and the Netherlands.

Miki Caul Kittilson is Associate Professor of Political Science at Arizona State University. She has received fellowships from the American Association of University Women and the German Marshall Fund, and was awarded the Carrie Chapman Catt Prize for Research on Women and Politics. Her recent book is entitled *Challenging Parties, Changing Parliaments: Women and Elected Office in Contemporary Western Europe*. Her research has appeared in journals such as the *American Journal of Political Science*, the *Journal of Politics*, *Party Politics*, *Perspectives on Politics*, *Politics and Gender*, *International Organization*, and *Comparative Political Studies*. Her research focuses on comparative political behavior, gender politics, and political parties.

Michael D. McDonald is Professor of Political Science and Director of the Center on Democratic Performance at Binghamton University, State University of New York. He has been a Research Fellow at the Netherlands Institute for Advanced Study, Essex University, and Free University Amsterdam. His recent publications include coauthored books on *Elections, Parties, Democracy: Conferring the Median Mandate* (2005) and *Mapping Policy Preferences* (2006). His articles have appeared in the *American Political Science Review*, the *British Journal of Political Science*, and elsewhere. His scholarly interests focus on political representation, with a particular emphasis on the role of political parties as policy agenda setters and distortions in the process from gerrymandering.

G. Bingham Powell, Jr. is Marie C. and Joseph C. Wilson Professor of Political Science at the University of Rochester. He is the author of *Elections as Instruments of Democracy* (2000), which was a cowinner of the Mattei Dogan Award for best comparative book of the year; *Contemporary Democracies* (1982), which won the Woodrow Wilson Foundation Award of APSA; and coauthor and coeditor of the textbooks *Comparative Politics Today* (9th ed. 2008) and *European Politics Today* (4th ed. 2009.) He is a former editor of the *American Political Science Review*. His current research focuses on election rules, party systems, and political representation.

Yuliya V. Tverdova is Assistant Professor of Political Science at the University of California, Irvine. She is also an affiliate for the Center for the Study of Democracy at the University of California, Irvine. Her scholarly interests include public opinion, comparative political behavior, and postcommunist transitions in East Central Europe. In particular, she has been intellectually drawn to such topics as the formation of economic evaluations and perceptions of corruption, support for democracy, and recently, candidate voting. Tverdova's work has appeared in the *American Journal of Political Science, Electoral Studies*, and *Comparative Political Studies*.

Introduction

1

Citizens, Context, and Choice

Russell J. Dalton and Christopher J. Anderson

We can illustrate the premise of this volume with a simple thought experiment. Imagine two people with identical characteristics, such as their age, education, social class, and gender. Also, assume that they hold identical political values. If these two individuals were deciding whether to vote in the next national elections or whom to vote for in that election, we expect they would make identical choices. But now, consider if they lived in two nations with different electoral rules, different numbers of parties, or sets of parties that offered divergent policy programs. How would these variations in political context affect their political behavior? And how would individual characteristics find expression in different political contexts?

We can imagine many differences that might occur. For instance, these two identical people might decide differently on whether to cast a ballot because of the party choices available to each. The voter who has many party choices in an election may be more likely to find a party that she believes merits her support – and thus also be more likely to vote. Previous research suggests that more party choices might improve the voter's ability to translate her policy views into voting choices. Furthermore, as the number of significant parties increases, information may become more important in shaping voters' choices, or voters may use information differently when sorting through the available options. Similarly, when incumbents and challengers can be clearly identified in an election, a voter may be more likely to hold governments accountable for economic performance. And all these effects might vary across subgroups of the population, creating additional and more complex contextual effects.

The point of our thought experiment and these various examples is simple, but fundamentally important: People make political decisions and act politically as individuals who are embedded in political contexts that can affect their choices and behaviors. Thus, the nature of democratic elections – even if electorates are identical – can be influenced by the institutional context.

This volume focuses on macro-political contexts and how they matter for citizens' electoral choices. We concentrate on three ways in which the macro-political environment might influence electoral outcomes. First, formal political institutions shape the options voters face, and this may affect *whether they participate in the election.* Second, the political context may also affect *how voters make party and candidate choices* in an election. Third, context may shape *parties' and candidates' incentives when communicating with voters* and the kind of information voters use to make their decisions. As a result, the nature and quantity of information sometimes creates divergent sets of choices in voters' minds. These three processes can affect electoral outcomes and public images of the electoral process. This volume investigates how formal institutions and the macro-political contexts they help create may affect citizen choices and how context influences political representation in modern democracies. Put simply, we examine how the political context affects the choices that voters make.

As others have noted (Anderson 2009; Klingemann 2009), modern electoral research regularly treats voters as autonomous political actors, often ignoring the effects of the political context. In part, this is a consequence of the methodology of national election studies. Public opinion surveys select respondents from many different sampling points to produce a nationally representative sample.[1] This makes it difficult to identify the immediate social and political context of each voter. What is more, many of the potentially most important differences in context – namely, the macro-political structures that delimit choices and define behavioral incentives – do not vary in a single national study.[2] The constitutional structure and the electoral rules broadly apply to all voters in a nation, and most of the variation is across nations. Thus, when we examine electoral behavior in a single nation, contextual effects are often hidden or constant because their impact is not apparent. The nature of party choices may change in a nation over time, as new parties enter the electorate or institutional structures change, but electoral research predominately focuses on one election in one nation.

Several pathbreaking studies have explored the impact of context in a variety of local settings.[3] This research typically required new sampling frameworks and additional data collection on local conditions. There have also been several significant steps forward in developing cross-national analyses of electoral behavior (Eijk and Franklin 1996; Thomassen 2005; Brug and Eijk 2007; Brug, Eijk, and Franklin 2007; Gunther, Puhle, and Montero 2007).[4] These studies present important theoretical questions and empirical evidence, and we rely upon them in the chapters that follow. However, this previous research is based on a relatively small number of nations with limited political and institutional variation across nations. Research on the effects of institutions requires broader cross-national comparisons with a large number of countries spanning significant variation in political contexts.

Our project compares citizens' political behavior across national political contexts with data collected by the Comparative Study of Electoral Systems (CSES). The CSES's primary goal is to collect standardized public opinion surveys and national macro-level data that allow researchers to study the effects of electoral systems and other cross-national variables. Because of the comparability of survey items across a large and diverse set of countries, we can examine how the political context affects the way that people make their political choices. Previous analyses of the first module of CSES illustrated the potential of this project (e.g., Klingemann 2009), and we now focus these resources on the study of contextual effects on electoral behavior. In other words, the CSES allows us to evaluate the thought experiment posed at the start of this chapter.

We believe the results of this volume can significantly expand our understanding of citizen decision making by describing and explaining how context shapes this process. The results also have broad implications for the study of democratic institutions by demonstrating how alternative institutional structures affect voter choices and electoral outcomes. Finally, our analyses can identify what is generally consistent in voting behavior regardless of context, and thereby determine the processes of choice that are common across nations.

A framework for connecting context and citizen choice

In some form or other, the political context has long been part of our theoretical understanding of how citizens make electoral choices (Huckfeldt 2009; Anderson 2009). But the impact of constitutional and electoral systems on individual behavior has not been fully investigated in previous research. To addresses this topic we need to create a framework for examining the effect of macro-level political contexts on voter behavior:

1. First, we must conceptualize how contextual factors may affect individual behavior.
2. Second, we need an empirical base for our analyses.
3. Third, we have to identify which aspects of context are important and how they can be measured.

Conceptualizing contextual influences

Contextual influences can be rooted in various social, economic, and political phenomena that structure people's political experiences. This volume focuses on the formal institutional characteristics and party systems of countries and their consequences. This definition of institutional influences implicitly excludes economic and social structures or informal factors (such as norms and habits). We also presume that institutions are exogenous to voter choice, at least in the short run. That is, while we know that voters' choices can affect the institutional environment, we presume that in any one election, institutions are defined and recognizable and thus shape voter behavior.

Political institutions can affect voters in three basic ways: via direct, indirect, and contingent effects.[5] *Direct contextual effects* result when formal rules directly act on citizens' decisions to vote or how to vote. For example, voting on a Tuesday in November rather than for a period of two weeks in October may mean that more people will vote during the longer October period. That is, turnout is higher with an extended voting period then than for the single Election Day. In this example, institutional features directly affect incentives to vote – that is, the costs of going to the polls. Many comparative studies of political context resemble a "direct effects" model, at least empirically. For example, several studies demonstrate how the electoral systems or seat allocations affect aggregate electoral outcomes (Grofman and Lijphart 1986; Taagepera and Shugart 1989; Lijphart 1994).

Indirect contextual effects imply that institutions affect some intervening variable, which is the proximate cause of the ultimate outcome. For example, electoral rules – such as a high electoral threshold – may affect the formation of particular parties by producing differential incentives for political elites. This influences elite behavior via the resulting formation of particular parties and thus the supply of party choices, which in turn affects voter behavior. Or a single-member district electoral system may affect the political norms of individuals, such as feelings of political efficacy or the accountability of political parties, which thereby influences their likelihood to participate.

Indirect effects can also influence citizens' voting choices. For instance, Duverger (1954) maintained that the electoral system has direct effects on voting outcomes, which he called a "mechanical effect," by decreasing representation for smaller parties that do not win districts in majoritarian electoral systems or past the representation threshold in PR systems. When voters realize these mechanical effects based on previous elections, they may be less likely to vote for a small party, even if that party is their preferred choice. This "psychological effect" in Duverger's terms is a micro-level example of the indirect effects of the electoral system.

In addition, institutions can have *contingent contextual effects*. This means that the effect of an institutional feature on voter behavior depends on the presence of some third variable. Alternatively, an institutional characteristic can affect the relative impact of an individual-level predictor of behavior. For instance, people with many resources are generally more likely to vote than people with few resources. However, the strength of this relationship will vary with institutional factors that affect the costs of voting. In this example, people with few resources may be more likely to vote if they live in a country with low costs of voting, compared to a country where the cost of voting is high. Conversely, individuals with many resources may be only slightly less likely to vote in countries where the cost of voting is high.

Our empirical base

To examine the effects of context on voter behavior requires data on individual voters across many political contexts. The CSES provides such data.[6] The CSES is a collaborative research program among election study projects and has been conducted in over fifty countries. Participating countries include a common module of survey questions in their postelection surveys. All surveys must meet certain quality and comparability standards, and all are conducted as nationally representative surveys. The resulting survey data are combined with district- and macro-level voting, demographic, and institutional variables.

The CSES conducted its first module of surveys between 1996 and 2001 in thirty-four nations (some with more than one election study). Table 1.1 lists the nations in this module and the year of the election. The survey focused on public orientations toward parties, political institutions, and the functioning of the democratic process. CSES fielded its second module between 2001 and 2006 with a thematic focus on representation and accountability. The rightmost column of Table 1.1 lists the thirty-eight Module II nations and the year of the election. Surveys from either or both of these modules are used in the chapters of this volume.[7] The CSES project also compiled ancillary data on the political systems, electoral systems, and parties in each election that we use in our analyses.

The CSES project is especially appropriate for the study of contextual effects for several reasons. It is includes a large number of nations to provide the empirical base for cross-national comparisons; previous cross-national projects were typically based on a dozen nations or less. More important, the CSES nations provide a rich variety in contextual characteristics. These nations include a mix of electoral systems and constitutional structures that were generally underrepresented in past European-based cross-national studies. The CSES nations also include a wider range of cultural zones, including North America, East Asia, and Latin America, and the ability to compare established and new democracies. Indeed, one of the core rationales of this large cross-national project was to enable the types of comparative analyses presented in this volume.

Dimensions of context

We do not presume that ordinary citizens can identify and analyze the design and consequences of various institutional features, such as the

Table 1.1 National elections included in the CSES

Nation	CSESI	CSESII
Albania	—	2005
Australia	1996	2004
Belgium	1999	2003
Belarus*	2001	—
Brazil	—	2002
Bulgaria	—	2001
Canada	1997	2004
Chile	1999	2005
Czech Republic	1996	2002
Denmark	1998	2001
Finland	—	2003
France	—	2002
Germany	1998	2002 (2)
Hong Kong*	1998, 2000	2004
Hungary	1998	2002
Iceland	1999	2003
Ireland	—	2002
Israel	1996	2003
Italy	—	2006
Japan	1996	2004
Korea, South	2000	2004
Kyrgyzstan*	—	2005
Lithuania	1997	
Mexico	1997, 2000	2003
Netherlands	1998	2002
New Zealand	1996	2002
Norway	1997	2001
Peru	2000, 2001	2006
Philippines	1998	2004
Poland	1997	2001
Portugal	2002	2002, 2005
Romania	1996	2004
Russia	1999, 2000	2004
Slovenia	1996	2004
Spain	1996, 2000	2004
Sweden	1998	2002
Switzerland	1999	2003
Taiwan	1996	2001, 2004
Ukraine	1998	—
United Kingdom	1997	2005
United States	1996	2004

Note: The nations with an asterisk were not included in this volume because the election was not clearly free, fair, and authoritative.

intricacies of electoral rules, the logics of coalition formation, or the dynamics of party systems. Instead, we assume that voters understand institutions in the form of recognizable outcomes that influence and constrain their electoral behavior. Viewed in this way, institutions exist in an objective form through citizens' perceptions of their choices and environments. This also implies that it is not the formal electoral system institutions, which commonly are the focus of comparative analyses of electoral politics, that affect the voter. Rather, voters may react to the more proximate and identifiable options existing in the party system that flows from these institutional structures.

We presume that the political context defined by the electoral system and party system shapes the voters' behavior in three ways: by determining the number of choices, the nature of the choices, and the predictability of choices. Each of these traits can influence both the party choices the voter faces in the election, and their images of the past and future government resulting from the elections.

The following sections discuss the general rationale for each of these contextual categories. Each of the individual analytic chapters more extensively considers the specific research literature and hypothesizes about the contextual effects directly relevant to their topic. Our goal here is to describe the broad contextual dimensions used throughout this volume, and describe how these characteristics are distributed across the CSES nations.

Party and candidate choice

Perhaps the most common contextual model presumes that the amount of choice available to voters influences their electoral behavior and election outcomes. Anthony Downs (1957) argued that multiparty systems were more likely to generate ideological or policy voting and more likely to have high turnout because more choices were available to citizens. That is, when people can identify parties with political views that are close to their own positions, they are more likely to feel that voting matters and they are more likely to choose a party on the basis of policy considerations. Reviewing this literature and the empirical findings from Module I of the CSES, Klingemann and Wessels (2009) maintain that the "supply of party choices" is a strong influence on electoral behavior. They argue that the greater the number of meaningful alternatives in an election, the greater the voter's motivation to invest and weigh such criteria in making their electoral decisions. We believe the potential effects for political choice are more varied, but the important factor is that scholars agree that the supply of electoral options should matter, and the literature offers several different dimensions of supply.

THE NUMBER OF OPTIONS

In simple terms, the diversity of choice is a matter of numbers. Baskin-Robbins offers thirty-one flavors to give more choices of ice cream to their customers. Similarly, a person who has multiple parties or candidates to select from at election time has more choice than the voter who has only two choices (or only one).

While it may seem apparent that the amount of choice can influence electoral outcomes and the electoral calculus of voters, actually measuring this trait is more complex. A natural starting place is to examine how institutions structure the choices available to voters. Duverger's Law (1951) spelled out the basic principle that the *rules of the electoral system* influence the number of significant parties competing in elections and winning legislative representation. Certainly one of the most consistently replicated analyses of electoral research demonstrates that proportional representation electoral systems have a greater number of competitive parties than majoritarian systems (Rae 1971; Grofman and Lijphart 1986; Taagepera and Shugart 1989). Proportional representation allows political parties to compete for the support of distinct social groups – or distinct policy views – and to successfully win seats in the legislature in proportion to their popular vote. Majoritarian systems, in contrast, prompt political groups to form coalitions and consolidate to win a plurality of the vote in these winner-takes-all systems. Arend Lijphart (1984, 1999) maintains that the structure of the electoral system, the number of parties, and other institutional characteristics create different structures of consensual and majoritarian democracy. Consensual and majoritarian systems influence participation patterns, electoral behavior, decision-making processes within government, and the outputs of the political process. This is one of the strongest arguments that institutions make basic differences in the workings of the democratic process, and which specific aspects of institutional structures are most important.

Rein Taagepera and Matthew Shugart (1999: 19) showed that *district magnitude*, which measures the number of parliamentary seats filled in each district, best predicts the proportionality of an electoral system and thus the number of parties competing in elections and winning seats in parliament. They also discuss how district magnitude affects citizens' voting choices, such as through greater strategic voting in systems where district composition may produce more "wasted" votes.[8] The electoral rules (majoritarian/PR) and district magnitude are occasionally used as proxies for the amount of party choice since both are readily available and stable traits of an electoral system. These institutional variables should affect the number of meaningful parties from which voters can choose.

A more direct indicator of the diversity of choice is the number of parties that actually compete in an election. Simply counting parties, however, is imprecise because many parties compete without a significant chance of winning representation. Even in majoritarian systems, many parties gain a position on the ballot but then garner very few votes. To account for this, Markku Laakso and Rein Taagepera developed a measure of the *effective number of parties* (Laakso and Taagepera 1979; Taagepera and Shugart 1999; Taagepera 2007). The effective number of parties weights the number of parties by their size, so that small parties count less than large parties.[9]

The CSES nations span a wide range of institutional contexts and the corresponding number of partisan choices (Table 1.2 and the appendix to this volume). Of the thirty-six democracies included in Module II, six have predominately majoritarian legislative elections, twenty-one are predominately proportional, and nine have mixed systems. District magnitude also widely varies across these nations.[10] Both Israel and the Netherlands use a single nationwide constituency to select members of parliament, which produces a district magnitude of 120 and 150, respectively (the number of seats in each parliament). In the Netherlands, for instance, it takes only 0.67 percent of the nationwide vote to win a seat in parliament, which should encourage even small parties to compete (and win seats). At the other extreme, the majoritarian electoral systems have district magnitudes near 1, which means that even receiving a large proportion of the vote in a district may not yield a seat in parliament if another party has a plurality.

The third data column in Table 1.2 describes the effective number of electoral parties (ENEP) based on the party vote shares in the legislative election. This ranges from 2.17 effective electoral parties in the 2004 election for the U.S. House of Representatives to 8.86 parties in Belgium's highly fragmented and regionalized election to the Chamber of Representatives. The next column presents the effective number of legislative parties (ENLP), based on the party seat shares in the parliament. Fewer parties typically gain representation compared to the number of parties who compete in the election, so the effective number of legislative parties is smaller than the effective number of electoral parties. These two variables are strongly related ($r = .90$), however.

As prior research suggests, the institutional structure of the electoral system is related to the effective number of parties. Based on the nations in Table 1.2, there is a strong correlation between a majoritarian/PR electoral system and the effective number of electoral parties (ENEP) and legislative parties (ENLP) ($r = .51$ and $.56$, respectively). In simple descriptive terms, majoritarian electoral systems average 2.4 effective legislative parties, and PR systems have 4.6 parties. Similarly, there is a positive relationship between district magnitude and the effective number of electoral and legislative parties (both are $r = .33$).

The nature of the electoral system may influence the content of electoral choice as well. The clearest example is the distinction between party-centered voting choices, such as in closed party list systems where voters choose between fixed party slates and a single transferable vote (STV) system where candidate-centered choices determine electoral outcomes. Presumably, party-based voting

Table 1.2 Diversity of choice in party systems

Country	Electoral system	District magnitude	Effective number of electoral parties	Effective number of legislative parties	Party-candidate centered	Polarization index
Albania	Mixed	11.10	2.76	2.25	3.6	4.47
Australia	Majoritarian	0.90	3.12	2.43	8.6	2.79
Belgium	PR	7.50	8.86	7.02	2.9	4.53
Brazil	PR	19.00	8.36	8.41	2.9	2.00
Bulgaria	PR	7.70	3.92	2.91	1.4	4.37
Canada	Majoritarian	1.00	3.76	3.03	4.3	2.06
Chile	PR	2.00	6.05	5.56	2.9	4.95
Czech Republic	PR	25.00	4.80	3.66	2.9	5.43
Denmark	PR	10.50	4.69	4.47	7.1	3.57
Finland	PR	13.33	5.91	4.93	7.1	2.85
France	Majoritarian	1.00	5.06	2.23	5.7	3.29
Germany	Mixed	11.20	3.86	3.37	3.6	2.70
Hungary	Mixed	1.96	2.80	2.21	5.7	5.85
Iceland	PR	7.90	3.92	3.71	1.4	4.08
Ireland	PR	4.00	3.94	3.30	10.0	2.20
Israel	PR	120.00	6.96	6.17	1.4	3.87
Italy	PR	23.70	7.73	7.70	1.4	3.89
Japan	Mixed	1.54	3.82	2.88	3.6	2.77
Korea, South	Mixed	8.60	3.36	2.35	3.6	3.55
Mexico	Mixed	16.60	3.40	2.98	3.6	2.10
Netherlands	PR	150.00	6.02	5.79	2.9	3.64
New Zealand	Mixed	24.00	4.09	3.75	3.6	3.35

Norway	PR	10.00	6.14	5.35	1.4	3.75
Peru	PR	4.80	6.36	3.72	2.9	1.71
Philippines	Majoritarian	1.00	3.19	4.94	3.6	0.46
Poland	PR	16.70	4.49	3.59	2.9	4.92
Portugal ('02)	PR	10.50	3.15	2.58	1.4	3.44
Romania	PR	7.80	3.79	3.31	1.4	2.43
Russia	Mixed	113.00	5.14	3.37	1.4	3.11
Slovenia	PR	11.00	5.91	4.89	2.9	3.15
Spain	PR	6.90	3.04	2.49	1.4	4.33
Sweden	PR	11.60	4.51	4.22	2.9	4.07
Switzerland	PR	9.10	5.46	4.99	7.1	4.01
Taiwan ('01)	Mixed	11.50	3.55	3.47	3.6	1.14
United Kingdom	Majoritarian	1.00	3.58	2.44	4.3	2.36
United States	Majoritarian	1.00	2.17	2.01	5.7	2.43

Source: See Appendix to this volume.

that focuses on party ideology or the accountability of parties should be stronger in the former electoral system and candidate image should have more weight in the latter. The next column of 1.2 presents a coding of electoral systems based on a framework developed by David Farrell and Ian McAllister (2006). Ireland's STV system rates a perfect 10 on their scale, while the closed party list systems receive a score of 1.4.

THE CLARITY OF CHOICES

With all due respect to Baskin-Robbins, the diversity of choice is more than just a count of numbers. Thirty-one flavors of vanilla would not represent meaningful choice. The choice thesis implies that choices are meaningful as well as numerous. Many of the consequences attributed to the number of parties actually are based on the presumption that parties differ and that more parties means more meaningful choice. To disentangle these, we need to distinguish between the quantity and nature of choices available to voters.

We might think of party choices as a function of the number of social cleavages that exist in a society and thus the number of parties that compete because they have a distinct constituency to represent (Lijphart 1984). Or, one can measure the diversity of choice by the number of distinct party families that exist in the party system (Sigelman and Yough 1978). Having the ability to choose between a socialist, green, and left-liberal party represents greater choice than selecting between three parties of a factionalized socialist bloc.

An alternative measure of party choice is based on the ideological polarization in a party system. Aside from the number of choices, we are interested in the extent to which the party choices are differentiated along some important dimension, such as Left–Right positions. Party system polarization reflects the dispersion of political parties along an ideological or policy dimension. Giovanni Sartori (1976), for example, compared the consequences of centripetal and centrifugal party systems. Similarly, many of Anthony Downs' theoretical arguments (1957) on the consequences of party system competition are based on parties' presumed distribution along an ideological continuum. Several cross-national empirical studies have demonstrated that the polarization of political parties can strongly influence the sources of electoral choice through indirect and contingent contextual effects (Thomassen 2005; Dalton 2008b; Wessels and Schmitt 2008; Klingemann and Wessels 2009).

We estimate party system polarization as the dispersion of parties along the Left–Right dimension (see Chapter 5). The use of the Left–Right scale does not imply that people possess a sophisticated conceptual framework or theoretical understanding of liberal–conservative philosophy. We simply expect that positions on this scale summarize the issues and cleavages that structure political competition in a nation. Ronald Inglehart (1990: 273), for instance, showed that people in most nations can locate themselves on the Left–Right scale and he described the scale as representing "whatever major conflicts are present in the political system" (also see Fuchs and Klingemann 1989; Huber and Inglehart 1995; Knutsen 1999).

Russell Dalton (2008*b*) presented a Polarization Index measuring the dispersion of parties along the Left–Right scale (the rightmost column of Table 1.2).[11] Low values indicate that the parties position themselves close together which limits ideological polarization or choice for the voters. This is the case in party systems such as in Australia, the United Kingdom, and the United States. Conversely, a system with a number of large parties including those at the political extremes is a highly polarized system that offers very diverse choices, such as Iceland, Poland, and Spain.

Previous research presumed that ideological choice was closely related to the effective number of parties in a political system. Surely, when larger numbers of parties compete because of numerous cleavages, ideological polarization was greater. Conversely, following Downs, a smaller number of parties in majoritarian systems will gravitate toward the median voter, reducing ideological polarization. As the legislative elections from CSES module II demonstrate, however, party system polarization and the effective number of electoral parties are in fact largely separate traits (Figure 1.1). Ideological polarization is not significantly related to the effective number of electoral parties ($r = .15$) or legislative parties ($r = .07$). For instance, most majoritarian systems – such as Australia, the United States, and Great Britain – have a relatively small number of effective

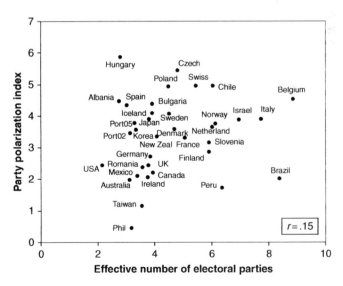

Figure 1.1 Effective numbers of parties and party system polarization

Source: Table 1.2

electoral parties, but their party system polarization is roughly equal to some nations with two or three times as many effective parties, such as Hungary, Albania, and Spain.[12] At the same time, Brazil and Peru have a relatively large number of effective electoral parties, but only modest levels of polarization.[13]

In the chapters that follow, one of our significant findings is the contrast in the impact of the number of choices versus the polarization of choices in contemporary electoral politics. While previous research on electoral politics has focused on the amount of choice, several contributions to this volume reveal that the clarity of options is also a strong contextual influence on many aspects of electoral behavior.

THE STABILITY OF CHOICES

Another contextual factor is the stability or institutionalization of the choice set. A consolidated democracy typically provides a context in which elections are recurring contests between essentially the same group of political parties. In this situation, institutionalized political parties are better able to build political ties to a distinct constituency, and then represent these groups within the political process. Voters who face the same party choices across elections should find it easier to vote based on past political performance and future policy goals (Duch and Stevenson 2008). Elections are not slates of unknown parties, but opportunities to evaluate the past policies of the incumbents and the future prospects of parties who are known, predictable entities.

Many of these characteristics are underdeveloped in new democracies. The social and political infrastructure for free and fair elections can be more tenuous. New political parties have to develop a programmatic identity and attract a stable core of voters on that basis. The degree of organizational structure, mass member support, and a party administrative elite is typically lower, which impedes the parties' ability to educate voters, mobilize supporters, and ultimately represent these voters (Mair and van Biezen 2001; Biezen 2003). Political parties are themselves less stable as new parties form and different parties compete across successive elections. Furthermore, transitional parties often appear more pragmatic than programmatic; or they compete based on valence issues, the personal charisma of the party leader, or clientelism and district service. Volatility in party offerings makes it difficult for voters to make meaningful choices, and to reward or punish political parties on programmatic grounds. Citizens in new democracies typically display weaker party identification and lower affect for parties overall –which might depress turnout and affect the correlates of vote choice (Dalton and Weldon 2007).

The CSES nations cover a wide range on many key elements of democratic and party system development (Table 1.3). One simple indicator is the amount of democratic experience a country has had over the past half century. The first column in the table counts the number of years a nation has been democratic

Table 1.3 Development of the political and party systems

Country	Years of democracy (1955–)	Freedom House score	Rank on Voice and Accountability	Press Freedom	Age of party system
Albania	8	3.0	48.6	51	10
Australia	49	1.0	94.2	14	86
Belgium	48	1.0	96.2	9	56
Brazil	17	2.5	57.2	32	18
Bulgaria	11	2.0	60.1	29	12
Canada	49	1.0	96.6	15	77
Chile	16	1.0	88.9	24	13
Czech Republic	9	1.5	76.4	25	12
Denmark	46	1.0	96.6	9	94
Finland	48	1.0	99.0	10	81
France	47	1.0	83.2	17	47
Germany	47	1.0	94.7	15	53
Hungary	12	1.5	88.5	23	12
Iceland	48	1.0	98.6	8	55
Ireland	47	1.0	90.9	16	54
Israel	48	2.0	64.4	27	11
Italy	51	1.0	85.1	35	12
Japan	49	1.5	76.9	18	20
Korea, South	16	1.5	69.2	29	9
Mexico	6	2.0	55.3	38	26
Netherlands	47	1.0	97.6	15	45
New Zealand	47	1.0	100.0	8	56
Norway	46	1.0	96.6	9	95
Peru	26	2.5	49.0	39	13
Philippines	17	2.5	50.0	34	23
Poland	12	1.5	84.6	18	9
Portugal ('02)	26	1.0	90.9	15	28
Romania	14	2.5	58.7	47	14
Russia	14	5.5	33.2	67	7
Slovenia	13	1.0	87.5	19	14
Spain	26	1.0	89.9	19	29
Sweden	47	1.0	98.1	8	47
Switzerland	48	1.0	95.2	10	99
Taiwan ('01)	9	1.5	76.0	21	14
United Kingdom	50	1.0	93.8	18	120
United States	49	1.0	89.4	13	152

Note: The scoring of variables is as follows: Freedom House, 1 is high; Voice and Accountability, 100 is high; Press Freedom, 1 is high. See Appendix for more information on each characteristic.

Source: See Appendix to this volume.

between 1955 and the year of the survey. Among the CSES Module II nations this ranges from six years to more than fifty years. Other indicators describe the level of democratic development in a nation. The second data column displays the widely used Freedom House scores, which ranges from 1 (highest level of democracy) to 7 (the lowest score). Most of these nations score relatively well on the Freedom House statistic, because it emphasizes the procedural framework of democracy. Only one nation (Albania) is ranked as partly free, and one nation (Russia) as not free in their rankings.[14] More refined measures of political development come from two other statistics. The World Bank's Voice and Accountability Index measures the extent to which a country's citizens are able to participate in selecting their government, as well as freedom of expression, freedom of association, and free media.[15] The Freedom House also calculates a Press Freedom index that considers the legal, political, and economic constraints on freedom of the press[16] The Press Freedom index ranks seven nations as having only a partly free press, and one nation as not free (Russia). Since Press Freedom taps the quality of freedom rather than just the institutionalization of elections, it may be even more important in identifying contexts where civil society groups can flourish, and free and fair elections can occur.

While these different characteristics of democratic development are strongly interrelated, these are also theoretically separate traits[17] Nations can possess a distinct mix of characteristics. This is seen in Figure 1.2, which plots the age of the democratic party system against the level of Press Freedom (reversed in low/high values to simplify the presentation). As one might expect, the United States, Britain, and other established democracies have long-established party systems and score high on Press Freedom. The other established democracies also score highly on Press Freedom, including Spain and Portugal that underwent their democratic transitions in the 1970s. The pattern is more varied among new democracies on the left side of the figure. Some of these new democracies have relatively high levels of Press Freedom despite their recent transition, such as Poland, Slovenia, Hungary, and the Czech Republic. But other transitional systems, such as Russia and Romania, score low on Press Freedom (and on the World Bank's Voice and Accountability Index). We might expect to find more structured and meaningful voting choices in the former set of postcommunist states, but inchoate party systems and voter choice in the latter.

Government choice

In addition to the menu of party choice available to voters, political institutions also structure the choice of governments. These two aspects of the institutional environment are related, but not coterminous. Partisan voting is choosing the political party that best represents one's ideological issue or group preferences in the parliament and possibly the government – this is *voting as an instrument of*

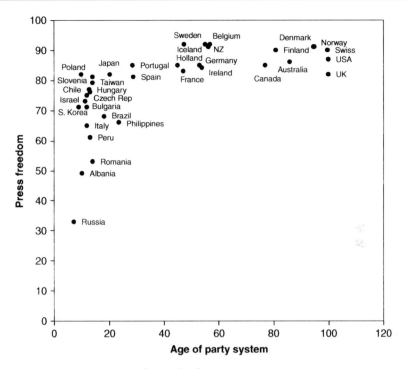

Figure 1.2 Party system age and press freedom

Source: Table 1.3

Note: The values for press freedom have been transposed so that higher values indicate more freedom.

partisan representation (cf. McDonald and Budge 2005). In addition, voting can be viewed as evaluating and influencing the composition of the government rather than simply a partisan choice, making *voting as a mechanism of democratic accountability*. In this latter case, people might choose parties with a goal of influencing the future government – prospectively selecting governors with the greatest future promise – or retrospectively rewarding and punishing (sanctioning) past holders of office. This shifts the logic of voting away from choosing the party that is most consistent with one's interests to evaluating parties or blocs of parties with a goal of assessing the performance of current government and influencing future ones.

Retrospective judgments are typically based on the so-called reward–punishment (or sanctioning) model, which lies at the heart of accountability evaluations (see Downs 1957; Anderson 2007*b*). The reward–punishment model often focuses on the government's performance in handling the economy (Lewis-Beck and Stegmaier 2000). But economic voting is an example of a broader category of performance voting that follows a principal–agent logic, where voters are the principals and governors act as their agents. Representation via accountability – rooted in performance voting – thus is an alternative vision of democracy that enables electorates to exert control because of their ability to "throw the rascals out."[18] In our framework, political institutions can structure government choice in ways that are analogous to party choice by influencing the number, clarity, and predictability of choices over alternative governments.

THE NUMBER AND CLARITY OF OPTIONS

The complexity of political institutions affects the ease with which voters can figure out which officeholders or parties are responsible for government policy performance. Fewer parties in the government produce a simplified choice. Britain has been the classic example of a country with simple governing choices. It has previously had a well-defined incumbent with a single party holding legislative and executive power. A simple reward–punishment mechanism should function most smoothly in such two-party, single-party incumbent executive systems. If British voters are satisfied, they can vote for the incumbent; if they are dissatisfied, they vote for an opposition party. Currently, however, this is not the case as the UK is being ruled by a two-party coalition.

As the number of parties within the government increases, parties may be better able to escape voters' attention or perhaps diffuse the blame for government policy outcomes. Coalition government in parliamentary democracies, or divided government (cohabitation) in presidential systems, makes the assignment of responsibility more difficult, even when government officials do not try to obfuscate responsibility. Thus, the simplest measure of the number of government options is the number of parties that form the governing coalition. As Table 1.4 shows, although most legislatures have a coalition of parties in the majority, the number of governing parties is typically small. Most legislatures in the CSES nations have only a single-party majority holding cabinet seats. Even if we exclude the nations with majoritarian electoral systems, a number of countries with proportional electoral systems had single-party government. At the other end of the distribution, Italy's six and Belgium and Finland's five governing parties represent a distribution of cabinet power unlike most others.

In reality, the definition of incumbency and alternative choices of governments is more complex than simply counting the number of parties in the cabinet. As a measure of the clarity of government responsibility, the CSES project collected data on the number (and percentage) of cabinet portfolios held by each governing party. These data can be used to calculate the *effective number of governing parties*, similar to the effective number of electoral parties described above. These data on parties' shares of cabinet responsibility also can show whether individual parties with greater governing responsibility are more likely to be singled out by voters for reward and punishment.

As Table 1.4 shows, there can be a significant difference between simply counting the number of governing parties and calculating their effective number. Japan's and Ireland's two governing parties, when weighted by their share of cabinet seats, really reflect a coalition of one large and one small party, resulting in an effective number of governing parties of 1.14. In contrast, the effective number of governing parties in the Netherlands (2.78) is quite close to the simple number of governing parties (3.0), reflecting a coalition of similarly sized, and thus similarly responsible governing parties.

Beyond the number of governing parties, a related approach investigates how formal institutional design and political contexts affect the assignment of credit and blame to incumbent governments, and how this shapes the choices voters have over alternative governments (Powell and Whitten 1993; Anderson 1995*a*; Powell 2000). This approach emphasizes the concept of "clarity of responsibility." There are two parts to clarity: First, does the government have the power to implement its policies? Second, is the government responsible for the outcomes that voters see? Some systems vest significantly more responsibility in the executive branch, relative to the legislative branch. When a unified national government is clearly responsible for performance outcomes, voters' choices should be simplified.

The nations in this volume display significant variation with regard to the clarity of (formal) government responsibility. The CSES project collected information on the type of executive authority spelled out in a country's constitution.[19] Executives whose formal powers make them dominant vis-à-vis the cabinet and legislature bear greater responsibility for political outcomes.

Table 1.4 reveals that the Anglo-American democracies like Australia, Canada, or the United Kingdom have a very powerful executive vis-à-vis the legislature. In contrast, the Netherlands, Denmark, the Philippines, and Sweden have relatively weak executives. Conversely, the parliaments in these nations are quite strong, thus sharing policymaking powers more equally among these different branches of government.

This is related to but not synonymous with the distinction between presidential and parliamentary systems. Presidential systems provide a particularly interesting group of elections because they ask voters to choose a single incumbent who, if not in reality, is at least perceived as being in charge of the government. Table 1.4 shows that the executive in some parliamentary systems (scored 2) have significant powers vis-à-vis the legislature (e.g., Australia), while others do not (e.g., Ireland).

Duch and Stevenson (2008) have recently proposed a summary measure for the distribution of responsibility, a variant of which we use for this volume. Our measure compares the actual distribution of cabinet portfolios among parties in a given legislature to the hypothetical case where portfolios are distributed evenly across all parties in the legislature (see Chapter 7 and the appendix to this volume). This measure is highly correlated with the effective number of

Table 1.4 Government characteristics affecting electoral supply

Country	# Parties pre-election government	Effective no. of governing parties	Type of executive	Power of executive vis-à-vis legislative branch	Concentration of responsibility	Government stability (months)	Government stability (percent)
Albania	2	1.11	2		0.88	67	47
Australia	2	1.37	2	4	0.60	103	95
Belgium	5	4.72	2		0.31	134	93
Brazil	4	3.84	0	1	0.45	118	82
Bulgaria	1	1.00	1	1	0.89	78	54
Canada	1	1.00	2	4	0.89	84	47
Chile	3		0		0.48	144	100
Czech Rep.	1	1.00	2	2	0.89	114	79
Denmark	2	1.22	2	0	0.76	86	60
Finland	5	3.16	2	1	0.38	98	68
France	2	1.49	1	4	0.63	85	47
Germany	2	1.31	2	1	0.72	141	98
Hungary	2	1.56	2	4	0.64	101	70
Iceland	2	1.80	2	0	0.55	143	99
Ireland	2	1.10	2	1	0.87	102	57
Israel	3		2	1	0.48	13	9
Italy	6		2		0.51	72	40
Japan	2	1.32	2	1	0.80	39	27
Korea, South	1	1.00	0	1	0.82	144	100
Mexico	1	1.00	0	1	0.82	216	100
Netherlands	3	2.57	2	0	0.48	141	98
New Zealand	2	1.39	2	2	0.87	57	53
Norway	1	1.00	2	2	0.94	60	42

Peru	1	1.00	0	0.86	120	67
Philippines	1	1.00	0	—	—	—
Poland	1	1.00	1	0.71	68	47
Portugal '02	2	1.27	1	0.73	105	73
Romania	1	1.00	1	0.89	73	51
Russia	1	1.00	0	—	—	—
Slovenia	3	1.86	1	0.65	46	32
Spain	1	1.00	2	0.95	108	75
Sweden	1	1.00	2	0.93	96	67
Switzerland	4	3.93	2	0.43	36	25
Taiwan '01	1	1.18	3		54	50
UK	1	1.00	4	0.94	157	87
United States	1	1.00	1	0.71	144	100

Source: See Appendix to this volume.

legislative parties, but it is derived from a different theoretical intuition. Table 1.4 shows that the concentration of responsibility can be quite low, both in presidential and parliamentary systems, as the scores for Chile and Israel demonstrate, or high as in countries as different as Norway, Spain, or Romania.

When parties have clearly delineated policies and identities, assessing responsibility for past policies is relatively straightforward. In other instances, the coalition party responsible for a specific policy is more difficult to identify. In simple numerical terms, presidential systems provide clear choices for and against a single incumbent executive, while parliamentary systems typically diffuse the focus on several parties. In addition, if voters seek to select governments prospectively rather than retrospectively, this increases the complexity voters' calculus because it implies that voters are choosing between alternative governments that might form after the election. In countries with coalition government, several alternative governing coalitions are usually plausible and the actual composition of the government occurs after the election, thereby decreasing the voters' ability to define the government by their votes.

STABILITY OF OPTIONS

The extent of performance voting should be a function of the predictability of the government choices. The stability of democratic institutions – and in particular the institutionalization of elections as part of this – should also affect voters' faith that elections matter and their ability to hold government accountable in the future. In this way, stability could have a similar effect: when citizens have not yet learned electoral politics, their motivation and ability to hold governments to account may be lower. How are voters to judge governments retrospectively when democracy has functioned for only a short while?

Even in countries with long histories of elections, stability can matter. Frequent government alternation and frequent elections should make it more difficult for voters to assign responsibility, as it becomes more difficult to connect government action and policy outcomes. This should diminish the likelihood that voters will turn out the incumbent government even when policy conditions are bad. And this, in turn, exacerbates any potential moral hazard problem inherent in the voter–government relationship (cf. Fearon 1999).

The measurement of government stability is complicated by the different length of electoral cycles, differences between presidential and parliamentary systems, and the complexity of defining when there is a significant change in government between elections (Conrad and Golder 2010). We define stability in two ways. First, we simply counted the number of months the three governments leading up to the CSES election had held office. This is presented on the right side of Table 1.4.[20] Because the length of the electoral cycle varies from three to five years, the total possible length of three governments varies widely.

Therefore, we also calculated the length of the last three governments as a percentage of three full electoral cycles, which is displayed in the next column in the table.

These two dimensions of government stability show considerable variation across the set of CSES nations. In addition, there is only a weak relationship between both measures, because the effect of differential electoral cycles greatly affects the simple count of months in a manner that distorts the results. Our analyses suggest that the percentage measure of stability is a more robust indicator of the stability of recent governments. This varies from full electoral cycles in several nations with constitutionally fixed electoral cycles, often coupled with presidential systems, such as the United States, Mexico, and Chile. At the other extreme are a set of highly fragmented parliamentary systems where governments are very transitory – on average lasting for less than a quarter of an electoral cycle (e.g., Israel and Italy). Lower stability means that voters may be frequently asked to evaluate the parties in frequent elections, or experience elections where control of the government has change in the interelection period. This greater instability may make it more difficult for voters to judge governments retrospectively when they have been in power only a short while, or when they can reasonably assume that the government they select will not celebrate an anniversary. Volatility blurs the responsibility of parties in government.

The various chapters in this volume use different subsets of the variables described in this section because certain contextual features are more relevant for certain aspects of electoral behavior. Information on the contextual variables described above are presented in this volume's appendix.

A note on methodology

To analyze contextual effects, most of the chapters rely on multilevel estimation techniques. These estimation models account for the multilevel nature of the data and remedy the statistical problems associated with traditional estimation techniques (clustering, nonconstant variance, underestimation of standard errors, etc.) (cf. Snijders and Bosker 1999). Because most chapters examine data at the individual level and the country level, they have a hierarchical structure, with one level (individual respondents) nested within the other (countries). The most complex multilevel models are presented in Chapter 6 by Yuliya Tverdova, who studies vote choice at three levels of analysis: individual-level, party-level, and nation-level effects.

In addition, identifying indirect and contingent contextual effects requires an examination of individual level behavior nested in a variety of political contexts. Using advanced multilevel modeling techniques allows us to examine the interaction of variables from both levels. For instance, we earlier discussed how the electoral system may affect the level of strategic voting in the electorate; who casts strategic votes is also likely to interact with the level of voter sophistication. Multilevel models can estimate such interactive effects, and each chapter details the specific methodological choices the authors have made.

The plan of the volume

This volume is part of a developing research program based on the CSES (Kedar and Shively 2005; Klingemann 2009). We assembled an international team of scholars, partly from the CSES principal investigators and partly from academic specialists on comparative electoral behavior. We developed a research plan for this project, and then met to discuss and compare our initial findings.[21] These findings led a revised and expanded research plan and ultimately to this volume.

We have organized our presentation around three themes. In the first part, individuals face an initial question of whether to become politically engaged, and whether the political context shapes that decision. Miki Caul Kittilson and Christopher Anderson examine how the range and diversity of choices available to voters affect voter engagement. They find that the electoral supply does not have a direct effect on turnout. Instead, it has a contingent effect by conditioning the effects of civic orientations and mobilization on people's decision to vote. Jeffrey Karp and Susan Banducci analyze citizen participation in election campaigns beyond vote turnout. They find that a nation's level of democratic experience, the polarization of the party system, and other contextual variables significantly influence campaign participation, as well as the individual level correlates of participation.

The second part of the volume looks at the correlates of voting choices and the impact of the institutional context. Robin Best and Michael McDonald introduce this part with a conceptual discussion of the principles required for individuals to be policy-directed voters. The long debate on the nature of mass belief systems makes presumptions about the public's political abilities, which Best and McDonald evaluate using the CSES. They conclude that the majority of electorates consistently vote with their broad policy orientations, but other factors also shape electoral choices. Russell Dalton extends this discussion by examining the influence of Left–Right orientations on voting choice. He finds that Left–Right attitudes are significantly related to voting in most nations, but with substantial cross-national variance. The diversity of choice, rather than the number of choices, most clearly enables voters to identify a party that shares their political preferences.

Yuliya Tverdova examines how the impact of party and candidate images on voting is shaped by contextual factors. She focuses in particular on contextual characteristics that highlight the importance of both predictors, such as presidential elections and type of elections (party-centered or candidate-centered). She shows that party images play a substantial role in determining vote choice, but candidate-centered voting is also significant. The strength of both party and leader effects are only weakly linked to context factors. Chapter 7 examines whether citizens hold government's accountable for their performance when they vote, and whether contextual factors influence this relationship. Timothy Hellwig finds that performance assessments matter more for the vote when responsibility is concentrated and when the party system provides for a wide range of policy choice. This second part closes with André Blais and Thomas Gschwend's study of partisan defections in voting and the ways in which contextual features – electoral rules and the nature of the electoral supply – affect defection rates. They find that formal electoral rules do not affect defection directly. Instead, the only significant contextual effect is a conditional one in which desertion occurs almost exclusively at the expense of weak parties in the most disproportional systems.

The third part of our volume considers the potential consequences of context for political representation and sources of democratic legitimacy. G. Bingham Powell addresses the question of democratic representation at the macro-level by investigating the fit between citizens' Left-Right positions and those of their government. He finds a high level of correspondence in the CSES nations, and other evidence suggests that voter–government agreement has increased in recent decades. Moreover, he shows that the Left–Right polarization of the party system increases the distance between the overall public and their elected governments. Finally, Christopher Anderson analyzes the impact of voter–party congruence at the level of individual voters. It shows that countries' macro-level electoral institutions and supply of choices together with individuals' predispositions interactively shape citizens' sense that their views are represented. While voters who locate themselves in the political middle generally have more negative views about democratic representation, the gap in feelings of representation between voters located in the middle of the political spectrum and away from it is larger in systems that provide polarized partisan choices and smaller in countries with proportional electoral systems.

Returning to the two "identical" individuals we described at the outset of this chapter, this volume's findings demonstrate that institutional context does matter in fundamental ways for the choices they make and, by implication, for the working of the electoral process in contemporary democracies. Many of the basic causal processes of electoral behavior are common across the diverse nations in the CSES. For instance, political skills and resources are strong predictors of participation in virtually all nations, and Left–Right orientations and evaluations of governmental performance are also strong predictors of vote choice across nations. At the same time, contextual factors shape the strength of these relationships and the efficacy of representative government in several ways. The characteristics of political choices and the structure of the institutional context affect whether and how individuals participate in elections. They shape the partisan choices voters make. And, the context for choice shapes the representativeness of government and popular images of the party system and electoral process.

Our empirical findings have important implications for students of political behavior, but also for political scientists interested in political institutions. They reveal that formal institutions – such as electoral systems or constitutional provision for allocating power – matter less for the choices voters make than the political contexts that flow from formal institutions as well as the dynamic interactions of political elites and voters. In particular, the nature and polarization of partisan offerings, rather than the mechanical properties of institutions or the count of parties, is often what voters perceive and respond to most clearly at the ballot box. This suggests that understanding the connection between institutions and political behavior requires a clear focus on the connecting tissue of political supply that flows from institutions and that voters react to.

These findings also have important implications for the quality of representative democracy, if the goal is to allow people to express their political preferences through elections. The findings also show which aspects of the political context are relevant for these processes, and the results often conflict with current assumptions in the literature on political institutions. Thus, rather than tinkering only with the formal rules, institutional designers of the electoral process should consider how to strengthen democratic representation and accountability through the diversity of the choices they produce.

Notes

1. Collecting contextual data on a large number of sampling points is somewhat difficult. However, a larger problem is that typical area-probability samples do not produce random, representative samples at the level of primary sampling units. So even if contextual data for a small geographic area (a zip code or a city) were available, it would not be linked to a representative public opinion sample for that area.
2. We do not mean that there is no subnational variation or that differences across subnational units are inconsequential, only that electoral rules and other institutional structures are generally uniform within a nation. Local contextual effects tend to involve other characteristics that are difficult to study in national surveys (see Huckfeldt 2009).
3. There are several important local studies of contextual effects (see the literature reviewed in Huckfeldt 2009). However, the generalizability of findings is often limited because these analyses are based on a smaller geographic area and typically one election. One example of a clustered national survey studying contextual effects is Beck et al. (2004).

4. *The European Voter* project (Thomassen 2005) compared voting patterns across six West European democracies. The European Election Study project described voting in European Parliament elections for the member states of the European Union, which were exclusively West European and a relatively small number of countries until the recent expansions of the European Union (Eijk and Franklin 1996; Brug and Eijk 2007). The Cross National Election Project is based on less than a dozen nations (Gunther, Puhle, and Montero 2007). Moreover, most of the research presented in these books does not focus on contextual effects explicitly.

5. For introductions to the politics of context, see Huckfeldt (1986, 2009) and Anderson (2007*a*).

6. We want to thank the principal investigators of the CSES member research groups for their efforts to collect these data and share with the international research community. The datasets used in this volume are available for free from the project website (www.cses.org).

7. We exclude Belarus, Hong Kong, and Kyrgyzstan because these were not free, fair, and effective elections. In addition, there are two surveys for the 2002 German Bundestagswahl, and we rely on the telephone survey as it is more representative of the population.

8. Other party systems' characteristics are potentially relevant to the number of parties that run in election and their likelihood of winning parliamentary representation. However, factors such as the formula used in calculating the PR distribution of seats or the threshold for sharing in the PR distribution of seats should have a minor influence compared to the two factors discussed above.

9. The volume appendix presents the formula for both the effective number of electoral parties (ENEP) and the effective number of legislative parties (ENLP).

10. This is the weighted mean district magnitude of the Lower House. This variable averages the number of representatives elected by each constituency size.

11. The calculation of the index is described in the volume's appendix. It has a value of 0 when all parties occupy the same position on the Left/Right scale, and 10 when all the parties are split between the two extremes of the scale. The index is comparable to the standard deviation of parties distributed along the dimension. We also examined several alternative measures of party dispersion and diversity, such as weighting or not weighting parties by their vote shares or measuring only the major parties (e.g., Kim and McDonald 2009). The initial polarization index appeared more robust in comparing these variables to various validity checks, and is more comparable to the ENEP measure, which also weights parties by their vote share. Thus, we use the initial index in this volume while recognizing that other aspects of party differentiation are worthy of consideration.

12. The form of the electoral system, majoritarian versus PR, is strongly related to the level of polarization in a party system ($r = .44$), but district magnitude is not significantly correlated with polarization ($r = .11$).

13. This does not mean, of course, that there are other lines of political division that are not captured by the left–right ideological polarization score.

14. The Freedom House treats nations between 1 and 2.5 as free, between 3.0–5.0 as partly free, and between 5.5 and 7.0 as not free. These scores are for the year in which the CSES survey was conducted.

15. The voice and accountability scale runs from 0 at the lowest level to 100 at the highest level.
16. The Freedom House treats nations between 0 and 20 as having a free press, 31–60 as a partly free press, and 61–100 as not free. These scores are for the year in which the CSES survey was conducted.
17. The following are the correlations between these items:

Freedom House	.58			
Voice	.66	.89		
Free press	.65	.89	.91	
Party age	.69	.46	.46	.58
	Years	Free H.	Voice	Press

18. This view of accountability is not uncontested. In fact, the concern over individuals and institutions as the sources as well as cures of democracy's imperfections is central to long-standing debates among political theorists. For a review of this literature in the context of economic performance voting, see Anderson (2007b).
19. These include powers the head of government has over the selection and dismissal of cabinet officers, as well as the executive's powers over policy in the form of setting the agenda and powers to dissolve the legislature and call for votes of confidence.
20. Our definition of a change in government is primarily derived from McDonald and Mendes (2002), with additional data collected by the authors for more recent election and nations not covered in their database. Also see Woldendorp, Keman, and Budge (2000). In a few presidential systems, such as Mexico and the United States, we calculated presidential governments rather than legislative majorities. Since presidential terms are typically fixed, this produces high stability scores compared to more fluid parliamentary systems, even if the parliamentary majority in a presidential system is equally (in)stable.
21. The initial findings were presented at a conference hosted at Cornell University in June 2009. We greatly appreciate the support of The Mario Einaudi Center for International Studies and the Cornell Institute for European Studies (CIES) at Cornell University and the Center for the Study of Democracy (CSD) at the University of California, Irvine for this conference.

Part I

Electoral Participation

2

Electoral Supply and Voter Turnout*

Miki Caul Kittilson and Christopher J. Anderson

Inclusive and vibrant voter participation is integral to the quality of representation in the democratic process. A large body of literature establishes that at the level of individual citizens, factors such as resources, social networks, and attitudes about elections and the political system are strong predictors of whether voters will cast their ballot on Election Day. Because it often focuses on individual countries and elections, this research places the onus for participation on citizens themselves – how they come to afford the cost of voting – but less emphasis on how the political context can facilitate or hamper participation. At the macro- (or cross-national) level, a variety of studies focus on how political context, and electoral institutions specifically, come to impose costs on citizens when deciding whether to vote. However, such studies are typically unable to elucidate the individual-level underpinnings of the vote or place the effects that individual-level factors have in the broader electoral and institutional context.

Drawing on the cross-national Comparative Study of Electoral Systems (CSES) data set, this chapter combines macro- and micro-level explanations of voter turnout by examining the confluence of individual-level characteristics such as resources and political attitudes alongside choices offered by the party system context in shaping voter participation across a set of democracies. We utilize statistical techniques appropriate for two-level data to combine individual and contextual levels of analyses into a single comprehensive model of voter participation. We argue and our findings show that party system polarization systematically affects voter engagement, but that these effects of the macro-political context are contingent: greater Left–Right polarization in the electoral supply conditions the effects of political beliefs (external efficacy) on voter participation. Importantly, the effects of party systems are not direct, and they do not impact citizens in an even-handed manner. Instead, citizens who already feel efficacious about their vote are more likely to vote if they live in countries where parties present more polarized policy profiles. Conversely, citizen who do not feel efficacious about their participation in the first place are substantially less likely to vote when political parties are located further apart ideologically.

We proceed as follows: we begin by reviewing the literature on voter turnout and describe the ways in which individual- and country-level differences may combine to shape patterns of participation. We then examine one particular aspect of the micro-macro-connection in voter turnout by examining how the supply of electoral choices and attitudes toward the political system affect voter turnout.

Existing explanations for voter participation

Because we cannot hope to do justice to the voluminous literature on voter participation here (for a review, see Blais 2006), we focus our discussion on the micro- (individual-level) and macro- (cross-national) foundations of voter engagement. Traditionally, research on voter turnout has proceeded along these two parallel tracks that rarely intersect. On one track, researchers have sought to establish what it is about individuals that makes some more likely to vote than others; on the other track, researchers have examined on why turnout is higher in some countries than others. Both approaches have commonly focused on the cost of voting and the ways in which individuals and institutions afford and lower them (Perea 2002).

Micro-foundations of turnout

Part of the parallel nature of the literature on voter turnout has to do with research design. Studies of individual voter behavior have traditionally been conducted within the context of one nation and one election where (national) electoral institutions and political context apply to everyone and are thus held constant. Such micro-level studies of voter participation are commonly motivated by questions of political equality, under the presumption that unequal turnout equals unequal representation. The most prominent explanations for what creates unequal participation at the level of individuals center on the unequal distribution of resources and orientations toward the political system, including elections (Powell 1986).[1]

Among these factors, the role of resources as an explanation for voter turnout has long been dominant, in part because differences in resources – especially material ones – are an easy shorthand for economic inequality in society and therefore the ways in which patterns of participation may favor one economic stratum over another. For example, Verba and Nie's seminal study (1972) of participation in the United States highlights the importance of education, income, and occupation for the propensity to participate in politics. While the empirical relationship between social status and voting participation holds strong, the causal mechanisms behind this relationship have proved more elusive. Verba, Schlozman, and Brady (1995) offer a convincing explanation: individuals' resources (time, money, and civic skills) help them to bear the costs of participation. Education is a key indicator of political skills and access to information, as well as a proxy for cognitive ability critical for processing political information (Dalton 2008a). Verba, Schlozman, and Brady find that formal education is, all things equal, related to political knowledge, interest, and sophistication, suggesting that "information costs might be lower for those of higher socio-economic status" (Verba, Schlozman, and Brady 1995: 287). A recent comparison of twenty-two European countries suggests that education is the most consistent cross-national influence on voter participation, and by extension a common source of inequality (Gallego 2007).[2]

Causally speaking, resources and other characteristics of individuals are expected to influence the decision to vote by shaping the calculus of the voting decision.[3] That is, resources do not "act," but they shape what people think; and attitudes, in turn, are the most proximate predictor of political action. Thus, aside from affecting the immediate and narrow cost–benefit calculus of the vote, researchers have long noted the importance of political orientations, broadly conceived, for shaping turnout. In particular, a sense of civic duty and other attitudes about the political system are powerful determinants of the vote and have helped to explain the so-called paradox of voting (Riker and Ordeshook 1968; Blais 2000).

Below, we focus on feelings of efficacy, which electoral researchers recognize as playing an important role for shaping the decision to vote. Political efficacy refers to "the feeling that individual political action does have, or can have, an impact upon the political process... the feeling that political and social change is possible, and that the individual citizen can play a part in bringing about this change" (Campbell, Gurin, and Miller 1954: 187). Existing research distinguishes between internal and external efficacy and defines the former as an individual's sense that he or she can personally affect the political process and the latter as beliefs about the responsiveness of the political system to the electorate (Lane 1959; Balch 1974; Miller and Listhaug 1990; Anderson et al. 2005: 42). While the connection between internal efficacy and participation perhaps skirts tautology, external efficacy is useful for our purposes because it measures citizens' sense that their participation matters to the political process – that elections lead to responsiveness to citizen demands, for example – and thus helps to overcome real or imagined hurdles to political engagement at the ballot box. Thus, citizens who have faith in elections and the political system are significantly more likely to vote than individuals with more cynical beliefs (Rosenstone and Hansen 1993; Leighley 1995).

Macro-foundations of turnout

By concentrating on resources, a great deal of the micro-level research has focused on how individuals come to afford the costs of voting (of time, knowledge, and so on). This mirrors the theoretical emphasis in cross-national aggregate studies of voter turnout. Thus, rather than focusing on the benefits of voting, which may derive from the perceived policy positions of candidates or parties, or from the intrinsic rewards of participating in the democratic process, past research explains cross-national variation in voter turnout primarily with the help of electoral institutions and how these shape the costs of casting a ballot. Speaking very generally, where the rules reduce the amount of time and effort required to cast a ballot, more citizens are likely to show up at the polls (Powell 1980, 1986; Jackman 1987; Jackman and Miller 1995). Several studies along these lines found that such features as automatic registration or weekend and holiday voting can lift some of the burdens of voting, while compulsory voting diminishes resource-based differences in the ability to afford the cost of voting.

Aside from facilitating the mechanics of casting a ballot, electoral systems are expected to influence aggregate patterns of turnout by shaping the structure of options voters have at the ballot box. Specifically, proportional representation (PR) electoral systems have long been assumed to increase turnout (Powell 1986; Jackman 1987; Banducci and Karp 2009). Yet, mapping out the theoretical foundations for this relationship has proved challenging (Blais 2006). To begin, we know that proportionality shapes the contours of the party system by encouraging a greater number of parties. While the connection between proportionality and a more numerous party system is well established, it is not altogether clear exactly how the number of parties may translate into a decision to vote.

On one hand, a greater variety of choices on the ballot may make it more likely that individual voters find a party that fits their policy preferences (Blais 2000, 2006). Moreover, because of the higher likelihood that one's vote affects a party's share of seats in parliament, proportionality may translate into a greater sense of efficacy that casting a ballot matters, which, in turn, may have a positive impact on turnout (Brockington 2004). A number of aggregate analyses, including Powell's classic study (1986), have corroborated this intuition, and a recent analysis of multilevel data from the CSES finds that greater proportionality indeed encourages turnout (Nevitte et al. 2009; see also Franklin 2002, 2004; Norris 2002; Gray and Caul 2000; Jackman 1987).[4]

On the other hand, Jackman (1987) argues that a greater number of parties increase the odds of coalition government (see also Kedar 2005). As a result, voters in multiparty systems may perceive their vote as disconnected from government formation and in fact make the election a lottery over alternative outcomes. And this, in turn, may alienate voters, rendering them less likely to cast a ballot. The bulk of the cross-national evidence supports the latter expectation, finding that a greater number of parties depresses voter turnout (Jackman 1987; Blais and Dobrzynska 1998; Gray and Caul 2000). Yet, in a recent analysis of CSES data, a greater number of parties – typically associated with PR systems – do not appear related to higher levels of voter participation (Nevitte et al. 2009).

Clearly, these expectations and findings are at odds, and some of them may be due to differences in methodology or the appropriateness of particular estimation techniques. Yet, understanding the mechanisms behind the relationship between proportionality, party systems, and turnout is essential to improving our understanding of how turnout varies across countries (Blais 2006). One key factor may be information costs in multiparty contexts. Indeed, Jusko and Shively (2005) find that the influence of the number of parties varies for low and high information voters. Recently, Karp and Banducci (2007, 2008) have also unpacked the relationship between proportionality and political involvement through a series of cross-national, multilevel analyses of turnout in old and new democracies. By utilizing individual-level survey data nested within contextual variables describing the number of parties in a country, they provide insight into how the number of parties can simultaneously hamper and facilitate turnout. Specifically, they find that voters have stronger party attachments in proportional systems, and these heighten political efficacy and voter participation. At the same time, they find evidence that coalition governments reduce political efficacy and therefore diminish incentives to turn out.

In addition to the number of parties, both Aarts and Wessels (2005) and Brockington (2009) highlight the role of the ideological spread of parties across the party system. While the former do not uncover clear links between the party system and participation, the latter finds a connection. Specifically, Brockington (2009) reports that a wider spread of parties along the ideological continuum is associated with a higher probability of turning out, thus suggesting that the relationship between macro-political context and the vote is direct (see also Dalton 2008*b*).

Below, we follow the general approaches taken by both Karp and Banducci and Brockington to consider how the nature of the macro-level electoral supply affects the choices individual voters make on Election Day. Taken together, these studies suggest that the number of parties and the ideological differences between them are important contextual influences, and that orientations at the individual level play an important role as well. At the same time, several questions remain: First, do ideological polarization and the number of parties have separable effects on turnout? Second, do they affect turnout directly or indirectly? Third, do the contours of the party system impact those who hold positive and negative attitudes toward the political process differently? And, fourth, can we confirm existing results once we model turnout simultaneously at two levels of analysis?

Connecting electoral supply, external efficacy, and turnout

Past research establishes clearly that faith in the political system – external efficacy – is one of the strongest and most proximate predictors of voter participation. We extend this insight by arguing that external efficacy also is key to understanding the link between macro-political context and the decision to cast a ballot on Election Day. We focus on electoral supply as the macro-political factor at play, and examine the following three dimensions of the political supply side: how many choices are presented to the electorate, how distinct these choices are, and how predictable those choices are. Simply put, our argument is that the electoral supply can make the election process worth investing in for potential voters, or it may make the vote even less attractive than they found it in the first place.

The mechanism by which political context exerts it influence is through the meaning of ballot choices. Where elections and parties present distinct choices and a higher probability of meaningful change via the electoral process, the act of voting becomes more important. Further, we introduce the idea that the electoral supply may both shape citizens' efficacy toward elections and interact with efficacy in important ways. In addition to the effects that the number and ideological spread of parties plays in shaping turnout, we argue that it is important to also consider the predictability of choices because stable choices lead to more discernable choices. The more stable the party system, the easier it is for citizens to make sense of their choice set. After all, the benefits of voting for one's preferred party, in part, stem from the assumption that parties offer clear distinctions to voters, and more specifically differentiated and therefore identifiable benefits to groups of voters, and that parties are around to provide them once in office.

How then, can we connect electoral supply, individual differences, and turnout? We build on cross-national work on turnout by arguing for the importance of combining micro- and macro-levels of analysis (Powell 1986; see also Franklin 2004). But in a departure from this work, we do not aim to pit individual and contextual variables against each other in a race to predict turnout. Instead, we hypothesize that the relationship between external efficacy and electoral supply on the one hand, and voter participation on the other, can take two different forms, as outlined in Figure 2.1 (see Anderson 2007b, 2009; and Chapter 1).

The figure presents two different theoretical models of indirect and contingent effects of macro-political context (electoral supply) on individual behavior (the decision to vote). The indirect effects work as a chain of causal factors, moving from the broader forces toward the more proximate influences on the decision to vote. In the first step, the electoral supply influences citizens' external efficacy toward electoral democracy. For example, with more choices (a greater number of parties) and greater Left–Right polarization among those choices, there may be a greater likelihood that there is a party that matches up with the preferences of any given voter. Great stability among these choices means that citizens can more easily identify them.

In such a causal chain, party system polarization and stability are expected to encourage citizens to feel that their vote makes a difference, and that the policy consequences will differ, depending on which party or candidate wins the election. In this way, discernible and predictable choices among parties encourage positive orientations toward the system and process of electoral representation. In turn, these orientations are among the most proximate and important determinants of political participation.

The second theoretical model depicted in Figure 2.1 maps a contingent relationship between electoral supply, external efficacy, and turnout. A contingent effect implies that the electoral supply moderates the effect of a voter's political efficacy – that is, whether they have faith in the political and electoral system – on participation. More choices may boost participation especially or

(a) Indirect effects:

(b) Contingent effects:

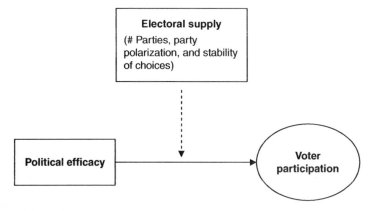

Figure 2.1 Models of electoral supply, individual orientations, and mobilization and voter participation

only among those who feel efficacious about the election process. Similarly, a more polarized electoral supply may especially heighten voter participation among those with high levels of efficacy. Because efficacious citizens already have a vested interest in the election outcome, clear choices raise the stakes for one team winning over another, increasing the potential regret if one abstains from voting. In contrast, even committed citizens may abstain in countries where the choices are less stark. The consequences of a rival candidate or party assuming leadership are obfuscated, dampening citizens' motivation to vote.

For those who do not feel efficacious, having more choices may be overwhelming and de-motivating and this, in turn, may dampen their propensity to vote. This would imply that a more numerous, stable, or polarized electoral supply should diminish turnout among inefficacious voters. Alternatively, the nature of the electoral supply may simply be beside the point for such individuals. Citizens who lack faith in the system may simply not be sensitive to variation in the macro-political context because they have given up on the game before the contest has even begun.

Finally, stability of the electoral supply may moderate the relationship between efficacy and voter participation. In the context of an entrenched, static choice set, the propensity to abstain from voting may be exacerbated for those who do not feel efficacious. By contrast, dynamism in the party system may introduce an incentive for politically inefficacious citizens to take a chance on voting for a new party.

Data and analysis

We utilize data from module II of the CSES project to examine these hypotheses. Specifically, for our purposes, we use data from thirty-one countries.[5] The pooled micro-level survey data are complemented by national-level contextual variables. In statistical terms, this means that individual respondents are nested within the different countries in our data set.

Our analysis requires three critical variables: turnout, efficacy, and electoral supply (see chapter appendix on question wording). Turnout is a standard question asking respondents to report whether they voted in the most recent election. To tap feelings of external political efficacy, we rely on questions asking respondents whether it makes a difference who is in power and whether one's vote makes a difference (cf. Brockington 2009). These measures are correlated, but they are not synonymous; while one is directed at the perceptions of the consequences of one's vote, the other gauges perceptions of the consequences of elections (their bivariate correlation is .41, indicating that they explain roughly 20% of each other's variation). Aarts and Thomassen (2008: 9) refer to the item measuring whether people believe that who one votes for makes a difference as a "perception of accountability."

Table 2.1 Gaps in voter participation, by country

Country	Election year	Aggregate turnout	Vote makes a difference	Who in power makes a difference
Albania	2005	49.2	8	10
Australia	2004	94.3	1	9
Brazil	2002	68.7	3	4
Bulgaria	2001	66.6	8	27
Canada	2004	60.9	17	11
Czech Republic	2002	57.9	30	61
Denmark	2001	87.1	4	4
Finland	2003	66.7	36	22
France	2002	60.3	18	15
Germany	2002	79.1	12	8
Hungary	2002	73.5	49	35
Iceland	2003	87.7	9	9
Ireland	2002	62.6	8	8
Israel	2003	67.8	26	10
Italy	2006	83.6	22	19
S. Korea	2004	60.0	15	20
Mexico	2003	41.7	9	9
New Zealand	2002	77.0	32	17
Norway	2001	75.5	4	15
Philippines	2004	45.3	15	−3
Poland	2001	46.2	40	21
Portugal	2005	64.3	4	4
Romania	2004	58.5	19	12
Slovenia	2004	60.6	20	3
Spain	2004	75.7	32	27
Sweden	2002	80.1	25	12
Switzerland	2003	45.2	46	25
Taiwan	2004	54.0	7	6
United Kingdom	2005	61.5	36	30
United States	2004	68.7	17	27

Note: Entries represent the difference in voter turnout percentages among those who do and do not feel their vote or who is in power makes a difference, by country.

Source: Comparative Study of Electoral Systems, module II. Voter turnout for parliamentary elections collected from IDEA represents the proportion of the total number of votes cast/registered voters.

To measure the party system context, we utilize three separate measures of the electoral supply (see volume Appendix for variable documentation). First, the effective number of parties measures the number of choices available to potential voters. Second, the degree of polarization in the party system taps into the distinctiveness of choices. Third, the age of the party system represents the stability of choices for the electorate. The older the party system, the longer potential voters have been exposed to the set of party choices, and their relative positions to one another.

Political efficacy and voter participation across democracies

Table 2.1 presents the CSES countries in our study, and the aggregate level of voter turnout for each country. Clearly, countries with compulsory voting laws such as Australia register higher rates of turnout than others. But beyond cross-national variation in levels of aggregate turnout, the forces that motivate citizens to cast their ballots vary substantially across countries as well. The final two columns of Table 2.1 display gaps in voter turnout among those who do and do not feel efficacious for the set of countries in this study. Those who believe that their vote or that who is in power makes a difference turn out in higher percentages. For example, in Switzerland the gap between those who strongly believe that their vote makes a difference and those who do not registers 46 percentage points. The United Kingdom, Finland, and New Zealand boast similar gaps of 36, 36, and 32 percentage points.

DECOMPOSING THE VARIANCE IN TURNOUT

Our indirect and contingent effects models imply that both a citizen's characteristics and the political context will shape voter participation. To gauge how much variance in voter participation is due to differences across individuals and differences across countries (contexts), we estimated a multilevel regression model that decomposes the variance in reported turnout for both levels of analysis. Table 2.2, which presents the variance components for voter participation, shows that over 80 percent of the variance (83.3%) is due to differences

Table 2.2 Variance decomposition in electoral participation

Parameter	Estimate
Fixed effects	
Constant	.863***
	(.012)
Variance components	
Country-level	.067***
	(.009)
Individual-level	.334**
	(.001)
−2 log likelihood	−8988.89

Note: Entries are maximum likelihood estimates; standard errors in parentheses.
*p < .05; **p < .01; ***p < .001.
Source: Comparative Study of Electoral Systems, module II.

across individuals, while macro-level variables account for less than 20 percent of the variance (16.7%). Both are statistically significant, suggesting that we need both to understand voter participation fully. While individual-level factors hold most of the explanatory power, political context plays a role as well. This is of substantive importance because it helps put macro-level effects in relief: these preliminary results suggest that macro-level variables play a relatively smaller role in shaping turnout, and this means that any one potential macro-level factor – of a wide variety that have been suggested in the literature – has only a relatively small chance at "coming out on top" in a statistical sense, relative to others and relative to individual-level differences in voter characteristics, when it comes to understanding why people vote.

THE EFFECTS OF ELECTORAL SUPPLY ON ORIENTATIONS AND VOTER PARTICIPATION

The relationships between political orientations and turnout may be influenced by a host of other factors identified by prior research, and certainly multivariate analyses are essential to improving our understanding of how these factors work together. One challenge in mixing aggregate and survey data comes in violating standard assumptions of OLS models – namely, that errors terms are independent. Respondents within nations are likely to have much in common with fellow citizens relative to those living elsewhere. Because the CSES allows one to merge data from both the individual and national levels, standard regression methods can create a number of statistical problems, perhaps most importantly that they typically underestimate the standard errors of the national-level variables (see Steenbergen and Jones 2002). To control for clustering error terms, researchers have adopted multilevel estimation models from education and sociological research (Bryk and Raudenbusch 1992; Kedar and Shively 2005) to study a wide range of political science topics. We utilize the xtlogit and xtmixed functions in STATA to estimate multilevel models, which allows for random intercepts across the panels (countries).

The indirect effects hypothesis displayed in Figure 2.1a posits that the contours of the party system shape individuals' orientations toward the system and processes of electoral democracy. Table 2.3 presents the results of the multilevel models estimating the direct effects of country-level contextual variables and the micro-level respondent characteristics on voter participation. This baseline model tests the first basic hypothesis, namely, that the number, differentiation, and stability of party choices directly influence an individual's propensity to vote, regardless of attitudes about electoral democracy. As the results show, party system characteristics do not appear to directly influence voter participation. In fact, none of the coefficients are close to statistical significance; even the variable measuring compulsory voting – while positive – fails to achieve

Table 2.3 Direct effects of electoral supply on voter turnout

	Turnout
Individual-level	
Vote makes a difference	.199**
	(.016)
Who in power makes a difference	.109**
	(.016)
Gender	.030
	(.038)
Age	.393**
	(.020)
Education	.184**
	(.028)
Income	.115**
	(.016)
Left/Right orientation	.006
	(.008)
Union member	.273**
	(.053)
Close to party	.747**
	(.041)
Contacted	.427**
	(.053)
Country-level	
Number of parties (ENEP)	−.040
	(.074)
Party system polarization	−.006
	(.122)
Age of party system	−.000
	(.004)
Freedom House	−.193
	(.250)
Compulsory voting	.424
	(.335)
Legislative election	−.437
	(1.14)
Constant	−.601
	(1.74)

Note: Coefficients from multilevel random intercept models, followed by standard errors in parentheses.

*p < .05, **p < .01. Respondent *n* = 26,033; Country *n* = 31.

Source: Comparative Study of Electoral Systems, module II.

conventional levels of significance (possibly because of the limited number of compulsory systems).

As hypothesized, at the individual level, individuals who feel their vote makes a difference and who feel that who is in power makes a difference are likely voters. In addition, as anticipated by prior research, several control variables are statistically significant. Age, education level, income, being a union member and feeling attached to a political party, and having been contacted by a party or candidate before the election are all strong predictors of voting.

While we can thus find no evidence to suggest that the effects of the party system are direct, they still may be indirect or contingent. In Table 2.4 we therefore step back in the causal chain to explain variation in the measures of efficacy, which the previous model showed to be critically important to explaining turnout. Specifically, we examine the influence of the electoral supply by regressing feelings of efficacy on the number of parties, the degree of party system polarization, and the age of the party system (stability).

Overall, the results indicate that the effects of the electoral supply on political orientations are weak, suggesting that the effects of macro-political context on turnout are neither direct nor indirect. In model 1, which focuses on the question of whether a respondent believes voting makes a difference, the results show clearly that the indicators of electoral supply have minimal impact on external efficacy. This stands in slight contrast to the results we obtain for model 2, which focuses on people's beliefs that who is in power makes a difference. We find that greater party system polarization is a statistically significant determinant of faith in the political system. Thus, there is some limited evidence that citizens are more likely to believe that it makes a difference who is in power if they live in a country where the electoral supply is more polarized.

Although our focus is primarily on the macro-level electoral supply variables, the established individual-level influences are statistically significant across the models: education, income, ideological orientation, party attachment, union membership, and having been contacted are important influences on political efficacy. This is important in the context of this study because it indicates that education, income, and social attachments have an indirect effect on turnout by boosting supportive attitudes, which, in turn, enhance turnout.

While the results so far suggest that the impact of macro-political context is not direct and that there is not much of an indirect effect, the question remains whether the effects of the electoral supply are possibly contingent. More specifically, is the effect of efficacy on turnout conditioned by the electoral supply? We investigate this possibility in Table 2.5 by adding several interaction variables to the baseline model of voter participation. The first model includes an interaction term between whether a respondent believes their vote makes a difference and each of the three electoral supply variables. In a parallel fashion, the second model includes three interactions between the electoral supply measures and whether a respondent believes who is in power makes a difference.

Table 2.4 Indirect effects of electoral supply on external efficacy

	Model 1	Model 2
	Voting makes a difference	Who is in power makes a difference
Individual-level		
Gender	.039**	.025
	(.014)	(.015)
Age	.001	−.001
	(.008)	(.008)
Education	.060**	.073**
	(.010)	(.010)
Income	.016*	.020**
	(.006)	(.006)
Left/Right orientation	.016**	.011**
	(.003)	(.003)
Union member	.085**	.019
	(.020)	(.020)
Close to party	.320**	.374**
	(.015)	(.016)
Contacted	.109**	.099**
	(.018)	(.019)
Country-level		
Number of parties (ENEP)	.033	.040
	(.028)	(.029)
Party system polarization	.038	.094*
	(.047)	(.048)
Age of party system	.000	−.001
	(.002)	(.002)
Freedom House	.105	.114
	(.096)	(.100)
Compulsory voting	−.120	−.111
	(.128)	(.132)
Legislative election	1.03	−.100
	(.443)	(.458)
Constant	1.93*	2.72**
	(.672)	(.695)

Note: Coefficients from multilevel random intercept models, followed by standard errors in parentheses.

*p < .05, **p < .01. Respondent n = 26,425; Country n = 31.

Source: Comparative Study of Electoral Systems, module II.

Table 2.5 Contingent effects of supply and efficacy on participation

	Model 1	Model 2
Individual-level		
Vote makes a difference	−.079	–
	(.060)	
Who in power makes a difference	–	−.089
		(.060)
Gender	.027	.033
	(.039)	(.038)
Age	.394**	.389**
	(.020)	(.020)
Education	.193**	.191**
	(.028)	(.028)
Income	.116	.115**
	(.016)	(.015)
Left/Right orientation	.008	.008
	(.008)	(.007)
Union member	.275**	.285**
	(.053)	(.053)
Close to party	.772**	.774**
	(.041)	(.042)
Contacted	.432**	.441**
	(.053)	(.053)
Country-level		
Number of parties (ENEP)	−.011	−.047
	(.081)	(.081)
Party system polarization	−.313*	−.223
	(.129)	(.130)
Age of party system	−.006	−.003
	(.004)	(.004)
Freedom House	−.175	−.166
	(.249)	(.253)
Compulsory Voting	.409	.389
	(.334)	(.339)
Legislative Election	−.410	−.194
	(1.14)	(1.15)
Micro–macro interactions		
ENEP * Vote makes a difference	−.004	–
	(.009)	
Polarization * Vote makes a difference	.087**	–
	(.012)	
Party age * Vote makes a difference	.001**	–
	(.000)	

(continued)

Table 2.5 Continued

	Model 1	Model 2
ENEP * Who in power makes a difference	–	.006
		(.009)
Polarization * Who in power makes a difference	–	.063**
		(.012)
Party age * Who in power makes a difference	–	.001*
		(.000)
Constant	.635	.427
	(1.74)	(1.76)

Note: Coefficients from multilevel random intercept logit models, followed by standard errors in parentheses.
*p < .05, **p < .01. Respondent n = 26,200; Country n = 31.

For the first model, both the interactions between polarization in electoral supply and the perception that voting makes a difference as well as the interaction between party system stability and the sense that voting makes a difference are statistically significant, and the coefficients are in the expected direction. A very similar pattern consistent with the first result emerges for the second model: the interactions between the individual-level perception that who is in power makes a difference and macro-level electoral supply in the form of polarization and stability are both statistically significant and in the expected direction.

If the effects of electoral supply on turnout are indeed mostly contingent, as our results suggest, how much do they matter? To answer this question, we next look at the joint effects of polarization and efficacy on voter participation. Figure 2.2 graphically illustrates the effect of party system polarization on voter participation among citizens who feel their vote makes a difference and those who do not. The top line shows that, for those who believe their vote makes a difference, greater polarization among parties slightly increases the likelihood of voting. In stark contrast, the bottom line in the graph indicates that those who do not feel efficacious are also sensitive to a polarized electoral supply, but in the opposite direction: increased polarization substantially decreases their likelihood of casting a ballot. Thus, a more ideologically polarized political supply turns efficacious voters out, and keeps voters who lack faith in the system home.

Figure 2.3 presents the substantive results for party system stability on voter participation among citizens with different levels of faith that their vote makes a difference. While the interaction term was statistically significant, the substantive results reveal little differentiation. In contrast to polarization, the effects for party system stability differ little across these two sets of respondents.

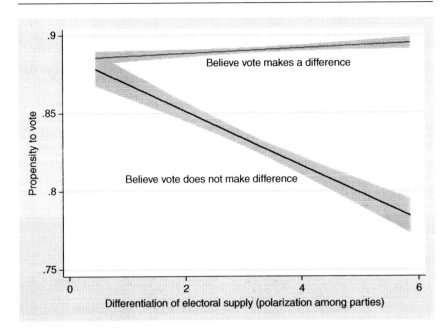

Figure 2.2 Effects of polarization and faith in voting on voter participation

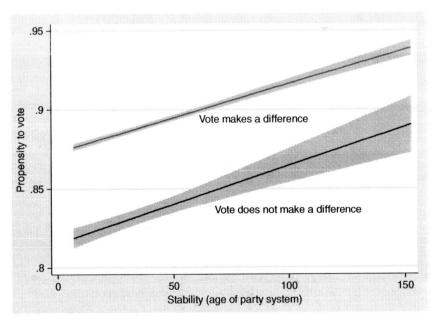

Figure 2.3 Effects of party system stability and faith in voting on voter participation

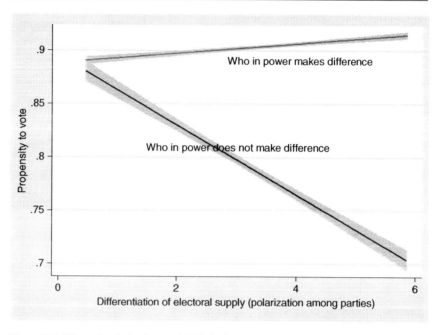

Figure 2.4 Effect of polarization and belief who is in power makes a difference in voter participation

Certainly those who do not believe their vote makes a difference are less likely to cast a ballot. However, for both those who have and those who lack faith in the ballot the influence of party system stability on turnout is positive.

The relationships for our alternative measure of external efficacy mirror those of the first. Figure 2.4 displays the effects of party system polarization on voter participation among those who believe that who is in power makes a difference and those who do not. As in the case of our other measure of external efficacy, we observe a positive slope for the former and a negative slope for the latter. In short, living in a country with a more polarized electoral supply makes those who feel efficacious more likely to cast their ballot on Election Day. In contrast, greater Left–Right polarization among parties substantially depresses the likelihood that citizens who do not feel efficacious will vote.

Finally, the relationship between party system stability and voter participation is depicted in Figure 2.5. The positive slope of the line for those who believe who is in power makes a difference parallels the positive slope of the line for those who do not. As before, although inefficacious citizens are less likely to vote, the effects of party system stability are similar for the inefficacious and efficacious citizens alike.

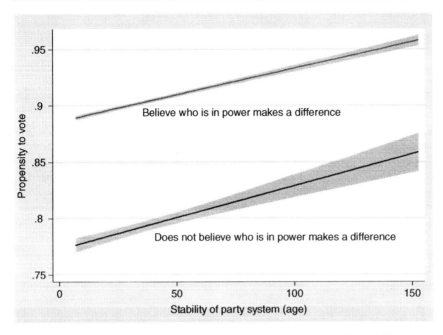

Figure 2.5 Effect of party system stability and belief who is in power makes a difference in voter participation

Conclusions

Over thirty years ago, Verba, Nie, and Kim set out to "explain differences across nations in the degree to which the participant population is representative of the population as a whole" (Verba, Nie, and Kim 1978: 19). Focusing on a limited number of countries, they argued that "the way in which institutional constraints on participation modify individual propensities to be politically active takes us a long way in explaining differences across nations in the representativeness of the participant population" (Verba, Nie, and Kim, 1978: 19).

While we depart from Verba et al. in our focus on the supply of electoral choices rather than examining the effects of countries' formal institutional characteristics, we (and our results) could not agree more. The structure of political conflict, as reflected in a country's party system, can provide a fundamental pull to participate in elections. This structure varies across countries and it has consequences. In particular, we find that the electoral supply plays a contingent role in influencing voter participation. Where the party system connects citizens to a more ideologically polarized set of choices, the efficacious are more likely to vote, while the inefficacious are less likely to vote. Put another way, the gap in turnout between efficacious and inefficacious citizens is largest in countries with more polarized party systems. In contrast, the simple number of parties competing in the election has little impact on turnout. Thus, the content of the electoral supply simultaneously strengthens and weakens the relationship between political orientations and the propensity to vote; while a more distinct set of choices propels efficacious citizens to the ballot box, it diminishes the odds that the less efficacious make the effort to turn out.

While these contingent effects are strong, the direct effects of the contours of the party system on voter participation are less so. And the electoral supply exerts little impact on respondents' feelings of efficacy, though we document that a more polarized choice set enhances people's sense that who is in power matters. This is broadly consistent with the findings by Anderson (Chapter 10) on system support attitudes. In this sense, the effects of the electoral supply are not truly compositional: the party system does not appear to strongly encourage feelings of efficacy in the first place. Rather, individual-level attributes play the most important role in shaping a citizen's sense of efficacy in the democratic process. Our findings support those of many previous studies: those with higher socioeconomic status and more social connections are more likely to feel efficacious.

In short, the context of elections does more than guide potential voters on who to vote for – it also shapes the likelihood that they will even cast a ballot in the first place. In this way, the structure of the party system can pull voters into the democratic process, or deflate whatever limited civic ambitions they had in the first place. We speculate that the strongly negative effect of polarization on turnout among citizens with low levels of external efficacy may reflect a deep cynicism among such voters to whom a polarized party system communicates conflict and division among self-interested political actors.

Regardless of the precise source of this effect, our results indicate that, among the indicators of the electoral supply, and in addition to the more commonly studied number of choices available to voters, the polarization among parties appears integral and most central to determining turnout. Among those who already feel isolated from parties and find the political system unresponsive, a wider gap among parties can further dampen their propensity to vote. As Sidney Verba reminds us, representativeness in citizen participation is "at the heart of political equality" (Verba 2003: 663). Recalling the image of diverging lines on a graph, a growing chasm between those who feel efficacious and engaged on the one hand, and those who feel ambivalent and disengaged on the other, may be troubling for the quality of the democratic process. Further, the lower levels of education, income, and social connectedness among voters who lack faith in politics portend important social and economic divisions in the political process. But as our results suggest, the nature of the electoral supply can narrow or widen that divide.

Appendix

Description of variables

Variable name	CSESII variable number	Coding
Gender	B2002 Gender	1 = male, 2 = female
Age	B2001 Age	Continuous variable
Education	B2003 Education	1 = lower, 2 = middle, 3 = upper
Left/Right ideological orientation	B3045 In politics people sometimes talk of Left and Right. Where would you place yourself on a scale from 0 to 10, where 0 means the Left and 10 means the Right?	Left/Right self placement, 0 = left, 10 = right
Union member	B2005 Union membership of respondent.	1 = union member, 0 = not member
Close to party	B3028 Do you usually think of yourself as close to any particular political party? [Some nations used different wording]	Are you close to a political party?, 0 = no, 1 = yes
Voting participation	B3004 Whether or not respondent cast a ballot (regardless of whether the ballot was valid).	Did respondent cast ballot? 0 = no, 1 = yes
Vote makes a difference	B3014 "Some people say that no matter who people vote for, it won't make any difference to what happens. Others say that who people vote for can make a difference to what happens. Using the scale on this card (where ONE means that voting won't make a difference to what happens and FIVE means that voting can make a difference), where would you place yourself?"	Who people vote for makes a difference; 0 = disagree, 1 = agree
Who in power makes a difference	B3013 "Some people say it makes a difference who is in power. Others say that it doesn't make a difference who is in power. Using the scale on this card (where ONE means that it makes a difference who is in power and FIVE means that it doesn't make a difference who is in power), where would you place yourself?"	Who is in power can make a difference; 0 = disagree, 1 = agree.

Notes

* We are grateful to Russell Dalton and the participants in the Citizens, Context, and Choice project for their valuable feedback on our chapter. Previous versions of this paper were presented at the 2009 American Political Science Association meeting and the Comparative Study of Electoral Systems conference at the University of Toronto on September 6, 2009. We would like to thank the panelists and participants, and especially André Blais and John Curtice, for their helpful suggestions.

1. We bracket the question of mobilization through social networks and by political parties and candidates (cf. Huckfeldt and Sprague 1987; Rosenstone and Hansen 1993; Leighley 1996). For a discussion of mobilization and campaign activities, see Chapter 3.

2. Age is another important individual-level difference that has long been considered a consistent predictor of voting participation, as young people are less likely to vote than their older counterparts. This finding holds in the United States (Miller and Shanks 1996) and across established democracies (Blais 2000; Franklin 2002; Norris 2002; Wattenberg 2006). Age is expected to work in two ways: first, it elevates levels of political knowledge acquired through a lifetime of experience with politics. This knowledge is a key resource for navigating the electoral landscape and can be called upon to understand the contours of an election campaign, thus reducing the amount of resources involved in the process of casting a ballot. In addition, age is a proxy for social connectedness and a sense of identification with one's community. Young people tend to be more mobile, increasing the amount of time and energy needed to make sense of the local issues and candidates, and to find the polling place on Election Day. Thus, age (as well as marriage, children, owning a home, etc.) is associated with more stable and extensive social ties and community roots and identification.

3. They also affect the calculus of other political actors to target particular groups of individuals for mobilization. As research suggests, individuals with desirable character-istics are more likely to be contacted during an election campaign. These include, in particular, those who are more likely to come out and vote (e.g., individuals with resources and attachments to parties), making the investment in mobilization on the part of parties and candidates more worthwhile (Karp, Banducci, and Bowler 2008; and Chapter 3).

4. A number of other macro-level factors have been examined. Among these, highly competitive elections, as measured by the margin of victory and how close the largest party is to achieving a majority, have consistently and prominently been found to increase voter turnout as well.

5. Some nations were excluded because the necessary predictors were not available. See Table 2.1 for a list of the nations included.

3

The Influence of Party and Electoral Systems on Campaign Engagement

Jeffrey A. Karp and Susan A. Banducci

It is widely known that political activity can vary substantially from one context to another. Some elections are characterized by a great deal of party activity and voter interest. Parties sometimes invest heavily in elections, and citizens sometimes appear to be deeply engaged in the political process. In other cases, voter apathy and disinterest characterizes an election. Often researchers turn to the unique characteristics of an election or party campaign strategies to explain variations in activity between elections. Studies of persisting participation patterns attempt to explain these results based on the individual characteristics of citizens. For example, age and education normally play an important role in determining whether citizens participate in the political process. Other explanations focus on political attitudes, such as an individual's belief that she will influence the outcome (a miscalculation in most cases) and the expressive benefits derived from participation, or values (e.g., social solidarity, civic duty, or post-materialism). These studies, however, rarely consider political context as a potential factor.

Studies that do take context into account often examine what institutional mechanisms are associated with higher voter turnout (see Chapter 2). Electoral systems are often a prominent explanatory factor (for a few examples, see Bowler, Lanoue, and Savoie 1994; Karp and Banducci 2008; Banducci and Karp 2009; Blais 2000). Proportional Representation (PR) electoral systems presumably motivate more citizens to vote because fewer votes are wasted. In addition, PR systems often produce more parties, which may lead to greater choice. In a more crowded electoral space with more parties competing for votes, parties may expend greater efforts in mobilizing voters. Of course these efforts are constrained by organizational resources (i.e., funds and membership) as well as the social connectedness of the party (Janda 1993). In addition, parties may be sensitive to the electoral rules and invest greater resources when the stakes are higher (i.e., under winner-take-all rules).

Despite the extensive research on electoral system and institutional features on voter turnout, we still know very little about how the political context motivates citizens to become engaged in the campaign process beyond voting. This chapter considers how political and institutional features encourage or inhibit more active forms of political participation.

By political context we mean features of the electoral system and the party system that specifically affect factors such as electoral supply and the ballot structure. For example, political parties can facilitate participation by encouraging citizens to become engaged in the political process and a greater supply of parties may also increase the chances that citizens come into contact with political parties. A greater diversity of choices, in contrast, might dampen campaign activity amongst those who do not have strong preferences because the choices may be overwhelming. Citizens may also be more encouraged to participate in systems where candidates feature prominently in elections.

In the following section we examine the ways in which the institutional context and micro-level variables might influence campaign activity. In particular we focus on the direct effects of the political context on campaign activity, the indirect effects, and then contingent effects. We examine these relationships with the objective of understanding how political context can influence political activity in three steps. In the following section, we first discuss the theoretical expectations for how the institutional context can affect political engagement. We then evaluate how party mobilization and the strength of partisan attachments – two intervening mechanisms associated with party activity – link the institutional context to campaign activity. Third, we examine how the political context can condition the relationship between our intervening variables and political activity. The results show that context matters, either directly or indirectly through party activity and strength of partisan preferences. Like other chapters in this volume, the effects of political context are also conditional. These conditional relationships are consistent with previous findings linking political institutions, attitudes, and behavior (see, e.g., Karp and Banducci 2008).

The institutional context

Although past research on contextual influences on political participation has focused on voter turnout, there are reasons to expect similar contextual factors to influence campaign activity (see Powell 1986). Many of the causal factors associated with voting turnout may carry over to broader participation in election campaigns.

One common contextual explanation for voter apathy focuses on the number of choices confronting voters. Plurality or "first-past-the-post" systems often reduce the number of choices to a few viable alternatives. In these systems, voters often face a simple choice between just two parties or candidates. If citizens are not satisfied with either alternative they may be less likely to become engaged in the process. In addition, in these types of systems, one party or candidate may often have a significant advantage. In such cases, where electoral choice is limited, voters may realize that the outcome is a foregone conclusion and thus will have less of an incentive to participate. Where there are more parties, voters may be more likely to be satisfied that one of the alternatives represents their interests. Furthermore these effects may be indirect as political parties may also have less of an incentive to campaign or mobilize voters when there is little competition (we discuss this below). Extensive research has demonstrated the relationship between the number of parties in the electorate and voting turnout (see Geys 2006) and the same general logic can apply to the direct effect of context on citizen's general activity in campaigns.

Another explanation for campaign activity and engagement focuses on the nature of choice. When there are greater differences between parties, electoral choices may be more meaningful and citizens may have a stronger incentive to be engaged in the process. Dalton (2008b) has argued that party polarization or the differentiation of choices offered to voters is another important variable linking electoral institutions to political behavior (also Aarts and Wessels 2005). While a larger number of parties implies greater competition, it does not necessarily mean that citizens are confronted by more meaningful and distinct choices. Thus party polarization reflects the diversity of choice rather than the simple number of choices. As Kittilson and Anderson find in Chapter 2, the variety of choices facing voters can alter the decision whether to vote. They find that when parties take on more ideologically distinct positions, citizens are offered clearer choices that can, at least indirectly, influence the decision of whether or not to vote. Classic pluralist accounts of democracy suggest that where differences of opinion exist, people and/or groups will be mobilized to represent the different views at stake (Dahl 1989).

While there are reasons to expect that party system polarization may lead citizens to be more engaged in the process, it is equally plausible that citizens may refrain from engaging in political debates when parties (and voters) are far apart from one another. Psychological models suggest that individuals are conflict-averse, and will avoid conflict wherever possible, whether by acquiescence or by silence (Noelle-Neumann 1993; Ulbig and Funk 1999). People may feel that there is no point engaging in political discussions with individuals with whom they disagree. Put another way, when there is broader agreement perceived in the opinion climate, citizens may be more engaged than when there is division.

A third factor that may affect participation is whether voters decide between candidates or parties. In candidate-based systems, voters can choose the person representing them, which provides a greater link between the voter and the choice of the representative. When choosing between or ranking candidates, the more personalized contests in these elections may engage voters more in campaign activity than the party appeals common in party list systems. Therefore, we might expect citizens to be more engaged in the process when they face a choice between candidates rather than parties. Evidence suggests that in candidate-based systems, citizens are more likely to report having been contacted by a party or candidate (Karp, Banducci, and Bowler 2008). Party mobilization efforts not only increase voter turnout (Rosenstone and Hansen 1993) but they can also influence campaign activity (Karp and Banducci 2007). We discuss this indirect relationship between candidate-based systems and campaign activity below.

When more is at stake in an election, citizens should be more active. When elections are more salient to citizens we know that they are more likely to vote (Franklin 2004) and we would also expect citizens to be more likely to become active in the campaign. However, there is some evidence that direct presidential elections can depress turnout (Norris 2004; Tavits 2009). But these studies are based on aggregate data and do not examine how presidential elections might influence campaign activity. When parliamentary elections are run concurrently with presidential elections, due to added salience, we would expect a boost in campaign activity.

Finally, we expect that a country's stage of democratic development influences levels of political activity. Faced with mounting economic hardships and slow governmental progress in addressing them, citizens in newer democracies may disengage from the political process out of feelings of dissatisfaction (Kostadinova 2003; Rose and Munro 2003). Furthermore, political activity, if characterized as a learned activity, may take time to develop and simply it is too soon in new democracies to expect high levels of campaign activity. The research demonstrating that voting is habit forming (Plutzer 2002) suggests that it may take time in newly established democracies to form a habit of campaign activity. Therefore, established democracies may be associated with greater campaign activity than emerging democracies.

Party preferences and mobilization as intervening variables

Aside from directly influencing campaign activity, the contextual factors discussed above are also likely to affect how voters relate to political parties and how parties interact with voters. Below we discuss how these two intervening variables – party mobilization and strength of partisan preferences – may vary by context and how they are understood to affect political behavior. To help the discussion of these complex relationships, we summarize our understanding of the links between contextual- and individual-level factors and campaign activity in Figure 3.1.

As discussed above, the electoral supply can affect how voters relate to political parties. When there are more parties, voters may find it easier to identify a party that speaks to them. Early studies of party competition assume that electoral rules can affect both the number of parties and where they locate themselves on the ideological continuum (see Downs 1957). Under plurality rules where preferences are normally distributed, Downs predicted that parties will have a disincentive to carve out a distinct ideological position and will instead position themselves closer to the median voter. In a polarized system, the larger number of parties should increase the diversity of the options from which voters can choose and result in greater involvement. Moreover, voters are more likely to have strong attachments to parties that cater more specifically to their needs as opposed to catch-all parties that appeal to the median voter. In addition to expecting polarized systems to produce stronger preferences for a party, we would expect people to develop a stronger dislike for other parties (e.g., those on the other side of the ideological spectrum).

The evidence suggests that features such as polarization are linked to stronger preferences and these stronger preferences increase campaign activity. For example, in systems that foster extreme parties, voters develop stronger attachments (Bowler, Lanoue, and Savoie 1994). Past research shows that voters with strong party attachments are more likely to be interested in politics and more likely to vote (Campbell et al. 1960; Verba, Nie, and Kim 1978). Having a policy connection to a party can also increase the likelihood of participating (see for example Blais 2000). One theory stresses the expressive benefits one derives from engagement; in other words, citizens derive satisfaction from expressing a preference for a political party or candidate. We might think strong partisans would derive greater satisfaction from expressing preferences through participating in politics.[1]

The other contextual variables of interest – democratic development and candidate-based electoral systems – may also affect the strength of partisan attachments. In terms of democratization, older democracies generally have institutionalized party systems, which encourages stable parties and trust in parties (Mainwaring 1998). Under such conditions, we expect stronger partisan attachments. Candidate-based systems likely work against strong partisan attachments because candidates generally make personal rather than partisan appeals (Samuels 1999). Similarly, we might consider presidential elections as the ultimate candidate-centered election and apply the same argument that when the election under consideration is a presidential one then we would expect partisan preferences to be weaker. Therefore, we expect that these contextual factors would affect campaign activity by influencing the strength of partisan preferences. These indirect effects of the contextual variables on party preference strength are illustrated in Figure 3.1 with the arrow connecting the series of macro-level factors to the strength of preference. The intervening relationship of the macro-level factors on campaign activity through strength of preference is further illustrated by the arrow connecting strength of preference to campaign activity.

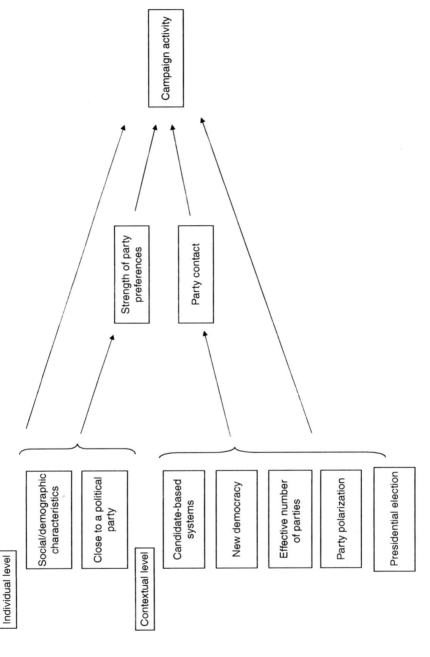

Figure 3.1 Electoral supply and campaign activity: direct and intervening relationships

Party mobilization serves as another intervening variable linking contextual factors to the probability of citizens engaging in campaign activity. Party contacting efforts are a reflection of the strategic considerations of the political parties; these efforts therefore will be influenced by features of the electoral and party system. For example, parties may contact more voters where the extra votes are more likely to produce extra seats (Cox 1999). Under winner-take-all rules, parties may have a much stronger incentive to mobilize voters because the stakes are much greater. In proportional systems that allow for a greater differentiation of parties, the incentives for engaging in mobilization may be low.

In polarized systems, parties may believe that they do not need to invest resources to mobilize voters who are already predisposed to participate. In addition, they may find it more difficult to convert other voters to their cause. As a consequence, parties may be less likely to mobilize voters in polarized systems. In new democracies, where partisan attachments are likely to be weak (see Dalton and Weldon 2007) or parties and elections may lack legitimacy, parties may need to exert greater efforts in getting potential supporters to the polls. Therefore, in new democracies there are reasons to expect greater levels of contact (Karp and Banducci 2007). These contextual effects are summarized in Figure 3.1 by the arrow connecting the group of indicators we use for electoral supply, ballot structure, and state of democratic development.

Past research has also demonstrated that candidate-based systems increase the likelihood of a respondent reporting having been contacted by a party (Karp, Banducci, and Bowler 2008). Candidates have a stronger incentive to campaign when they are directly selected by voters. While parties may adopt a national focus to their campaigns, local candidates may still think it worthwhile to canvass support for their own campaign rather than remain complacent and rely on the national party to campaign on their behalf (see Karp, Banducci, and Bowler 2003: 212).

In contacting potential voters, parties will devote resources either to mobilize those who are already predisposed to support them or to expand their base by converting other citizens to support their cause. Of the two strategies, party mobilization to increase turnout or generate campaign activity is generally a more effective strategy since converting voters generally requires more resources. It is far easier to get citizens to the polls or active in the campaign when they are inclined to support a party, rather than converting voters who prefer another party. Moreover, parties generally target their own supporters in order to ensure that they show up at the polls. Cross-national studies thus demonstrate that party contacting does increase the probability of citizens voting. Other studies demonstrate that party mobilization can extend beyond voting to other campaign activities (Huckfeldt and Sprague 1992; Pattie et al. 2003). This relationship is illustrated in Figure 3.1 with the arrow connecting party contacting and campaign activity.

Conditional relationships

We have identified how macro and micro factors may influence political engagement. We now place the effects of the individual-level variables in relation to contextual-level effects. There are reasons to understand that electoral supply, for example, conditions how the strength of partisan preferences influences campaign activity. These conditional effects are seen in addition to the main effects of both the contextual- and individual-level variables. These effects are illustrated in Figure 3.2. We proceed by discussing how the nature and extent of electoral supply, the type of ballot (candidate-based systems), democratic development, and the saliency of the election might condition the effects of strength of partisan preferences and party contacting.

First, the influence of party contacting on campaign activity may be conditioned by the different incentives that face political parties. For example, when the party system is highly fragmented and/or ideologically polarized, mobilization efforts will be less costly as voters will be more committed to a particular party that more closely matches preferences.[2] Therefore, under these conditions, the effectiveness of being contacted by a party may lead to an increased impact on campaign activity. In terms of a conditional relationship, the coefficient representing the influence of party contact on campaign activity may be higher when the electoral supply is greater both in the amount and diversity of choice.

Second, polarization effects should be conditioned by the strength of partisan preferences. As explained above, polarization affects citizens' willingness to engage in activities that are intended to change the minds of others. People may want to avoid conflict or may feel an inhibition about expressing opinions that might be contrary to those around them when party positions are polarized and commitments are stronger. However, this negative effect of polarization may only apply to those with weak preferences who are more susceptible to

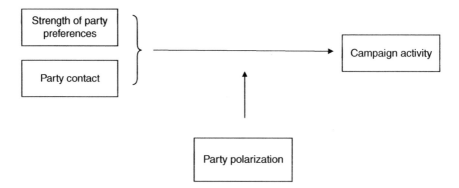

Figure 3.2 Electoral supply and campaign activity: conditional effects

influence. In other words, those with strong preferences will be more likely to act on those preferences even when party positions are polarized. Figure 3.2 provides a summary of this and other possible conditional relationships.

Data and methods

The Comparative Study of Electoral Systems (CSES) provides a valuable source for testing these hypotheses. To date, the CSES makes available over forty election studies conducted between 2001 and 2004 through the project website.[3] We use thirty-six elections in our analysis spanning a variety of electoral systems and both established and new democracies. Our contextual indicators of electoral supply, as in the other chapters in this volume, include the effective number of parties and party system polarization (see volume Appendix for details). In addition, we include a variable distinguishing between established and new democracies, and the candidate versus party-centeredness of the electoral system (Farrell and McAllister 2006).

Our ultimate dependent variable is citizen participation in election campaigns. We measure this activity using two questions administered in module II of the CSES. The first asks whether a respondent reports trying to persuade others to vote for a particular party or candidate. The second, representing more active political engagement, asks whether a respondent attended a meeting or put up a poster or showed their support for a campaign in some other way (see chapter Appendix for details).

Table 3.1 summarizes campaign activity across thirty-six countries. On average, about 20 percent reported trying to persuade others how to vote while about 11 percent reported having campaigned in some way. Canada and the United States have unusually high levels of activity, with over 40 percent reporting having tried to persuade others to vote and more than a third reporting campaigning in some way. In comparison, less than 10 percent reported trying to persuade others in Slovenia, Bulgaria, Poland, Spain, Italy, and Mexico. Where persuasion is high, as in Canada and the United States, campaign activity is also generally high.[4] There are, however, some exceptions. In Albania, the Philippines, and Mexico, the proportion reporting campaign activity is relatively high compared to the proportion reporting persuasion.

We measure the strength of party preference with a series of questions that ask respondents to rate political parties on a scale ranging from strongly like (10) to strongly dislike (0) (see chapter Appendix). In multiparty systems, respondents may have rated as many as six political parties. The strength of party preference is calculated by taking the highest value a respondent gives to any party (see Karp and Banducci 2008). In some cases, where respondents rated parties equally, the measure represents attitudes about more than one party. Two-thirds of the respondents rated parties between 5.6 and 9.6 with a mean

Table 3.1 Campaign activities by country

	Persuade	Campaign
Canada (2004)	65.0	34.6
United States (2004)	44.1	29.9
Brazil (2002)	36.6	18.0
Albania (2005)	33.6	45.5
Australia (2004)	32.4	16.3
Israel (2003)	32.3	10.9
France (2002)	29.0	6.9
Peru (2006)	28.9	16.2
Germany (2002)	27.7	6.5
Czech Republic (2002)	26.0	20.4
Russia (2004)	25.8	3.4
Philippines (2004)	25.7	27.2
Chile (2005)	22.6	12.0
Denmark (2001)	22.1	7.8
Iceland (2003)	22.1	16.2
New Zealand (2002)	21.5	5.8
Korea (2004)	20.6	4.2
Taiwan (2001)	19.7	11.9
Britain (2005)	18.2	13.1
Norway (2001)	17.5	6.6
Romania (2004)	17.2	7.5
Hungary (2002)	15.4	9.8
Switzerland (2003)	15.0	6.0
Ireland (2002)	13.2	8.2
Sweden (2002)	12.9	3.1
Finland (2003)	12.6	11.4
Netherlands (2002)	12.4	7.0
Japan (2004)	12.2	4.4
Belgium (2003)	12.0	7.2
Portugal (2002)	10.3	7.3
Italy (2006)	9.1	8.4
Mexico (2003)	8.9	12.8
Spain (2004)	7.7	5.7
Poland (2001)	7.2	4.1
Bulgaria (2001)	7.0	6.5
Slovenia (2004)	6.6	5.3

Source: Comparative Study of Electoral Systems (CSES), module II.

score of 7.6. To measure party mobilization we rely on the question: "During the last campaign did a candidate or anyone from a political party contact you to persuade you to vote for them?"[5] On average, 24 percent reported having been contacted by a political party in the campaign. The proportion is highest in Ireland, where 55 percent said they had been contacted by a political party or candidate during the campaign and is lowest in Spain, Poland, and Russia where 6 percent or less reported any contact.

The contextual variables are measured as follows. As discussed in other chapters of this volume, polarization is a measure of the ideological dispersion of parties along the Left/Right scale. The effective number of parties is based on the measure devised by Laakso and Taagepera (1979) which takes into account both the number and the size of parties within any given nation. New democracies are classified as those with less than twenty years of continuous democratic rule. Most of the elections in the sample are legislative elections; only three of the thirty-six elections are only presidential while six held presidential elections concurrent with legislative elections. Candidate-based systems are those where voters have the opportunity to select candidates running either in single-member districts or appearing on open lists (see volume Appendix for details).

Contextual effects

To begin our analyses we consider how the political context affects both the strength of party preferences and party contacting. Table 3.2 summarizes the relationships between the contextual, the intervening variables, and the two measures of campaign activity. Several strong relationships are apparent. As expected, more polarized systems generally have stronger preferences for parties. Polarization, however, is negatively related to contact. In addition, greater polarization is associated with lower levels of campaign activity. While contact, strength of preferences, and persuasion appears to be lower in new democracies, campaign activity appears to be higher. Candidate-based systems

Table 3.2 Contextual correlates of campaign activity

Variable	Contact	Strength	Persuade	Campaign
Strength of preference	—	—	0.12	0.12
Contact	—	0.02	0.17	0.21
Effective number of parties	−0.17	−0.11	−0.12	−0.32
Polarization	−0.53	0.42	−0.33	−0.23
New democracy	−0.06	−0.02	−0.10	0.13
Candidate-based system	0.32	−0.08	0.26	0.23
Presidential election	0.13	−0.18	0.35	0.19

Note: Table entries are aggregate level correlations among variables ($N = 36$).

Source: Comparative Study of Electoral Systems (CSES), module II.

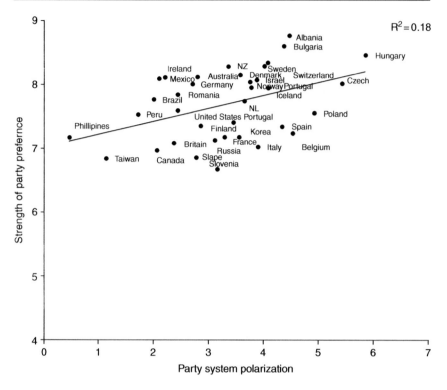

Figure 3.3 Party system polarization and strength of preference

Source: Comparative Study of Electoral Systems (CSES), module II.

have higher levels of contact, stronger party preferences, and greater levels of campaign activity. Presidential elections appear to be associated with higher contact and greater campaign activity but party preferences are weaker.

To illustrate these effects, Figures 3.3 and 3.4 show how strength of preferences and party contact varies with polarization across the countries. The most polarized systems include Hungary, the Czech Republic, and Poland whereas the Philippines and Taiwan are the least polarized. The most polarized countries had some of the highest average levels of preference strength. For example, Hungary has the highest level of polarization in the party system, and it has one of the highest strength of preferences (8.5 on the 10-point scale). In contrast, Taiwan has one of the lowest polarization rating and the average rating of preferred parties is almost two points below that of Hungary. Figure 3.3 shows that most of the countries are scattered around the regression line with few outliers. The regression line is not steep but there is a clear relationship between polarization and strength of preferences which is consistent with our expectations.

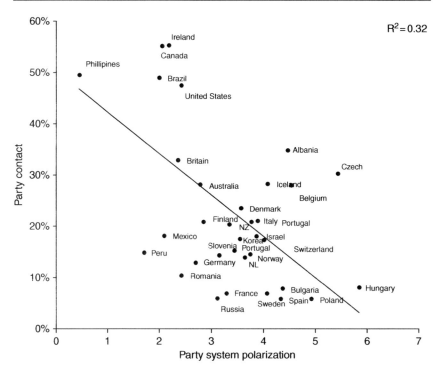

Figure 3.4 Party system polarization and party contact

Figure 3.4 shows the proportion of respondents reporting contact (by a political party) by level of party system polarization across all of the countries in our set. There is a strong negative relationship indicating that parties are reluctant to engage in broad based canvassing efforts in polarized systems. In comparison, party contact is very high in low polarization systems such as the Philippines, Ireland, Canada, Brazil, and the United States. Given the evidence in Figure 3.3, as we expected, parties find it difficult to convert voters who have strong attachments to other parties. This suggests that parties in polarized systems may follow a more targeted strategy by contacting only their own supporters in order to mobilize them to participate. (Unfortunately, follow-up questions asking which party contacted the respondent are not included in the CSES module.) On the one hand, countries such as Ireland, Canada, and the United States (all candidate-based systems) exhibit high levels of party contact but relatively low levels of polarization. On the other hand, several proportional systems with high party polarization such as Hungary and Poland have low levels of party contacting. As these figures illustrate relationships at the country level only, our next step is to examine whether at the individual level and using party polarization as a contextual variable the same relationships hold.

Multivariate analysis

Our further empirical analysis proceeds in two steps. First, we examine the intervening impact of party mobilization efforts and the strength of partisan preferences on campaign activity. We consider how contextual effects and individual-level variables influence both the strength of party preference and party contact. Second, we examine the impact of context, party contacting, and party strength (and other individual-level factors) on campaign activity.

The model includes the five contextual variables that we discussed above: the effective number of parties, party system polarization, established/new democracy, the candidate-party orientation of the electoral system, and whether the election is only legislative, presidential, or both.[6] The model also includes several standard individual-level predictors of campaign activity that are routinely identified in the participation literature, such as age, gender, and education. We expect these variables to also affect both our intervening variables and campaign participation. In addition, we control for whether an individual is close to a political party which is analogous to the traditional measure of party identification (Barnes et al. 1988). Not only would we expect partisans to have stronger preferences but we also expect parties to be more likely to contact partisans than nonpartisans if their strategy is to mobilize voters. In contrast, if parties adopt a conversion strategy they should be contacting nonpartisans who are more easily persuaded to change their minds.

We use an OLS model where strength of preference is the dependent variable and a logit model for party contact, since the variable is dichotomous. To account for the multilevel structure of the data, we use an analysis method that allows for random intercepts across countries.[7] To ease the interpretation of the logit coefficients in the model, we also report the expected probability of being contacted for each of the independent variables holding all other variables constant at their mean values.

The results are displayed in Table 3.3. As expected, partisans are more likely to have stronger partisan preferences than nonpartisans. In addition, women have somewhat stronger preferences than men. One might expect education to facilitate stronger preferences, but the sign is negative and significant indicating that those with higher education have weaker preferences. As we have seen above, polarization remains a positive influence while presidential elections are associated with weaker preferences.

As expected, partisans are more likely to be contacted which suggests that parties are adopting a mobilization strategy rather than a conversion strategy when they contact voters. The sign for education is also positive, indicating that those with higher education are more likely to be contacted. Moreover, the effects are considerable; a person with the highest level of education is about twice as likely to be contacted as a person with the lowest level of education. Together these results indicate that parties are more likely to contact those who are already predisposed to vote.

The contextual variables continue to exert a strong influence. Citizens in the most polarized systems have little chance of being contacted; while in the least polarized systems, the probability of being contacted is .41. The coefficient for the effective number of parties fails to reach significance indicating that electoral differentiation is more important than the quantity of choices. Candidate-based systems are associated with greater contact but the difference between party-based systems is only modest and fails to reach statistical significance. People have little chance of being contacted in elections where the president is the only contested race. In comparison, citizens have a probability of being contacted of .20 in legislative contests. Most likely this reflects the fact that citizens are more likely to come into contact with parties or candidates competing within local geographic districts than candidates competing on a national basis.

Table 3.3 Model predicting intervening variables for campaign activity

	OLS model			Logit model				
	Strength of preference			Contact				
	Coef.		Std. error	Coef.		Std. error	Min.	Max.
Individual-level								
Close to a party	1.31	***	(0.02)	0.39	***	(0.02)	0.16	0.22
Age (in decades)	0.01	**	(0.01)	0.00		(0.01)	0.18	0.19
Female	0.14	***	(0.02)	−0.13	***	(0.02)	0.19	0.17
Education	−0.06	***	(0.00)	0.09	***	(0.01)	0.13	0.24
Country-level								
Party system polarization	0.21	**	(0.08)	−0.37	**	(0.18)	0.41	0.07
Candidate-based system	0.09		(0.21)	0.49		(0.48)	0.13	0.20
Effective number of parties (ENEP)	−0.05		(0.05)	0.07		(0.11)	0.14	0.15
New democracy	−0.05		(0.18)	0.20		(0.40)	0.17	0.20
Presidential election	−0.45		(0.32)	−1.55	**	(0.73)	0.20	0.05
Presidential election (concurrent)	0.28		(0.29)	0.08		(0.65)	0.18	0.19
Constant	6.75	***	(0.41)	−1.61	*	(0.93)		
Number of countries	36			36				
Number of individuals	52,705			56,064				

Note: Coefficients from multilevel random intercept models.

*** $p < .01$; ** $p < .05$; * $p < .10$

Source: Comparative Study of Electoral Systems (CSES), module II.

These findings lead us to conclude that parties have little incentive to contact voters in systems where there is a high degree of differentiation between the parties. In such cases they may see little point in trying to convert voters from opposing parties that offer substantially different policy proposals from their own. Parties may also be more confident that they can rely on their distinct platforms to mobilize voters. In contrast, where parties compete in a more narrow issue space, a more competitive environment may exist where voters may be more easily courted. This would give parties a stronger incentive to reach out to their potential supporters in order to mobilize them. In addition, these might be systems with highly personalistic politics, which leads to patron/client networking. The Philippines is a classic example along with Ireland, which combines small districts in terms of population with the single transferable vote (STV), creating strong incentives for extensive door-to-door canvassing (Marsh et al. 2008). Single-member district elections in the United States and Canada also encourage more personalistic politics and individual contacting.

Explaining campaign activity

Our next step is to examine the cumulative processes leading to campaign activity. This model includes the two intervening variables as predictors of campaign activity along with the contextual- and individual-level variables identified above. In addition, we include two cross-level interactions to examine whether the effects of polarization are conditional on either the strength of preference or party mobilization. As illustrated in Figure 3.2, the effects of polarization may vary depending on party strength and party contact. Those with strong party ties or those who are mobilized in a campaign may be less affected by polarization.

To gauge how much cross-national variance in political participation can be explained by individual and contextual factors, we initially calculated the variance components for an intercept-only model predicting the probability of persuading others and engaging in campaign activity. For the variance components in the model predicting persuading others, the variation at the country level is reduced by 36 percent (from 14 to 9 percentage points) when comparing an intercept only model to the model presented in Table 3.4 with the individual- and contextual-level variables. For campaign activity, the variance is reduced by 46 percent (from 13 to 6 percentage points) after adding the contextual- and individual-level variables to the intercept-only model. Therefore, a significant proportion of the variance in the variables at the country level is accounted for by individual- and contextual-level factors.

The full model results are shown in Table 3.4. We first consider whether there are any direct effects of our contextual variables on campaign activity. Party

Table 3.4 Explaining campaign activity

Predictor	Persuasion				Campaign			
	Coef.		Std. error	Min.	Max.	Coef.		Std. error	Min.	Max.
Individual-level										
Contact	0.69	***	(0.07)	0.15	0.26	0.87	***	(0.08)	0.07	0.14
Strength of preference	0.09	***	(0.02)	0.09	0.21	0.14	***	(0.02)	0.03	0.11
Close to a party	0.75	***	(0.03)	0.13	0.24	1.07	***	(0.03)	0.05	0.13
Age (in decades)	−0.05	***	(0.01)	0.20	0.14	0.04	***	(0.01)	0.07	0.09
Female	−0.29	***	(0.02)	0.20	0.16	−0.26	***	(0.03)	0.09	0.07
Education	0.11	***	(0.01)	0.12	0.24	0.09	***	(0.01)	0.06	0.11
Country-level										
Party system polarization	−0.19	**	(0.10)	0.28	0.11	−0.19	*	(0.11)	0.14	0.05
Candidate-based system	0.41	*	(0.23)	0.13	0.19	0.22		(0.26)	0.07	0.08
Effective number of parties (ENEP)	−0.03		(0.05)	0.20	0.19	−0.07		(0.06)	0.11	0.10
New democracy	−0.38	**	(0.19)	0.20	0.15	0.08		(0.22)	0.08	0.08
Presidential election	0.79	**	(0.35)	0.17	0.30	−0.14		(0.40)	0.08	0.07
Presidential election (concurrent)	0.90	***	(0.31)	0.16	0.31	0.66	*	(0.35)	0.07	0.13
Polarize x strength	0.02	***	(0.01)	0.12	0.27	0.01	**	(0.01)	0.06	0.11
Polarize x contact	0.02		(0.02)	0.17	0.19	0.07	***	(0.02)	0.08	0.11
Constant	−3.06	***	(0.46)			−4.38		(0.53)		
Number of countries	36					36				
Number of individuals	52,388					52,314				

Note: Coefficients from multilevel random intercept models.

*** $p < .01$; ** $p < .05$; * $p < .10$

polarization appears to have a negative effect for both persuasion and campaign activity, indicating that all other things being equal, polarized systems produce less campaign activity. Specifically, in the least polarized system, an individual has a .28 probability of engaging in a persuasive activity compared to a probability of just .11 in the most polarized system. However the positive sign on the interaction term indicates that these negative effects are conditional on partisan strength. As can be seen from Figure 3.5, there are significant differences between respondents who have strong preferences versus those that have weak preferences. Strong identifiers are more likely to presuade others overall but as the positive sign on the coefficient indicates, the negative impact of polarization is attennated for these strong identifiers. Specifically, those who are contacted in the most polarized system have a .12 probability of campaigning while those not contacted have only a .04 probability of campaigning.[8]

Multiparty systems also appear to have a negative impact on campaign activity. This suggests that fewer parties may produce a more competitive electoral environment that mobilizes campaign activity. However, there appears to be no relationship between the number of parties and the likelihood of engaging in persuasion. Citizens in new democracies are also less likely to engage in persuasion than in old democracies. Presidential elections appear to

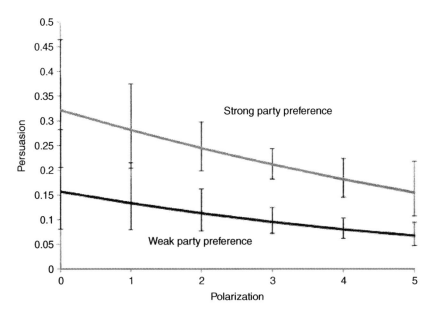

Figure 3.5 Conditional impact of polarization and strength of partisan preferences on probability of persuading others

Source: Comparative Study of Electoral Systems (CSES), module II.

have a substantial positive influence on both persuasion and campaign activity (when run concurrently with legislative elections). Finally, candidate-based systems have a modest positive impact on both forms of engagement.

In terms of the intervening variables, consistent with past research and with the findings on voter participation, party contact and strength of preference have positive impacts on these two types of campaign activity. These effects are substantively large. Party mobilization can substantially increase the likelihood that citizens engage in campaign activity. All other things being equal, citizens who are contacted are twice as likely as those who are not contacted to engage in both forms of campaign activity.[9] The strength of preferences has a similar impact for campaign activity but fails to reach statistical significance in the persuasion model. However, as discussed above, the interaction between polarization and party strength indicate that the effects of party strength are considerable particularly in polarized systems. As expected, education is also positively associated with campaign activity although age appears to have little effect.

Conclusions about engaging the public

This chapter explored the mechanism by which the political context shapes campaign activity. We tested a two-step process by which strength of partisan preferences and party contacting served as intervening variables linking the political context and the likelihood of an individual becoming active in a campaign by either trying to persuade someone to vote a particular way or by participating in a campaign event.

Our main interest has been two-fold: first, how does the political/institutional context influence two intervening characteristics – strength of preferences and party contacting. Second, how does the political context condition the relationship between these two factors and citizens' engagement in the campaign. To provide greater clarity on the role of electoral supply, as in the rest of the volume, we distinguished between the number of choices that citizens face (effective number of parties) and the clarity of those choices (polarization).

Three main points summarize the implications of our findings for both campaign activity and the effects of electoral supply on individual behavior:

1. Similar to the act of voting, campaign activity is influenced by the political context.
2. The distinction between the number and type of partisan choices facing voters is an important difference when explaining campaign activity.
3. In addition to the electoral supply, other features of the political context are important influences on campaign activity.

First, turnout is similar to campaign engagement or at least there are similar influences at work (see Chapter 2). In particular, party contacting efforts explain substantial variation in campaign activity. When contacted by a party, people are more likely to try to persuade others as well as participate in campaign activity. Likewise, polarization depresses the probability of campaign activity although this impact is conditioned by the strength of preferences and party contacting. In addition, despite the differences in activities – persuading others versus showing support for a party or candidate during the campaign – the predictors of each are generally consistent across these two activities with a few exceptions (new democracies specifically).

Second, the distinction between the amount of electoral supply and the clarity of electoral supply is important for understanding the relationship between the political context and political participation. Downs (1957) and others expected more committed partisans when there is greater diversity of ideological positions in the electoral marketplace, but equated diversity with the number of parties. However, by taking into account that the quantity and clarity of choices are conceptually different, we demonstrate that it is the diversity of choices that is more important. This difference is most striking when looking at the impact of polarization on the strength of preferences. Indeed, where there is greater electoral supply citizens do have stronger preferences for parties, but this is due to increased diversity of choices not simply having more parties from which to choose. This suggests that the number of parties performs as a proxy in any understanding of how quantity in the electoral supply influences the strength of attachment to a party. In addition, the ideological diversity of choices is a better mechanism for understanding the dynamic of strong attachments to parties in multiparty systems. Furthermore, while polarization has a small but positive impact on campaign activity by strengthening preferences, the direct effects of polarization are negative reflecting the idea that people are less likely to engage in persuasive activities when other citizens have strongly committed preferences. However, the negative impact of polarization is lessened amongst citizens with the strongest preferences and those that have been contacted by a party.

Finally, this chapter confirms and builds on the other work presented in this volume. The political context matters for individual political behavior. We have uncovered both intervening and conditional effects. In particular, in addition to party polarization, our results indicate that the structure of the ballot influences campaign activity. In many ways, the structure of the ballot, like electoral supply, is an indication of the choices voters have in an election. Where voters are choosing between candidates rather than political parties, both the likelihood of persuading others to vote and campaign participation are higher. This suggests that the choices voters face within the electoral environment are important contributing factors directly contributing to whether citizens actually participate in the electoral process. Of course, we should also keep in mind that candidate-based systems have an indirect impact by producing high levels of party contacting and that this in turn influences participation.

Appendix

Variable name	CSESII variable number	Coding
Gender	B2002 Gender	1 = Female; 0 = Male
Age	B2001 Age	Continuous variable
Education	B2003 Education	1 = None; 2 = Incomplete primary; 3 = Primary completed; 4 = Incomplete secondary; 5 = Secondary completed; 6 = Postsecondary trade/vocational school; 7 = University undergraduate incomplete; 8 = University undergraduate degree; 9 = See notes
Close to party	B3028 Do you usually think of yourself as close to any particular political party? [Some nations used different wording]	1 = Yes; 0 = No
Party contacting	B3003 During the last campaign did a candidate or anyone from a political party contact you to persuade you to vote for them?	1 = Yes; 0 = No
Strength of party preference	B3037a-i Please rate the ___ Party on a scale from 0 to 10, where 0 means you "strongly dislike the ___ Party," and 10 means you "strongly like the ___ Party." Strength of preference is the value of the ranking given to the most preferred party.	0–10, with 10 being strongest preferences.
Persuade others	B3001_1 Here is a list of things some people do during elections. Which if any did you do during the most recent election? Q1a. . . . talked to other people to persuade them to vote for a particular party or candidate?	1 = Yes; 0 = No
Campaign activity	B3002_1 Q1b . . . .showed your support for a particular party or candidate by, for example, attending a meeting, putting up a poster, or in some other way?	1 = Yes; 0 = No

Source: Comparative Study of Electoral Systems (CSES), module II.

Notes

1. Whiteley (1995) similarly argues that those who hold radical ideological beliefs gain greater satisfaction from political protest because they can express deeply held political beliefs alongside like-minded citizens.
2. While researchers have often used the number of parties as a proxy of ideological differentiation, Dalton (2008*b*) suggests that the more appropriate measure is party polarization.

3. See www.cses.org We are using release 3 of the data with some modifications.

4. The cross-national correlation between the two campaign activity measures in Table 3.1 is very high ($r = 71$). However, campaign activity is only weakly related to cross-national levels of voting turnout. If we combine both campaign activity items into a single index, this is essentially unrelated to turnout ($r = .03$). This is a significant finding because it implies that the national characteristics related to turnout may differ from those affecting actual participation in the campaign.

5. Unfortunately, the question does not specify the nature of the contact, whether it was a personal visit, telephone call, or campaign letter. The question asks about contact from a candidate or party; therefore, we are likely to capture campaign contacts in candidate-based and party list systems. However, we will not be able to distinguish who made the actual contact in order to test whether more candidate (vs. party) contacts are made in candidate-based systems or whether parties were contacting their own supporters.

6. New democracies, candidate-based systems, and presidential elections are measured as dichotomous variables taking on a value of 1 and 0.

7. The procedure to estimate the models in STATA is xtmixed (for the OLS model) and xtlogit.

8. In the least polarized system, the probability of campaigning is .23 when contacted and .11 when not contacted holding all other variables constant at their mean values.

9. Another conditional relationship may exist between new democracies and party contact. In new democracies, due to mistrust in parties or a perceived lack of legitimacy, being contacted by a political party will have less of an impact on persuasion and campaign activity than in established democracies. We tested for this but find no significant relationship.

Part II

Electoral Choice

4

The Role of Party Policy Positions in the Operation of Democracy

Robin E. Best and Michael D. McDonald

Long ago E. E. Schattschneider suggested that political scientists more seriously take the proposition that a nation's political party system is the keystone to the successful operation of democracy. His suggestion came in the form of this strong assertion: "parties are not . . . merely the appendages of modern government; they are at the center of it and play a determinative and creative role in it" (Schattschneider 1942, 1). Our purpose is to follow Schatteschneider's suggestion by considering why parties are thought to be central to democracy, by evaluating what sorts of creative roles parties play in the democratic process, and by investigating to what extent parties help to determine the quality of self-governance.

Evidence for or against a party systems' centrality in the democratic process rests on whether it is farfetched to think a citizenry can control public policy without substantial reliance on parties. Otherwise, if it is not farfetched, modern democracy is thinkable without parties and lofty assertions about their roles are much overstated. As for our second consideration, claims about the creative roles played by parties focus attention on whether parties supply vital support in the bridge between voter preferences and government policy. Evidence on this score involves evaluating a set of three conditions: asking whether parties offer manageable, recognizable, and distinct policy choices to voters. The number of parties in a system has to be small enough for the individual party brands to form a manageable choice set for voters; otherwise voters are liable to be left adrift. The choices have to be recognizable in policy terms; otherwise voters cannot make policy choices. Recognizable policy options have to be distinct from one another; otherwise there is no policy choice. Of course, meeting these conditions only establishes preconditions along the road to self-governance. Our third and final consideration is whether electorates use elections to control policy. Evidence for or against citizen control of policy through elections depends on whether voter preferences can find their way across the bridge that parties support. Voters have to use the policy options parties place before them as a basis for making a choice; otherwise the choice of the electorate as a whole is not identifiable as a policy choice.

This is a feasibility study in three steps. Is it feasible to think democracy can operate without parties? Is it feasible to think parties can organize elections so that voters can make policy choices? Is it feasible to think voters actually use elections to make policy choices? The next section establishes the logical predicate for thinking parties are central, more than appendages. It recounts what we have come to understand about the problems facing electoral democracies, and it leads to a conclusion that parties are needed to confront and surmount them. Sections three and four lean heavily on the trove of evidence coming available through the *Comparative Study of Electoral Systems* (CSES). Section three checks on whether the three-pronged conditions could give rise to a realistic possibility of parties connecting public preferences to public policies. Our results indicate that they do, especially in long-established democracies. Section four turns to the question of whether voters actually use what parties put on offer to make an election a policy statement. The evidence shows they do not. Relatively low proportions of voters cast pure policy-based votes. Thus, while party systems with distinct offerings are essential for public control over policy, they are not enough – at least not with respect to any single election. We conclude by summarizing our findings and offering a speculative thought about what else might be needed to bring public policy in line with public preferences.

Problems facing electoral democracy

A long-term strain of political thinking, probably the predominant strain among commentators on democracy, assumes policy choices are supposed to emanate from the interests of the people unadulterated by political institutions. As "should implies could" Schattschneider warned against going down this path.

Predemocratic philosophers...took it for granted that the sovereign will of the people would be translated into governmental action more or less automatically and inevitably just as the owner of a piece of property might be expected to administer it in his own interest....The sovereign elector was expected to produce the most enormous effect in government simply by voting.

The fact [is] that this assumption involves a colossal oversimplification of the democratic process...[It makes] the very natural mistake of underestimating the difficulties arising from the numbers, preoccupation, immobility, and indifference of the people. (Schattschneider 1942, 13–14)

Despite this warning, it came as a surprise when Duncan Black and Kenneth Arrow (Black 1948, 1958; Arrow 1951) made clear the inexorable possibility of incoherent decision making by collective bodies in the absence of institutions, such as the extra-constitutional institutions of political parties. The inexorableness remained surprising, and doubted, at least until William Riker put the theoretical capstone on the point in his review and pronouncement of the "disequilibrium of majority rule" (Riker 1980).

The 1950s and 1960s offered another surprise when *The American Voter* suggested that public opinion on particular issues is ill-formed and that electoral decision making depends in important ways on party identification (Campbell et al. 1960; see also Converse 1964, 2000; Campbell et al. 1966). Qualifications have been needed (e.g., Budge et al. 1976; Fiorina 1981; Page and Shapiro 1992; Caplan 2007), but the principal points have not been overturned.

Upon reflection it is now easy to recognize that democracy's prescribed method of governing is fraught with feasibility problems, three in number and each intertwined with the others. First, elections are needed to solve an efficiency problem of large-group decision making. Second, agenda-setting groups, such as political parties, are needed to give coherence to the exchange of multidimensional information that takes place through elections. Third, familiar agenda setters associated with recognizable policy content, such as political parties, are needed to overcome the disincentive voters have for getting themselves informed about political issues. Or, as Schattschneider made the point, parties are needed to "organize the electorate and channelize the expression of the popular will" (Schattschneider 1942, 14).

The scale problem

The scale of contemporary democracies makes the ballot box the essential democratic institution. The need for the ballot box to solve the scale problem is demonstrated by Bertrand de Jouvenel (Jouvenel 1961). Under a philosophy that calls for equal inclusion of all adult citizens in decision making, the ballot box is the institution that allows all to express themselves efficiently, in a timeframe of a day or two. Looking at the problem from the standpoint of *reductio ad absurdum*, with 200 million eligible voters each given one minute to state her or his position, in sequence so each can hear and appreciate the reasons behind all others' thinking, it would take more than a thousand years of ten-hour-per-day sessions held five days a week to reach the end of the discussions — [(200,000,000/60 minutes)/10 hours per day]/260 days per year = 1282 years. The ballot box cuts the time required by permitting large numbers of people to express their viewpoints simultaneously. For this reason, elections are not to be seen as a venerable way of making decisions but as a necessary compromise that squares the principle of universal adult inclusion with the practical need for an efficient process (Dahl 1998, 105–13).

The dimensionality problem

Using elections to address the efficiency problem creates its own difficulty for how information is to be conveyed in a coherent form. If millions of people go to the ballot box to say what is on their minds without reference to what is at issue, there is no telling what one could make of what the people are saying. This leadership and agenda setting need is a second argument pressed by Jouvenel (1961, 369–70). It has been given a more cogent and familiar formulation by Richard Niemi when he showed that democracy's tendency to produce incoherent results is strongly mitigated by having a small number of options on an agenda (Niemi 1969). Kenneth Shepsle later gave an even more general formulation with his concept of structure induced equilibria (Shepsle 1979; see also Shepsle and Weingast 1981). Put simply, the orderly use of the ballot box toward coherent ends calls for some sort of leadership and agenda-setting person or organization to specify what is at issue.

The knowledge problem

Given the prospects that elections might be only a rough guide to what the people are thinking in policy terms, it cannot be surprising to learn that that mass publics are not well informed. As one example, survey responses to a question about post-2002 U.S.–Iraq war show that as late as 2006 more than 20 percent of self-identified Independent and Republican survey respondents were saying weapons of mass destruction actually had been found (Shapiro and Bloch-Elkon 2008). This has no factual basis, and Iraq is not a one-off situation. Only about one-third of the American electorate know which branch of government has the constitutional authority to declare war; only about 30 percent can name their representative in the House of Representatives; and something close to the same 30 percent is able to identify the two Senators from their state (Delli Carpini and Keeter 1996, 94). And, while political knowledge levels among U.S. respondents are generally below those in other Western nations, the limited data available suggest the United States public is not much of an outlier (Delli Carpini and Keeter 1996, 89–92).

The body of work on the quantity and quality of political knowledge among citizens is a glass that can be viewed as half-full or half-empty, partially due to cross-national and institutional variations in political knowledge (e.g., Kuklinski and Petyon 2007). Nevertheless, when the specific concern is whether citizens are capable of directing public policy, the levels of factual knowledge among mass publics has led some to despair (see e.g., Somin 1998, 2006; Hardin 2009).

The despairing argument goes like this. Under-informed voters have the wherewithal neither to direct government to do something new – they do not have much knowledge of what their government might do next – nor to hold government responsible for its missteps; they do not have much knowledge of what their government has done. Still, the generally low levels of political knowledge are unsurprising if we consider that voters have easy to understand reasons for not trying to be fully informed. The value of an expected policy benefit from voting is between miniscule and nil. And, even if voting is induced through other mechanisms, such as an appeal to civic duty (Riker and Ordeshook 1968) or as an exhibition of trustworthiness (Nelson and Greene 2002), voters still have little reason to keep themselves informed. Thus, despair, among those who have it, gives leave to the under-informed voters and indicts what it considers the pretension of democratic theory that government can be run in the people's interest through elections (Somin 2006; Hardin 2009).

An indictment of democracy on this score is premature, however. It harkens back to the pre-democratic theorists Schatteschneider criticized, back to those who thought about democracy without parties. Factual knowledge is relevant, but so too are shortcuts in the form of long-term preferences that match up with the options on an electorate's agenda. Heuristic devices can allow citizens to make political decisions that are both reasonable and efficient (e.g., Sniderman, Brody, and Tetlock 1991; Mondak 1993; Lau 2003). Citizens may know little but still know enough to make decisions *as if* they were politically informed. Indeed, among the myriad pieces of information with which voters might be armed, the critical piece is the one that that says something important about the available options.

To summarize, the situation appears to be this. As fundamental as the scale problem is, as undeniable as the aggregation problems are, and as indisputable as the low levels of fact-based political information are, an important point is that much of the time in many of the places it has been tried democracy appears to work, by which we mean policies appear in general alignment with public preferences (Powell 1982, 154–200; Erikson, MacKuen, and Stimson 2002, 325–80; Wlezien 2004; Soroka and Wlezien 2004, 2005; McDonald and Budge 2005, 203–26). Therefore, we want to know this. Given that politics and governments are not under close and constant scrutiny of the public, do parties supply what is needed to surmount the problems facing democratic policy making?

Preconditions for popular control through parties

Political parties organize elections and in doing so, if they do so as needed, bring three important elements to the process:

1. Parties concentrate attention on a limited number of policy packages.
2. Parties present policy ideas in packaged forms that are describable along a recognizable single dimension, Left–Right.
3. Parties offer voters a variety of choice options along the Left–Right dimension.

The effects are to limit the number of options to a manageable array; to organize the highly structured, multiple-choice based communication in intelligible form; and to offer a variety of policy choices.

The analyses that follow examine evidence on the existence of these preconditions within thirty-five democracies around the world. The thirty-five countries include those listed in Tables 1.2–1.4, except for Belgium.[1]

Number of options

An appealing intuition holds that the more choices available the more refined and satisfying are the choices made. And, if one's intuition does not suggest as much, analyses by Russell Dalton (2004) and Christopher Anderson (Chapter 10) show that support for a political system is connected in meaningful ways to the number and variety of choices on offer. But, we hasten to add, however true this is within the ranges of choice options of interest to Dalton and Anderson, it almost certainly comes with a limit. For instance, Sheena Iyengar and Mark Lepper report the results of three experiments showing an *overload of choices*, somewhere in the neighborhood of more than a half-dozen, undermines a chooser's motivation and satisfaction (Iyengar and Lepper 2000).

In the electoral realm, parties are the vehicles for focusing choice on a manageable number of options. Figure 4.1 shows a histogram for counts of the effective number of electoral parties, from the calculations reported by Dalton and Anderson (Table 1.2). Just over half the countries, eighteen of thirty-five, have less than four effective electoral parties – a set of numbers clearly within the range suggested as manageable by the Iyengar and Lepper study. Only Brazil and Italy have more than seven effective electoral parties.[2]

Parties alone do not fix the reported count. Voters, choosing within the confines of electoral systems, concentrate their support on a limited number of political parties. For example, while upward of fifty parties appeared on the 2007 UK general election ballot, the effective party count is 3.58. For the most part, British voters ignore all but a handful of parties and concentrate their attention and votes on the three major parties and a few regional ones. The effect, in Britain and elsewhere, is for political discussions, debates, and decisions to take place around a limited number of effective, and in that sense relevant, political parties. Is this concentration of votes a behavioral indicator, present as well in countries other than Britain, that the people are satisfied with a limited number of choices under the circumstances of the electoral rules? We think so.

Citizens, voters, and parties along the Left–Right dimension

A count of options is merely a count of nominal choices. When it comes to policy choice qua parties, two characteristics are needed. First, there has to be some meaningful way to convert parties as nominal choices into parties as policy

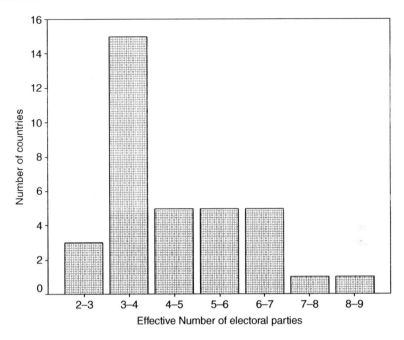

Figure 4.1 Histogram of the effective number of electoral parties

Note: Categories run from 2 up to but not including 3, 3 up to but not including 4, etc.

Source: Table 1.2.

choices. Second, the conversion must be in a form recognizable and relevant to voters. The likely candidate with these characteristics is the abstraction commonly called Left–Right. Left–Right is a matter of convenience, which is a large part of the problem giving rise to objections to analysts constructing a Left–Right measure and imposing it for their own analytical purposes (e.g., Benoit and Laver 2006, 129–48). In the context of electoral politics, however, convenience is precisely the point. No one is imposing it, so its value depends on widespread understanding and usage within each country at a given point in time.

To see where the organization of elections by parties, in association with reliance on Left–Right policy preferences, could lead democracies, we ask four questions:

1. Is Left–Right a convenient policy concept voters understand?
2. Can voters apply Left–Right to parties?
3. Can voters apply it to parties accurately?
4. If voters use Left–Right party locations to make a choice, would the available options permit the electorate as a whole to produce an outcome congruent with the median citizen's Left–Right preference?

If all four questions can be answered in the affirmative, electorates can use elections to control policy – assuming parties in parliament and government act in accord with their Left–Right positions.

CITIZENS AND THE LEFT–RIGHT DIMENSION

CSES surveys ask respondents to place themselves on a zero-to-ten Left–Right dimension. In more than half of our thirty-five countries over 90 percent did so. The precise percentages are reported in the first column of Table 4.1. Electorates in seven other counties have between 80 and 90 percent of respondents self-identifying a Left–Right position. Another eight countries have percentages only between seventy and eighty. The eight include five newer democracies – namely, Brazil, Mexico, Poland, Romania, and Russia – and three long-standing democracies – Ireland, New Zealand, and the United Kingdom. Finally, Taiwan comes up considerably shorter than all the others, with only 45.6 percent of respondents self-placing.

Percentages in countries where fewer than eight out of ten citizens can place themselves in a Left–Right position could be cast in an unfavorable light. However, considered relative to the levels of factual information about politics and government, 70 to 80 percent is a reasonably good showing and 80 to 100 percent is a very good showing. Everywhere but Taiwan a sizable majority of citizens say they can describe themselves in Left–Right terms – where their Left–Right standing has to be taken to mean a position with respect to whatever Left–Right means within the context of their country.[3]

Table 4.1 also reports summary statistics for respondent Left–Right self-placements. One feature of the distributions is immediately apparent, and important. The mean and median values are near the midpoint of the zero to ten metric. Only Mexico and the Philippines have means outside the range of positions 4 to 6, and only Mexico has a median citizen at a position other than 4, 5, or 6.[4]

The dispersions of citizen locations indicate something approximating normal distributions. Thirty of the thirty-five nations have standard deviations between two and three. Some distributions are skewed slightly left or right compared to others, where negative skew indicates more clumping than normal on the political right and a relatively long thin tail on the political left – as in, notably, Israel and Mexico. Also, many of the citizen distributions are slightly more or less peaked than normal. This is indicated by more than half the nations with kurtosis values statistically significantly different from 3.0, the normal distribution standard value. Peakedness is revealed perhaps more tellingly by nations where less than 55 percent (usually flatter than normal) or more than 80 percent (usually more peaked than normal) percent of respondents are below position 3 or above position 7 on the zero to ten metric – these include only the six countries, that is, Albania, Brazil, Israel, Japan, Mexico, and Taiwan.

Table 4.1 The distribution of voter self-placements along the Left–Right dimension

Country	% Place L–R[a]	Median	Mean	Std. dev.	Skew	Kurtosis	% at positions 3–7
Albania	97.9	6	5.71	3.88	−.24*	1.47*	26.2
Australia	100.0	5	5.37	2.17	.06	3.08	75.6
Brazil	76.5	5	5.26	3.49	−.09	1.76*	41.9
Bulgaria	100.0	5	5.72	2.24	−.16*	3.05	69.9
Canada	100.0	5	5.15	1.92	.01	3.25	79.6
Chile	89.7	5	4.80	2.61	.16*	2.58*	63.0
Czech Rep.	91.7	5	4.68	2.55	.12	2.39*	63.2
Denmark	96.3	5	5.56	2.24	−.18*	2.66*	70.2
Finland	90.4	5	5.59	2.02	−.20*	2.68*	73.8
France	98.1	5	5.12	2.55	−.14	2.65*	67.0
Germany	96.0	4	4.22	2.28	.29*	3.12	70.3
Hungary	91.5	5	4.88	2.87	.02	2.23*	56.9
Iceland	93.5	5	5.41	2.22	−.13*	2.92	71.9
Ireland	77.9	5	5.83	2.11	.01	3.09	71.8
Israel	96.1	6	5.77	2.99	−.34*	2.15*	47.5
Italy	85.3	5	5.14	2.70	−.10	2.33*	61.0
Japan†	91.1	5	5.40	1.76	.05	3.30*	82.1
Korea	88.0	5	4.55	2.44	.05	2.83	70.9
Mexico	75.2	7	6.49	3.13	−.58*	2.44*	43.4
Netherlands	98.4	5	5.22	2.25	−.04	2.37*	73.3
New Zealand	79.1	5	5.16	2.31	.01	2.74*	69.2
Norway	96.3	5	5.51	2.09	−.14*	2.77*	75.3
Peru	82.6	5	5.12	2.76	.05	2.55*	61.8
Philippines	100.0	5	6.06	2.49	−.07	2.75	64.7
Poland	77.5	5	4.59	2.74	.17*	2.40*	59.2
Portugal	89.5	5	5.10	2.53	.01	2.88	68.9
Romania	73.0	6	5.79	2.27	−.24*	3.02	69.6
Russia	72.1	6	5.90	2.32	−.03	2.71*	67.3
Slovenia	100.0	5	5.01	2.33	.05	3.14	71.3
Spain	87.9	4	4.14	2.11	.14	2.90	74.3
Sweden	96.0	5	4.79	2.50	−.06	2.30*	64.8
Switzerland	96.7	5	5.05	2.34	−.21*	2.91	71.2
Taiwan	45.6	5	5.76	2.02	−.01	4.23*	81.0
United Kingdom	74.1	5	5.23	2.12	−.04	3.2	77.5
United States	86.7	6	5.85	2.35	−.13	2.60*	66.1

Notes: * Statistically significant difference from a normally distributed variable at the 95% confidence level.
†Respondents in Japan were asked to locate themselves along a 0–10 progressive to conservative dimension.
[a] Percentage of respondents placing themselves on a Left–Right dimension, 0–10, treating those who "refused" to self-place as missing data – that is, number self-placing as a percentage of those self-placing and responding "don't know," with refusals and those denoted "missing" not included in the calculation.

Source: Comparative Study of Electoral Systems, module II.

The usual image is a distribution of citizens self-placing along a Left–Right dimension in a form something similar to a normal distribution. Central tendencies are between 4 and 6; standard deviations are between 2 and 3; and usually 55 to 80 percent of the citizens locate themselves between 3 and 7. Stated in familiar political terms, sizable majorities of voters are at Left–Right positions between where one would normally find a social democratic party on the left and a conservative party on the right. This depiction holds for thirty of the thirty-five nations, with Albania, Brazil, Israel, Mexico, and the Philippines standing as exceptions – and with the reminder that a majority of Taiwanese respondents did not self-place along the Left–Right dimension.

PARTY SYSTEM VARIETY ALONG THE LEFT–RIGHT DIMENSION

For voters to be able to use their Left–Right positions to choose the policy direction for governing there have to be various Left–Right policy options on offer from the parties. Figure 4.2 shows the Left–Right variety as recorded by a CSES expert in each country. The presentation is divided into two groups. Figure 4.2a illustrates the Left–Right party options for long-standing democracies. All of them offer alternatives on both the left and right of the country's median citizen position. Only the United States leaves a gap in the middle by not having a party that an expert sees as located at positions 4, 5, or 6. Similarly, in all but two of the seventeen newer democracies, Figure 4.2b, parties stand to the left and right of the median citizen position. The exceptions are Mexico, where the median citizen is on the right and no party is farther right, and the Philippines where citizens – there is no expert score reported – see all the parties very near the middle. Also, as in the long-standing democracies, only one country – the Czech Republic – does not offer a middle-range alternative. In summary, taking the expert placements of parties as accurate, we can conclude that voters almost everywhere can choose from a variety of Left–Right policy choices.

The next two questions are whether the voters, too, see variety in the policy position on offer and, if so, whether their perceptions are accurate. Table 4.2 offers evidence to address both questions, noting with emphasis that the focus here is on voters and not citizens more generally, as voters are the people who could be using the Left–Right perceptions when recording a choice. Because we suspect that the ability to use Left–Right in application to national politics could depend on how long a democracy has been operating, we again organize the presentation in two groups, with older democracies in the top half and newer democracies below.

The first column of Table 4.2 reports the percentage of voters who would not or could not place either themselves or the parties along the Left–Right dimension. The calculations include voters who did not place themselves and, among those who did place themselves, those who either did not place the parties or placed all the parties and themselves in the same location. Surprisingly, to us,

(a)

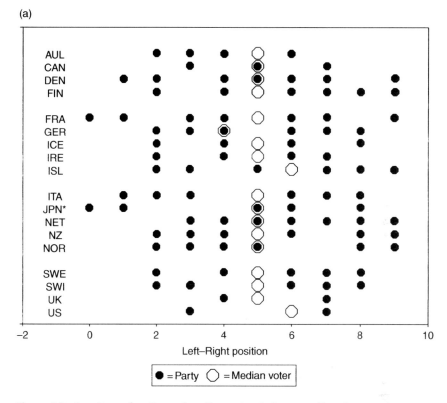

Figure 4.2a Locations of parties and median voters in long-standing democracies

• = Party O = Median voter

Note: Entries are positions for parties provided by the expert data in the CSES and the median position for voters.

* Respondents in Japan were asked to located themselves along a 0-10 progressive to conservative dimension.

Source: Comparative Study of Electoral Systems, module II.

more than 20 percent of voters in the United Kingdom and three of its one-time possessions – viz., Australia, Ireland, and New Zealand – are unable to use Left–Right as a reference point for themselves, their national parties, or both. This result is surprising because these are countries with electoral systems that tend to encourage development or relatively small party systems – present-day New Zealand excepted – and makes one wonder whether the focused attention that comes from a somewhat compressed party system makes the voters task any easier than it is in larger party systems. Less surprisingly, the four systems where voters have the greatest difficulty using Left–Right are newer democracies. Korea, Russia, Slovenia, and Taiwan each have more than 29 percent of their voters unable to place themselves, the parties, or both.

(b)

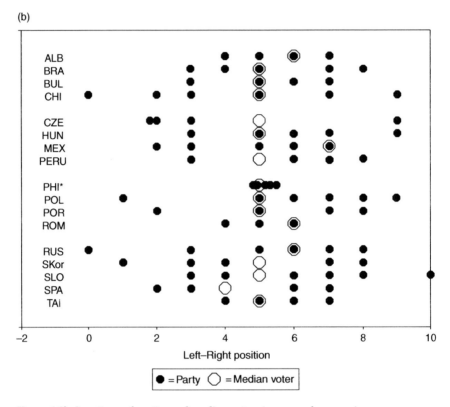

Figure 4.2b Locations of parties and median voters in newer democracies

• = Party O = Median voter

Note: Entries are positions for parties provided by the expert data in the CSES and the median position for voters.

* CSES expert scores are not available for the Philippine political parties. Average positions assigned by Filipino respondents are shown in the graph.

Source: Comparative Study of Electoral Systems, module II.

In most countries the percentage of voters able to deal with Left–Right for themselves and the parties is double or more compared to citizens who are able to accurately described facts about politics and government in their countries. In that sense, decisions organized around Left–Right decisions surely have more meaning to voters than most other bases, perhaps any other basis, for policy decision making. Nevertheless, three important cautions have to be noted. It may be a dubious enterprise to read decisions by electorates as a whole as saying something expressly about Left–Right policy when as many as three in ten or more cannot be part of the conversation.[5] Also, some of the voters' Left–Right self-placements might amount to little more than doorstep responses. Third,

Table 4.2 Relationships and differences between voter and expert party placements

Country	% of voters unable to use L–R[a]	Difference[b]		Linear relationship[c]	
		Absolute	Average	Intercept	Slope
Australia	20.3	1.22	1.22	1.01	.74
Canada	10.3	.46	.10	−.05	.70
Denmark	13.8	.58	.27	.25	.87
Finland	11.9	.87	−.36	−.09	.63
France	3.2	1.02	.37	.17	.64
Germany	13.5	.70	−.70	−.69	.78
Iceland	8.7	.23	.03	.03	.99
Ireland	24.5	.83	.47	.28	.62
Israel	2.5	.50	−.25	−.21	.94
Italy	12.1	.67	.57	.50	.88
Japan†	6.7	~~~	~~~	~~~	~~~
Netherlands	3.3	1.00	−.80	−.75	.96
New Zealand	27.2	.74	−.41	−.36	.77
Norway	8.1	.77	.47	.52	.75
Sweden	11.1	.50	−.14	−.27	1.20
Switzerland	1.9	.51	−.08	−.05	.86
United Kingdom	22.6	.35	.14	.07	.82
United States	12.3	.71	.39	.39	.65
Albania	3.5	1.50	.98	.83	1.45
Bulgaria	6.1	.94	.40	.25	1.75
Brazil	15.4	1.33	.93	.60	.45
Chile	6.1	.79	.79	.74	.93
Czech Republic	2.1	2.17	1.33	.74	.93
Hungary	10.9	1.33	−.30	−.47	1.20
Korea	29.1	1.25	.95	.81	.65
Mexico	24.1	1.16	−.50	−.64	.57
Peru	16.2	1.63	−1.52	−.88	.36
Philippines†	8.6	Missing	Missing	Missing	Missing
Poland	18.2	1.31	−.24	.62	.40
Portugal	9.9	.66	−.10	−.26	.94
Romania	24.9	.78	.32	.36	1.26
Russia	43.2	1.38	.27	.19	.51
Slovenia	30.7	.99	−.63	−.15	.44
Spain	4.5	.30	−.25	−.11	.99
Taiwan†	~~~	~~~	~~~	~~~	~~~

Notes: [a] The percentage unable to use the Left–Right dimension refers to voters who did not respond to the Left–Right question for themselves or for parties and to voters who placed themselves and all parties at the same position. [b] Differences are absolute and average calculations of voter minus expert placements. Absolute differences indicate the magnitude of voter and expert disagreement. Negative and positive average differences indicate, respectively, the general tendency of voters to place parties to the left and right of experts. [c] The linear relations are estimated after subtracting 5 from both average voter placements of parties and expert placements of parties. Y = voter placement; X = expert placement. A negative/positive intercept indicates voters tend to place a centrist party to the left/right of expert placements. A slope below or above 1.0 indicates voter placements are, respectively, more or less centrist.

†Respondents in Japan were asked to locate themselves along a 0–10 progressive to conservative dimension while experts used a Left–Right dimension. No expert placement of parties is reported for the Philippines. Only a minority of Taiwanese could self-place on Left–Right.

Source: Comparative Study of Electoral Systems, module II.

voters' use of their own Left–Right positions depends on not just assigning Left–Right positions to parties but doing so accurately.

Do voters accurately perceive party positions? The CSES offers a unique opportunity for addressing this question. Expert placements can be set as a standard against which to evaluate the accurate perceptions of the average voter.[6] Columns 2 through 5 of Table 4.2 report on four qualities of the relationship between voter average party placements and the expert identified party locations in thirty-two of the thirty-five political systems. Because voter and expert placements are designed to be on the same metric (except in Japan, see Table 4.2 note), one indicator of accuracy comes from looking at two forms of simple differences. Absolute differences tell us the magnitude of disagreement; average differences tell us whether the disagreements tend to be biased leftward or rightward. Additional details about accuracy can be gleaned for an analysis of the linear relationship between the voter–expert placements, reported in columns four and five. By subtracting five from both voter and expert scores, an intercept indicates whether bias (displacement to the left or right) exists at the center. A positive intercept indicates citizens have displaced the center of the party system to the right, relative to the expert placement; a negative intercept indicates the opposite. Information from each slope indicates whether voters see their parties standing in more or less polarized positions compared to the expert perception. A slope greater than 1.0 indicates citizens see their parties as more polarized than the experts; a slope less than 1.0 indicates a voter perception of parties less polarized than an expert sees them.

Among the eighteen long-standing democracies, three systems have absolute differences at or above 1.0 – Australia, France, and the Netherlands. Two of the three have large biases as well. Australians see the center of their party system more than a point to the right, compared to the expert perception, and the Dutch see the center of their party systems eight-tenths of a point to the left of where the Dutch expert sees them. Two additional nations have intercept magnitudes above .5. In Germany respondents place the center to the left of what the expert sees, and in Norway respondents see the center relatively more to the right than the expert reports. With or without any noticeable displacement of the center, all citizenries but Sweden's see their party systems as relatively less polarized than they probably are. That is, all but Sweden's slope value is less than 1.0.

Citizen perceptions in newer democracies are less accurate than in long-established ones. A majority of newer democracies, nine of fifteen, have absolute differences above 1.0, and the two newer democracies with most accurate citizen perceptions are Portugal and Spain, which are not all that new given their twenty-five to thirty years of continuous democracy.[7] Notice also that more than half of the electorates have biased perceptions, taking as an indication of bias an intercept outside of a ±.5 interval. There is also quite a mix of citizens seeing their party systems as more or less polarized compared to expert perceptions. All in all then, it is not clear that newer democracies have familiar enough party systems to use them to gain and retain control over policy.

Our tentative thinking is that citizen perceptions rest on party reputations. Not only do we see differences in accuracy between long-standing and newer democracies, but among the long-standing democracies an analysis of citizen placement of parties as predicted from each party's "family" – Communist, Green, Social Democrat, Liberal, Christian Democrat, Agrarian, Conservative, Regional, and Nationalist – shows that over three-quarters of the variation in citizen average placements are accounted for by party family.[8] This is similar to the finding that experts, too, assign party positions based on reputation more so than on individual party maneuvering from one election to the next (Klingemann et al. 2006, 63–85). We do not have good information on party family affiliations among the newer democracies, but that which we do have suggests party family is not nearly as good a predictor. Thus, within the limits of the results we have in hand, it appears that party reputations developed over a relatively long period of time usually contain enough recognizable policy information for the voters to make a policy choice.

HYPOTHETICAL RESULTS FROM PARTY CHOICE SETS

In the final analysis the quality of a party system involves whether voters can use the policy options on offer from the parties to produce a policy disposition in parliaments and governments that is to their collective liking. Keeping in mind the information presented in Table 4.2, we press forward and ask what electoral decisions would look like if all voters who are willing and able to use the Left–Right dimension cast a policy deterministic vote did so. The point is to see whether policy deterministic voters could produce a parliament and government to their liking. If the answer is "no," then that must be because the Left-Right options available through the party system are not granting an opportunity for elections to produce congruent representation. If the answer is "yes," then discrepancies – at least major discrepancies – in representation reside elsewhere than what the parties put on offer to voters.

One way to characterize the match between an electorate's vote distribution among parties and the likely governing position of parliaments and governments is by looking at the potential congruence between a median citizen Left–Right position and the Left–Right positions of the median and plurality parties. In countries using mixed or proportional rules over 80 percent of governments include the median party, the plurality party, or both (Müller and Strøm 2000, 563–9), and therefore they can stand-in analytically for the Left–Right position from which governance would likely emanate. Under SMD rules, the plurality electoral party alone often controls of both parliament and government with manufactured parliamentary majorities.

Column 1 of Table 4.3 repeats the listing of median citizen positions from Table 4.1; column 2 adds information on the position of median voters. The

Table 4.3 Median citizens, median voters, and the hypothetical median and plurality parties assuming policy deterministic voters

Country	Median citizen Left–Right	Median voter Left–Right	Median party Left–Right	Plurality party Left–Right
PR & mixed				
Albania	6	7	7.26	8.86
Brazil	5	5	5.35	3.70
Bulgaria	5	6	5.90	5.12
Chile	5	5	5.07	5.07
Czech Republic	5	4	2.70	2.70
Denmark	5	5	4.61	4.61
Finland	5	6	6.12	6.12
Germany	4	4	3.34	3.34
Hungary	5	3	2.92	1.90
Iceland	5	5	5.49	5.49
Ireland	5	5	4.34	4.34
Israel	6	6	7.00	4.88
Italy	5	5	5.70	5.70
Japan	5	5	6.33	6.33
Korea	5	5	4.44	4.44
Mexico	7	7	5.59	5.59
Netherlands	5	5	5.90	5.90
New Zealand	5	5	5.59	5.59
Norway	5	6	5.90	8.05
Peru	5	5	5.24	5.24
Poland	5	5	4.63	1.32
Portugal	5	5	4.68	4.68
Romania	6	6	6.77	6.86
Russia	6	6	5.40	3.12
Slovenia	5	5	5.35	5.35
Spain	4	4	3.30	3.30
Sweden	5	5	5.74	5.74
Switzerland	5	5	4.48	4.48
Taiwan†	~~	~~	~~~	~~~
SMD				
Australia	5	5	4.41	4.41
Canada	5	5	5.07	6.28
France	5	5	4.62	4.62
Philippines	5	5	4.93	5.47
United Kingdom	5	5	4.65	6.71
United States	6	6	6.68	6.68

Note: † A majority of Taiwanese could not self-place on Left–Right.

Source: Comparative Study of Electoral Systems, module II.

median voter position helps to take account of any effect of turnout differentials along the Left–Right continuum as a possible source of not matching the hypothetical governance and median citizen positions. Columns 3 and 4 show the positions of the median and plurality party positions *if* all voters cast Left–Right deterministic votes.[9]

Twenty-one of the twenty-eight countries with proportional or mixed electoral systems have median parties within one point of the position of the median citizen (also see Chapter 9). The seven exceptions are Albania, the Czech Republic, Finland, Hungary, Israel, Japan, and Mexico. In three of the seven – Albania, Finland, and Hungary – the median electoral party lies within one point of the median voter, and thus the mismatch with the citizen median is possibly attributable to turnout differentials. Adding the consideration that governments in mixed and proportional systems are often influenced by the plurality party, we notice that the median and plurality parties are most often one and the same. In the nine countries where they are not, only in Bulgaria and Israel does the plurality party's position have the potential to move the governing outcome nearer to the median citizen than if the median party position were entirely controlling.

The six majoritarian systems all have median electoral parties within one point of their median citizen. Here, however, the plurality electoral party is almost sure to have full responsibility in governing. Plurality parties in both Canada and the United Kingdom are more than a point away from the median citizen. Elsewhere, the plurality party position is within one point of the median citizen (and voter) location.

It appears that the party offerings of national party systems are usually capable of producing a governing disposition near to a country's median citizen and/or voter. Party systems in over four-fifths of the countries do so (twenty-eight of thirty-four, Albania, Finland, and Hungary included). Do voters actually behave in ways that take advantage of the possibility? That is the next and final question to be addressed.

Voter choices

The percentage of voters who make policy deterministic choices along the Left–Right dimension can be calculated in two ways. One way measures the percentage voting for the party a voter places closest to her or his own position.[10] A second measure is the percentage voting for the closest party when party positions are scored by mean voter placements. The first calculation tells us what the voter personally is thinking; the second tells how voters are coordinating on policy choices that they as a collective body see as the available policy options. We report both of these calculations of policy deterministic voters in Table 4.4. A caveat is in order, however, since voters may have supported a party not placed along the Left–Right dimensions in the CSES surveys. We report the

Table 4.4 Percentage of policy deterministic and policy conscious votes

Country	% voting for party not listed	% Choosing closest party: self-placement	% Choosing closest party: mean-placement	% Policy conscious voters
PR & Mixed				
Albania	10.1	60.9	45.9	80.7
Brazil	30.2	~*~	~*~	~*~
Bulgaria	21.3	64.7	27.4	46.6
Chile	14.0	68.6	28.3	66.4
Czech Republic	26.8	~*~	~*~	~*~
Denmark	1.7	55.3	19.5	76.8
Finland	3.8	55.3	27.5	78.4
Germany	0.9	53.4	23.0	62.1
Hungary	46.0	~*~	~*~	~*~
Iceland	1.6	66.9	35.9	82.8
Ireland	11.8	59.8	29.9	93.2
Israel	23.8	60.5	31.7	69.0
Italy	56.0	~*~	~*~	~*~
Japan	10.1	52.3	37.1	54.3
Korea	1.4	58.5	19.1	71.0
Mexico	21.2	65.4	33.9	79.2
Netherlands	1.3	57.7	26.5	71.8
New Zealand	3.3	61.5	19.4	73.6
Norway	3.6	54.0	38.4	71.0
Peru	6.4	45.9	27.3	58.2
Poland	1.1	54.0	34.4	70.3
Portugal	4.7	68.4	43.4	60.0
Romania	88.5	~*~	~*~	~*~
Russia	83.3	~*~	~*~	~*~
Slovenia	0.0	56.1	19.6	52.4
Spain	12.0	82.7	67.0	86.9
Sweden	8.3	65.3	33.5	82.5
Switzerland	12.0	61.6	38.7	71.4
Taiwan	***	***	***	***
SMD				
Australia	2.9	61.3	34.7	64.7
Canada	15.4	72.3	45.9	68.6
France	13.1	51.7	21.5	78.7
Philippines	53.2	~*~	~*~	~*~
United Kingdom	4.1	75.2	47.7	61.5
United States	0.8	76.4	56.5	67.8

Notes: ~*~ Entry excluded because vote choice information on Left–Right is missing for more than 25 percent of respondents.
*** A majority of Taiwanese could not self-place on Left–Right.

percentages of voters casting a ballot not scored on Left–Right in column 1 and withhold reports on policy deterministic voters where the percentage exceeds 25.[11]

Judged on the basis of what the voters think they are doing in their personal assessment of both themselves and parties (column 2), usually 50 to 70 percent report voting for their most closely aligned party. Only in Spain does this percentage of policy deterministic voting exceed 80 percent, and only in the majoritarian Canada, the United Kingdom, and the United States is it between 70 and 80. These modest levels are somewhat of a high water mark for policy deterministic voting. When we use mean placements of parties (column 3), only two countries have a majority of policy-deterministic voters, namely, Spain and the United States. These are two of the countries with wide gaps between parties in the middle. Percentages of policy deterministic voters drop below one-third in just about half the countries. These figures are too low to support the notion that voters generally choose the closest policy package on offer, in their own minds and especially as perceived by their fellow citizens.

Does all of this mean policy concerns are very often irrelevant to voters? No. As Russell Dalton shows in Chapter 5, policy positions of voters and the parties they support are correlated, strongly so in some contexts. The last column in Table 4.4 supports his evidence. Everywhere but Bulgaria a majority of voters cast what we call policy conscious ballots. We define a policy conscious vote as

1. voting for the party standing lower than 4.5 for voters self-placing at Left–Right positions 0–3;
2. voting for a party between 3.5 and 6.5 for voters at positions 4–6, or the closest party where no party is placed between 3.5 and 6.5;[12] and
3. voting for a party standing above 6.5 for voters at positions 7–10.

Most voters appear to take Left–Right policy into account to at least to some extent when casting their ballots. Nineteen of the twenty-seven countries have more than 65 percent of their voters casting a ballot for a party in their Left–Right vicinity.

The combination of the low levels of policy deterministic voters and nothing more than reasonable levels of policy conscious voting strongly suggests party systems do not resolve the multidimensionality problem facing voter choice. Scholarship that puts emphasis on policy positioning alone tells us that part of the reason voters stray from their Left–Right position likely rests with policy multidimensionality itself. A voter may place a great deal of policy weight on one particular issue – for example, the environment, crime, taxes, immigration – and vote for a party that bests advocates their single issue position regardless of where the party stands in Left–Right terms. Additionally, behavioral research tells us that many voters are likely to have concerns that mix their policy considerations with other politically important concerns. Affection for a party on grounds other than pure policy concerns could play a determinative role (Adams 2001).

Also, a strong liking or disliking of party leaders can carry weight in voting decisions, as Yuliya Tverdova shows (Chapter 6). Another important consideration is strategic voting; voters often abandon small parties they prefer in policy terms in favor of a larger party that has governing potential (see Chapter 8). As well, the large literature on economic voting and performance evaluation voting more generally tells us that recent performance likely weighs enough on some voters' minds to have them cast a ballot to reward or punish incumbent parties, as Timothy Hellwig shows (Chapter 7).

That voters respond to, among other things, singular policy interests not precisely correlated with Left–Right, to more and less appealing qualities of leaders, to strategic calculations about party legislative strength and government potential, and to incumbent performance evaluations are well-established facts about elections. Almost any review of an election campaign will record parties know as much and appeal to voters on non-policy grounds. Parties compete by pressing accusations against their opponents and ballyhooing their own positive qualities on policy grounds *and* for many other reasons.

Whatever the reasons and as intriguing as they are, an essential point to take away from the analysis in this chapter is that policy deterministic voting is not so widespread as to think that voters, functioning as a collective electorate, are actively and consciously using their votes to pull and push parliaments and governments left, right, or toward the center. Policy-conscious considerations are in play, but, on the evidence here, it is impossible to say with respect to any one election how much they are in play or how determinative they are.

Summary and conclusion

This has been a feasibility analysis in three parts. In part one we find it is not feasible to think that electoral democracies on the scale of nation-states could operate without substantial reliance on political parties. Parties are needed to focus attention on a limited number of options so that citizens can be involved in a conversation about how to govern. Parties are needed also to give widespread and common substantive meaning to the policy matters at stake. Finally, parties are needed to overcome the disincentives citizens have for becoming informed decision makers.

That parties are needed does not imply they do what is needed, but the empirical analysis in part two tells us they do, at least in most countries surveyed here. Party systems are small in their effective number and implicitly present themselves in a policy language most citizens understand, Left–Right. What the parties stand for in Left–Right terms is also widely recognized, although on this score the understanding by voters appears to have a good deal to do with long-standing party reputations. In the final analysis, voters casting ballots exclusively in terms of policy proximity could usually produce governing positions reasonably congruent with a country's median citizen, which in a single dimension is the position favored by a majority.

Voting decisions are often more complex than this. This is what we find in part three. In the best light, when we ask how voters actually react to the choices presented by parties given their personal assessment of their own and party Left–Right positions, often a majority but less than two-thirds decide exclusively in Left–Right terms. These no more than modest levels depend on letting each voter set the terms personally. When we look at whether voters are casting ballots that have nationwide Left–Right meaning, often as little as one-third are doing so. The evidence does not indicate that this low fraction is because most voters are not at all policy conscious. To the contrary, most often voters appear to have a policy consciousness in mind. Of the twenty-seven nations considered, twenty-three have electorates with 60 percent or more of their voters casting a ballot consistent with their own Left–Right position.

Voters are policy conscious, but they take other considerations into account. Leadership matters, advocacy on single issues matters, the prospect of a party being significant player in parliament and government matters, and past performance matters. This is true of economic consumers too, we would have to think. Like voters, not every consumer shops exclusively at a local supermarket that offers the best price for an overall basket of goods. Cleanliness matters, stocking a particular product matters, convenience matters, and predictable quality matters. Voters, like consumers, take into account and weight their various considerations according to how important non-price considerations strike them under the particular circumstances of the day.

Does this leave democratic policy making unanchored by the policy preferences of citizens? Perhaps, but the evidence we cited earlier, which finds policies to be in general alignment with public preferences, suggests it is not so (i.e., the evidence from Powell 1982, 154–200; Erikson, MacKuen, and Stimson 2002, 325–80; Wlezien 2004; Soroka and Wlezien 2004, 2005; McDonald and Budge 2005, 203–26).

We conclude with this speculative thought. Maybe the way we think about the operation of democracy has too much to do with viewing it through a lens that does not fully correct the myopia induced by the data at hand. Democracy in its representational form is a process, not a one-off affair. Often, as we have done here, the evidence brought to bear on the operation of democracy looks at one-off situations by focusing on one election per country. What if we were to extend the time horizon, to look at a series of elections? Would the ebb and flow caused by electorates giving extra weight to leadership this time, focusing almost exclusively on Left–Right next time, reacting to incumbent performance the next time, and then highlighting one particular issue the time after that produce governing arrangements with parties of the left, the right, and the center rotating in office and thereby, in the long run, produce policy outcomes that reflect the settle preferences of citizens? Given both the typically near-normal distribution of citizens on policy matters and parties spanning a wide left–center–right berth, it could. If that turns out to be the case, then party systems are playing a more significant role in the democratic process than even Schatteschneider had in mind.

Appendix

CSES survey variables

Variable	Question wording	Coding
Left–Right self-placement	B3045: In politics people sometimes talk of left and right. Where would you place yourself on a scale from 0 to 10, where 0 means the left and 10 means the right?	0 = Left to 10 = Right
	In Japan, B3046: Regarding the government, sometimes the terms Progressive and Conservative are used. Please rank yourself on a 0–10 scale with 0 being most progressive and 10 being most conservative.	
Left–Right party placement	B3038: In politics people sometimes talk of left and right. Where would you place Party A on a scale from 0 to 10 where 0 means the left and 10 means the right?	0 = Left to 10 = Right
	In Japan, B3040: When referring to politics, the terms Conservative and Progressive have occasionally been used. On a scale from 0–10 with 0 being Progressive and 10 being Conservative, please rate where you think the [party] would stand.	
Left–Right expert party placement	B5018: Parties' positions on the Left–Right scale (in the expert judgment of the CSES Collaborator):	0 = Left to 10 = Right
Vote choice – legislative election	B3006_1/LegVT_Nat: This variable reports the vote cast by the respondent in lower house elections.	Country-specific
Vote choice – presidential election	B3017: This variable reports the presidential candidate or party affiliation of the presidential candidate for whom the respondent voted.	Country-specific

Notes

1. The Comparative Study of Electoral Systems (CSES) module 2 covers thirty-six nations, but Belgium has to be excluded because Belgian respondents were not asked to place the parties along a Left–Right dimension.
2. We can add that Belgium also has more than seven effective electoral parties when counted nationwide – 8.86 in the Dalton and Anderson count (see Table 1.2). Outside of the Brussels area, however, counting nationwide ballot choices in Belgium is artificial. Each language community has its own party system. In 2003, parliamentary balloting Flanders had 4.35 effective electoral parties and Wallonia had 3.82.

3. We cannot assume that the meaning of Left–Right is the same in all countries. When the respondents are country "experts" there is good reason to think the meaning of Left–Right varies cross-nationally (Huber and Inglehart 1995; see also Benoit and Laver 2006). We have no reason to think this would be different for mass survey respondents.

4. There appears to be no particular rhyme and reason behind the country means. While Ireland and the United States have means values on the right, which have face validity to most observers' mind's eye, Norway's mean citizen is also standing relatively far to the right and Germany's is relatively far to the left, neither of which have face validity to our mind's eyes. A reasonable inference to draw is that the citizens are norming their positions to the politics within their own country. This has no important consequences for the analyses in this chapter, which make within-nation comparisons, but norming does serve a warning to be cautious about using Left–Right self-placement in these data for cross-national comparisons. Likewise, caution is advised with respect to cross-national comparisons of citizen dispersion. The standard deviations are essentially uncorrelated, in the statistically significant sense, with majoritarian-mixed-proportional systems ($R = .218$), the effective number of parties ($r = .144$), and with party system polarization ($r = .198$). Thus, dispersion values, too, may be reflecting a nation-specific norming. (Note: the values of the three variables used are from Anderson and Dalton – Tables 1.2 and 1.3 – and the proportional-mixed-majoritarian multiple correlation is from the regression on two dummy variables.

5. This is not to say these voters are not policy-minded voters. They might have some policy important to them in mind when they think about themselves and the parties – for example, a strong environmental concern. However, if that is the type of a policy concern they have in mind, it is not something that effectively communicates policy meaning when aggregated for choices made by an electorate as a whole.

6. A potential shortcoming of using the CSES expert as the standard for accurate perception is that only one expert per country is recorded. We have checked on the reliability of these single-individual reports by evaluating their accuracy against a battery of national experts in the 2003–4 survey by Kenneth Benoit and Michael Laver (Benoit and Laver 2006). The CSES and Benoit-Laver surveys have 240 common placements of parties. The correlation is .88, which in this type of application is a reliability coefficient. On this evidence we have confidence that the CSES single expert is a reasonable standard by which to evaluate citizen accuracy.

7. Expert scores for the Philippines are missing.

8. Party family affiliations in these countries are taken from the assignment in the Comparative Manifesto Project (Klingemann et al. 2006).

9. Our data here include those who placed themselves and the parties along the Left–Right dimension and excludes Taiwan.

10. In the case where more than one party is tied for closest, we count a vote for any of the tied parties as a vote for the closest party. With the exception of Russia, where we only have data from the presidential election, all percentages in Table 4.4 are derived from legislative elections.

11. In several countries more than a quarter of the voters report supporting a party the CSES survey did not place on the Left–Right dimension. This could be either because a nation has so many parties that the CSES did not ask about all of them or because voters responded by referring to an electoral coalition they supported. For either reason, we do not have Left–Right information for more than a quarter of the votes cast in seven countries, and for those seven we do not report percentages that characterize voting as more or less policy deterministic. Also, Taiwan is again excluded due to its low percentage of voters placing themselves or the parties.

12. This condition applies only to Spain once the CiU is dropped for its regional standing.

5

Left–Right Orientations, Context, and Voting Choices[*]

Russell J. Dalton

In the 2000 U.S. presidential elections, the *American National Election Study* asked people what they liked and disliked about the two major political parties (Lewis-Beck, Jacoby, et al. 2008, ch. 10). When asked about the political parties, one voter said:

(Likes about the Democrats): Lots of things. They are trying to help middle class families. They want to do some things that will make us a better America. We need government and people together to make it work.

(Dislikes about the Democrats): Sometimes they get a little carried away, and they need to be reined in. It would help if they were just a little more conservative in their views and programs.

(Likes about the Republicans): Sometimes I like the fact that they are a little conservative. Still, I don't really agree with them on most issues.

(Dislikes about the Republicans): They don't have a clue about what America is all about. All they think about is themselves.

Although most people are not as articulate as this example in expressing their likes and dislikes about political parties, we think that most people have opinions about the issues that are most important to them – and views about the parties' positions on these issues. The democratic process should provide a means for the public to express their views by choosing a political party that shares their preferences, and the party then represents their preferences in the policy-making process (Dahl 2002). Elections presumably give people an opportunity to evaluate the policies of the incumbent parties and make judgments about the desired course of government in the future. Indeed, during campaigns the parties ask the voters to give them a mandate to implement their programs, and claim such a mandate when the ballots are counted. Whether it is Barack Obama requesting a mandate for change in the United States, or the National Front campaigning against past public policies in France, elections are the vehicle for such policy debates and choices. Thus, a policy-centered view of electoral choice is closely linked to the theoretical concept of democracy and representation.

There is continuing academic debate on the public's understanding of public policy and thus the role of such policy preferences in electoral choice.[1] The contribution by Best and McDonald in this volume effectively summarized this literature. This chapter engages in this debate by examining how the public's political preferences, based on the Left–Right scale, influence their voting choices. Even if many voters lack the political sophistication that political theorists and electoral scholars expect, the basic fact is that people do make electoral choices when they cast their ballots. Political judgments about government programs past and future are part of this calculus. Thus, this chapter asks to what extent do policy positions shape electoral choices.

Furthermore, policy positions may differentially affect voting behavior depending on the context of electoral choice – which is the core research focus of this volume. For instance, longitudinal studies of voting behavior show that the impact of issue voting or Left–Right voting ebbs and flows over time (Nie, Verba, and Petrocik 1979; Miller and Shanks 1996; Van der Eijk, Schmitt, and Binder 2005). In addition, the extent of Left–Right voting may vary as a function of the political and institutional context of elections (Anderson 2000; Thomassen 2005; Dalton 2008a; Wessels and Schmitt 2008). For instance, it is easier for voters to see ideological choices when the parties range from the French Communist Party to the National Front, than when the election pits less extreme choices such as George H. W. Bush against Bill Clinton.

This chapter proceeds in four steps. First, we discuss the Left–Right scale as a summary measure of voters' policy preferences and their perceptions of the parties' positions on this same dimension. This leads to an empirical analysis of the relationship between Left–Right orientations and vote in the CSES nations. Second, we consider how contextual factors may affect this relationship, and integrate contextual influences into our analysis. Third, we develop a multilevel statistical model to estimate how context and individual voter characteristics combine to determine the level of Left–Right voting. Finally, we discuss the implications of our findings for the underlying question of whether elections are sufficient vehicles for voter direction and control of democratic governments.

Policy voting and the Left–Right scale

As the other chapters in this volume demonstrate, many factors can potentially influence the electoral choice of voters. However, if elections are to be meaningful guides to democratic government, there must be substantial policy content to electoral choices. Elections should provide a means for people to express their policy preferences and to seek representation for these views within the democratic process. For example, in the 1998 German Bundestag elections, Gerhard Schröder encouraged the voters to judge his administration (if elected) by its policy record by the time of the next election. Voters should have used these judgments in making their decision in the 2002 Bundestags-wahl, which Schröder won. Similarly, in the 2009 elections Germans should have evaluated the performance and policy positions of the German parties since 2005. Voters may also consider the prospects for governing and opposition parties after the election. If citizens' voting choices lack this political content, then democracy is a mirage.

There is a large and rich literature on the impact of issue voting in specific nations or in specific elections (e.g., Anderson and Zelle 1998; van Wijnen 2001; Abramson, Aldrich, and Rohde 2005; Thomassen 2005; Clarke et al. 2008). Contemporary issue voting often involves long-standing economic or religious cleavages. Economic cycles inevitably stimulate concerns about the economic role of government and individual economic security. Similarly, political events can revive latent conflicts, such as the recent debate over immigration in several Western democracies, or renewed regional tensions in many of these societies. Contemporary democracies are also grappling with new foreign policy issues: the post-Cold War international system, the global economy, the threat of Jihadist terrorism, and other international events. Faced with a diversity of issues across elections and nations, it is difficult to systematically and meaningfully compare the impact of specific issues (e.g., Wijnen 2001; Aardal and Wijnen 2005). Indeed, the impact of specific issues should shift across time since they are a dynamic part of elections. One cannot simply draw up a set of common issues and include in a cross-national survey because no list is sufficiently detailed to include all the possible themes of debate, and the themes even change in the midst of campaigns.[2] With partial or incomplete coverage of the issues of the campaign, estimates on the overall level and content of issue voting will be biased in unknown ways. Yet, our goal is to compare the level of policy-based voting across nations and identify the factors that systematically affect these correlates of voting.

We therefore assess the impact of political preferences on voting behavior by examining the relationship between Left–Right attitudes and vote. We do not assume that most voters have an understanding of "Left" and "Right" in terms of sophisticated ideological concepts, such as socialism, liberalism, or other philosophical concepts.[3] Instead, the Left–Right scale is a *political identity and policy orientation* that helps individuals make political choices (Fuchs and Klingemann 1989; Inglehart 1990).

The political content of Left–Right orientations can vary across time, space, and individuals (Dalton 2006; Mair 2007). Historically, the terms Left and Right were most commonly linked to contrasting positions on economic and social class issues. A leftist citizen generally supported more extensive social services, a larger role of government in managing the economy, and policies to ensure the well-being of the working class. The Right was synonymous with a smaller government, modest social programs, and the advocacy of middle-class economic interests. To other voters the terms signify positions on issues derived from religious and moral conflicts.

While economics and cultural issues are still important elements of the Left–Right framework in many nations, the content of these orientations has expanded. A variety of other issues has entered the contemporary political agenda – such as environmentalism, gender equality, and multiculturalism – and are integrated into the Left–Right scale. For instance, a recent survey of the German public asked respondents to select those issues that they identified with "the Left" and those that they identified with "the Right" (Noelle-Neumann and Koecher 2002, 709). People linked the term "Left" to voting rights for foreigners, support for more asylum-seekers, and limitations on German military participation in UN missions (limitations on social programs was fourth on this list). Germans described opposition to foreigners, a desire for more law and order, opposition to an environmental tax, and opposition to a shorter work week as Right issues (the issue of social programs was fifth on this list). Thus, to a German blue-collar worker, Left may still mean social welfare policies; to a young German college student it may mean environmental protection and issues of multiculturalism. This illustrates how Left–Right orientations can represent a range of very different issues.

Other research shows that the content of Left–Right systematically varies across nations (Benoit and Laver 2006; Rohrschneider and Whitefield 2009; Rovny and Edwards 2009). This cross-national variation can reflect the specific issues of the campaign, as well the longer-term cleavages that structure party competition. Analyses from the World Values Survey indicate that traditional class and economic issues are more strongly related to Left–Right orientations in established Western democracies, while religious values, national identity, or democratic orientations display stronger correlations in Latin America and East Asia (Dalton 2006).

In summary, the value of the Left–Right scale derives from its inclusive nature. Ronald Inglehart describes the scale as a sort of super-issue dimension that represents the "major conflicts that are present in the political system" (Inglehart 1990, 273; also see Gabel and Huber 2000, 96; Knutsen 1999; Dalton 2006). Even if the specific definitions of Left and Right vary across individuals and nations, the simple structure of a general Left–Right scale can summarize the political positions of voters and political parties. Then, these political views should guide voting choices.

The extent of Left–Right voting

We begin our analyses by assuming that party competition is structured along a Left–Right dimension. This is a simplifying assumption, but it is reasonable if we accept that the Left and Right scale encompasses different political issues in a comparable political scale. We expect that positions on this scale generally summarize the issues and cleavages that define political competition to individuals in a nation. In keeping with Downs' logic, these labels provide reference points that help people interpret and evaluate political parties and other political actors and policies. Thus, the Left–Right dimension provides the metric for our cross-national comparisons.

We analyze Module II of the Comparative Study of Electoral Systems (CSES).[4] The CSES asks respondents to position themselves along a Left–Right scale using the following question:

In politics people sometimes talk of left and right. Where would you place yourself on a scale from 0 to 10, where 0 means the left and 10 means the right?

| 0 | 1 | 2 | 3 | 4 | 5 | 6 | 7 | 8 | 9 | 10 |

As Best and McDonald show in Chapter 4, the majority of the public in most CSES nations can locate themselves on this Left–Right scale (nearly 90 percent on average). This ranges from 46 percent in Taiwan to 98 percent in The Netherlands. This fulfills the first general criteria about policy voting: that people have a position.

The next question is the degree to which Left–Right orientations are correlated with party choice. We examine the relationship between citizens' Left–Right orientations and vote in two ways. First, as a baseline we use the nominal level Cramer's V correlation to measure the basic relationship between Left–Right self-placement and legislative vote. This nominal-level statistic does not require we make assumptions about the Left–Right ordering of parties, and it uses all parties in the legislative vote choice question. In other words, it tells us if the two variables are related, but without making assumptions about the nature of the relationship.

Second, the CSES survey asked respondents to place the major political parties on the same Left–Right scale. In most party systems, a large majority of the voting public can locate the parties on the Left–Right scale, even if individuals differ in their judgments.[5] We use the entire public's mean value for a party to determine the party's Left–Right score. In France, for example, the Communist Party receives an average score of 2.42 on the Left–Right scale, while the National Front is placed at 7.85. We recoded the party categories on the legislative vote variable into their Left–Right scores. Then we calculated a Pearson's r correlation between a voter's own Left–Right position and their Left–Right legislative vote. This is a more demanding measure of association because it presumes an ordered relationship between Left–Right orientations and voter choice. (It excludes voters who select parties without a Left–Right score).[6] Both of these methods are reasonable alternatives that use different assumptions to assess the relationship between Left–Right orientations and vote. In practical terms, we want to demonstrate that these two correlations generate very similar cross-national patterns in the level of Left–Right voting and so our analyses are not dependent on the choice of statistics.[7]

Table 5.1 The strength of Left–Right legislative voting by nation

Nation	Nominal correlation (Cramer's V)	Interval correlation (Pearson's r)
Albania	.29	.78
Australia	.20	.50
Belgium	.19	.40
Brazil	.21	.28
Bulgaria	.37	.70
Canada	.18	.37
Chile	.27	.59
Czech Republic	.35	.83
Denmark	.30	.63
Finland	.27	.54
France	.34	.64
Germany	.19	.46
Hungary	.33	.67
Iceland	.36	.68
Ireland	.20	.36
Israel	.32	.75
Italy	.36	.79
Japan	.18	.32
Korea (S.)	.24	.46
Mexico	.12	.14
Netherlands	.28	.68
New Zealand	.24	.58
Norway	.31	.68
Peru	.13	.21
Philippines	.14	.06
Poland	.25	.65
Portugal 2002	.38	.67
Portugal 2005	.28	.54
Romania	.21	.33
Slovenia	.32	.57
Spain	.32	.74
Sweden	.35	.70
Switzerland	.26	.66
Taiwan	.12	.16
United Kingdom	.27	.46
United States	.33	.38
Average	.26	.52

Notes: The table displays the relationship between respondent's Left–Right self-placement and their legislative vote choice. Vote is coded as nominal categories in the first column (Cramer's V correlation), and as quasi-interval Left–Right positions in the second column (Pearson's r correlation)

Source: Comparative Study of Electoral Systems, module II ($N = 36$).

Table 5.1 displays a considerable relationship between citizens' Left–Right orientations and their voting choice in almost every national election. The Cramer's V correlations average .26, with a range from .12 (Mexico) to .38 (Portugal). Similarly, the Pearson's r correlations display strong relationships with an average correlation of .52 with substantial variability across party systems (from .06 in the Philippines to .83 in the Czech Republic).

Best and McDonald stress the limits of "deterministic" Left-Right voting in Chapter 4. To the extent that this is not a perfect relationship, we agree. By measuring Left–Right voting in deterministic terms, Best and McDonald set a standard that overlooks the stochastic and multivariate aspects of voting choice.[8] Nothing in mass political behavior research is deterministic. Compared to most social cleavages as predictors of vote (such as class, religion, or other characteristics) or even economic voting (see Chapter 7), Left–Right orientations are routinely a stronger predictor of vote choice – as we would expect if they represent the policy concerns of voters.

Furthermore, these simple correlations presumably underestimate the actual degree of congruence. An individual's own perceptions of a party's Left–Right placement may vary from the overall average because of the person's own issue interests. For instance, the British Labour Party and Liberal Democrats have different relative positions if one defines Left–Right in terms of traditional social services issues versus a Left–Right position based on environmental policy or the war in Iraq. People thus place parties differently on the Left–Right scale – which are then averaged together in these correlations.[9] In Chapter 4, Best and McDonald thus showed greater agreement when the respondent's own positioning of the parties is used instead of the electorate's average.

Voters in multiparty systems typically also have more than one party that is close to their own position, and all these parties might be reasonable choices, leading voters to decide on other factors such as party experience, leadership, or the capacity to govern. For instance, across the CSES nations, more than three-quarters of the public perceive at least one party as within one point of their own position on the Left–Right scale. Among this group, more than half see at least two parties within this range, which gives them multiple, ideologically consistent choices.[10] Thus, the degree to which voters translate their political views into appropriate party choices is probably stronger than the correlations of Left–Right voting in Table 5.1.

National context and Left–Right voting

We have shown that voters generally select a party that is close to their own position on the Left–Right scale. However, the variation in this relationship leads us to examine the factors that might explain this cross-national variability. The relationship might depend on factors at either the macro or the micro level; we consider macro-contextual factors in this section, and then individual-level factors in the next section.

Several aspects of the macro-level context might affect the strength of Left–Right voting. The most prominent theory in the literature argues that the *amount of choice* facing the voters directly affects the likelihood of Left–Right voting (or issue-based voting). Anthony Downs claimed, "voters in multiparty systems . . . are given a wide range of ideological choice, with parties emphasizing rather than soft-pedaling their doctrinal differences. Hence regarding ideologies as a decisive factor in one's voting decision is usually more rational in a multiparty system than in a two-party system" (Downs 1957, 127). Similarly, Giovanni Sartori (1976) maintained that party systems with high levels of polarization can intensify ideological debates, which strengthens voting choices based on Left–Right or other relevant policy orientations. Furthermore, with parties spread across the Left–Right spectrum, it may be easier for voters to identify differences between parties, and thereby select a party more representative of their own views. In simple terms, it should be easier for an environmentalist or a nationalist to find a party closely representing their views in a varied multiparty system than in an election with a few large catch-all parties.

Previous research often resorted to the shorthand of counting the number of parties as a measure of diversity, because scholars assumed that the number of parties reflected the amount of choice (e.g., Taagepera and Shugart 1989; Klingemann and Wessels 2009). However, the underlying theoretical logic implies that the diversity in the parties' policy positions or Left–Right positions is more important than the simple number of parties.

Several recent cross-national electoral studies validate these predictions. Van der Eijk, Schmitt, and Binder (2005, 178–180) found that the greater the Left–Right polarization of party systems, the stronger the effect of Left–Right orientations on voting choices in six European democracies. Dalton (2008*b*) demonstrated that the level of Left–Right polarization in a party system was strongly related to the levels of Left–Right voting (also see Wessels and Schmitt 2008; Kroh 2009; Lachat 2008).[11]

In addition, we might presume that the type of electoral system is relevant. In part, the type of electoral system is an indirect indicator of the number of parties likely competing for votes, with more parties winning seats in proportional representation systems. The nature of the electoral system also may affect voting choices in another way. In majoritarian systems, the electoral logic might encourage voters to make satisficing choices by strategically voting for a party that can win rather than a party that most closely reflects their political views (Blais et al. 2009; Gschwend 2009). In contrast, proportional-representation systems enable individuals to vote for the party that most closely agrees with their views with less regard to strategic calculations. David Farrell and Ian McAllister (2006) have also categorized the degree to which the voting procedures of the electoral system are party-centered or candidate-centered. We expect stronger Left–Right voting in party-centered systems where the party provides a unified focus for vote choice.[12]

Another potential contextual factor is the institutionalization of the democratic system (Dalton 2008b). The CSES nations span a range of established and new democracies where such a comparison may be relevant. We expect that Left–Right orientations are more likely to influence voting in established democracies where electoral competition produces clear Left–Right party frameworks. These societies also have more sophisticated electorates who are more likely to vote on the issues and candidates of a campaign. In contrast, in new democracies the partisan choices are often less clearly defined. Voters in new democracies are also less likely to have complex and sophisticated issue beliefs because they are learning the democratic electoral process. In short, a nation's history of democratic elections may affect the level of Left–Right voting.

Similarly, the institutionalization of the party system can be a separate aspect of political development. Party systems typically become more institutionalized as democracy develops, but this is an imperfect relationship. Some party systems experience continuing fluidity in the number and identities of the competing parties, which would make it difficult for voters to identify the political orientations of a party that exists for a single electoral cycle or two. South Korea, for example, has experienced continuing turnover in the major political parties since the democratic transition, while Taiwan's democratic transition occurred at roughly the same time but has produced a relatively stable partisan landscape. British voters face a relatively stable and predictable party landscape, while French voters routinely see old parties rebranded and new parties entering the electoral fray. Consequently, the overall institutionalization of the party system may affect the strength of Left–Right voting.

Other macro-level factors might influence the level of Left–Right voting, such as the political discourse of the campaign or the competitiveness of an election.[13] Timothy Hellwig (2008) presents evidence that Left–Right voting will decrease in postindustrial societies because of the changing structure of their labor forces. There are also basic questions of how these contextual factors interact with the personal characteristics of voters. For instance, in what contexts is Left–Right voting more dependent on the political sophistication and knowledge of voters, or when does Left–Right voting overlap with partisan identities? We consider these additional questions below, but the first step is to consider how the macro-level context influences overall patterns of Left–Right voting.

We begin our empirical tests of contextual effects by examining the impact of the electoral system. Table 5.2 shows a modest tendency for Left–Right voting to be stronger in proportional representation systems for both measures of Left–Right voting ($r = .31$ and $r = .40$).[14] Yet this is only a modest difference; the average Cramer's V between Left–Right orientations and legislative vote was .29

Table 5.2 Contextual correlates of the strength of Left–Right voting

Predictor	Nominal correlation	Left–Right correlation
Electoral system		
Proportional representation	.31	.40*
District magnitude	.14	.29
Party-centered electoral system	.26	.21
Party fragmentation		
Effective number electoral parties	.02	.11
Effective number of legislative parties	.02	.10
Polarization		
Party system Polarization Index	.67*	.84*
Democratic development		
Established democracy	.24	.25
Years of democracy (1955–present)	.13	.16
Freedom House rating	.33*	.33*
Voice and Accountability	.34*	.38*
Press Freedom	.24	.23
Party system institutionalization		
Age of the party system	.08	−.03
Socioeconomic development		
GNP/capita	.19	.18
UN Human Development Index	.29	.34*

Notes: The table presents the Pearson's r correlations between national characteristics and the strength of the relationship between Left–Right attitudes and legislative vote (Table 5.1). The first column is based on a nominal level Cramer's V to measure the relationship of Left–Right to vote; the second column uses a Pearson's r to measure the relationship with parties coded according to their Left–Right position. Most relationships are based on thirty-six nations; relationships significant at .05 level are denoted by an asterisk.

Source: Comparative Study of Electoral Systems, module II

for PR systems and .24 for majoritarian systems. Similarly, researchers often use district magnitude as a more refined measure of the proportionality of the voting system, but it yields only a weak relationship with either Left–Right voting correlation. There is a slight but statistically insignificant tendency toward stronger Left–Right voting in party-centered electoral systems.

Despite the theoretical literature on the importance of multiparty competition, neither the effective number of parties competing for votes (ENEP) nor holding legislative seats (ENLP) is related to the strength of Left–Right voting. Having many parties simply does not ensure that voters can find one that represents their political orientations.

The third panel of Table 5.2 shows the extent of Left–Right voting based on the diversity of party choice as measured by party polarization along the Left–Right dimension. The Polarization Index uses the public's estimates of the parties' positions on the Left–Right scale (weighted by party vote share) to measure the dispersion of choice available to voters.

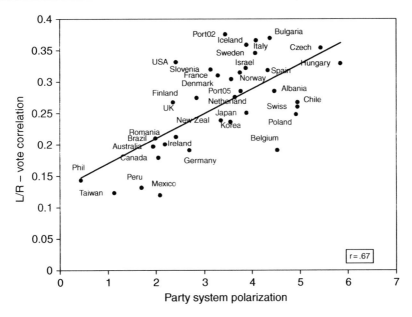

Figure 5.1 The relationship between party system polarization and Left–Right voting

Note: The table presents the relationship between the Left–Right polarization of the party system and the strength of the Cramer's V correlation between Left–Right attitudes and legislative vote ($N = 36$).
Source: Comparative Study of Electoral Systems, module II

There is a very strong relationship between party system polarization and the strength of Left–Right voting.[15] More diverse Left–Right party choices make it easier for voters to find a party that represents their position. One can gain a better sense of this relationship from Figure 5.1, which plots the Party Polarization Index on the X-axis and the strength of the correlation between Left–Right attitudes and legislative on the Y-axis (Cramer's V correlations). For instance, Bulgaria and Ireland have roughly the same effective number of electoral parties, but the Bulgarian parties are much more dispersed along the Left–Right dimension. Consequently, Left–Right attitudes are more strongly related to legislative vote choice in Bulgaria ($V = .37$) than in Ireland ($V = .20$).

The next panel of Table 5.2 examines the impact of the institutionalization of the democratic system or the party system. Left–Right attitudes are a slightly stronger predictor of legislative vote in established democracies than in new democracies. Similarly, the level of democratic development – measured by either the Freedom House scale, the World Bank Voice and Accountability Index, or the Press Freedom scale – is positively related to Left–Right voting. In a similar vein, Left–Right voting tends to be stronger in nations with a higher GDP per capita or a higher score on the United Nations' Human Development index (but not always a statistically significant correlation). This may partially be spurious correlations with democratic de- velopment, but it also likely reflects a more educated and politically knowl- edgeable public in affluent societies. As we expected, democratization and social modernization are accompanied by a stronger link between voter atti- tudes and their party choices.[16]

These results may seem unsurprising and inevitable: with more varied elec- toral choice, voters can more clearly translate their Left–Right orientations into a party preference. Indeed, this is the theoretical logic we are testing. *However, the important factor is not the number of party choices*, which is what previous research has primarily discussed, *but the diversity of choice* as measured by the dispersion of parties along the Left–Right scale. If democracy is about voters making political choices, then the party system needs to offer meaningful choices for this process to function most effectively.

Citizen characteristics, context, and choice

In addition to contextual variation, the extent of Left–Right voting varies as a function of the characteristics of individual voters. As Martin Kroh notes, "individual processes leading to vote choice do not uniformly apply to all voters in the electorate" (2009: 221). We focus on two micro-level characteristics – political knowledge and partisanship – that may affect the strength of Left– Right voting across individuals. In addition, we expand the analyses to deter- mine if contextual effects interact with individual characteristics to alter their impact on vote choice.

We expect that a voter's level of political sophistication affects the strength of Left–Right voting. Voters that are more sophisticated should be better able to determine their own political preferences and express them in Left–Right terms – and then link these preferences to an appropriate party choice. Conversely, less sophisticated voters may have weakly formed political opinions, or have difficulty drawing the connection between their own preferences and the party that best represents these positions. An extensive literature has discussed the theoretical basis of such expectations (Converse 1964; Zaller 1992; Lachat 2008; Kroh 2009).

We examine the relationship between political knowledge and Left–Right voting using a political knowledge index available in the CSES.[17] Each election survey included three knowledge questions that were designed to divide the public into roughly equal quartiles. As we would expect, the first row of Table 5.3 shows that the correlation between Left–Right self-placement and Left– Right legislative voting choice rises with the level of political knowledge. Left–Right voting is weakest among those lowest in knowledge ($r = .48$) and strongest among those who answered all three questions ($r = .62$). The com- plications of measuring political knowledge might have even attenuated these contrasts.[18] Still, political knowledge does enhance the ability of people to use Left–Right orientations as a basis of voting choice.

This finding leads to the more complex question of the role of individual political sophistication in different political contexts – a contingent contextual effect. Nations with highly polarized political parties make it is easier for all voters to distinguish between the political parties and thus make electoral choices based on Left–Right orientations. However, does this facilitate knowledgeable voters making choices more strongly on Left–Right terms, or does the clarity of party choice mean that individual level knowledge becomes less important? Ensley (2007) and Lachat (2008) both find that the impact of issues and ideology on vote increases among sophisticated voters when there are highly polarized party choices, while claiming that political knowledge may be less valuable in less polarized systems where the choices are ambiguous. In contrast, there are reasons to expect that a citizen's knowledge may be even more important in low polarization systems. In this environment, political knowledge may help voters to link their preferences to an appropriate party choice because of the blurred nature of party cues makes this a more difficult task.

The second row of Table 5.3 displays the Left–Right voting correlation by the level of political knowledge in high polarization party systems. In these party systems, the individual's level of political knowledge (or presumably other measures of political engagement) has only a limited impact on the strength of Left–Right voting. Because party choices are clear, most voters – even those with limited knowledge – can identify a party that comes close to their own Left–Right position. In contrast, an individual's political knowledge is more relevant in low polarization party systems where voting is complicated by the ambiguity of party choice. In less polarized systems, the gap in the voting correlation between low knowledge (.21) and high knowledge (.44) voters is substantial. The impact of context is so important that the *most knowledgeable* voters in low polarization systems are less likely to make Left–Right voting choices ($r = .44$) than the *least knowledgeable* in high polarization systems ($r = .62$).

Partisan attachment can also shape voting choice in multifaceted ways. Partisanship normally incorporates political values that reinforce the link between voter and party, and prior research stressed the overlap of partisanship and Left–Right positions (Inglehart and Klingemann 1976). Thus, stronger partisans may display a stronger relationship between their Left–Right position and vote. In addition, partisans are typically more interested and engaged in politics, which might further strengthen the relationship between Left–Right orientations and vote.

In contrast, the influence of Left–Right attitudes on voting is more ambiguous for nonpartisans. On the one hand, research traditionally maintained that nonpartisans were minimally involved in politics and thus less likely to employ a Left–Right calculus or other policy views in making their voting choices. On

115

Table 5.3 The correlation between Left–Right orientations and Left–Right vote choice

Party system polarization	Level of political knowledge			
	Low	Low-mid	Mid-high	High
All voters	.48	.55	.62	.61
High polarization (N)	.62 (1718)	.65 (4153)	.71 (5456)	.70 (4609)
Low polarization (N)	.21 (1348)	.34 (2983)	.41 (4039)	.44 (3325)
	Closeness to political party			
	No partisanship	Not very close	Somewhat close	Very close
All voters	.51	.52	.63	.69
High polarization (N)	.59 (7236)	.60 (3017)	.71 (6671)	.81 (3089)
Low polarization (N)	.23 (3692)	.33 (1821)	.44 (5029)	.41 (1838)

Note: Table entries are the correlation between the respondent's Left–Right self-placement and Left–Right legislative vote choice (parties coded by their Left–Right score).

Source: CSES, module II.

the other hand, a new type of sophisticated nonpartisan may place more reliance on Left–Right orientations and other evaluative criteria as a basis of voting choice because they lack standing partisan predispositions.[19]

The second panel of Table 5.3 describes the Left–Right voting relationship as a function of the strength of partisanship (see chapter appendix on coding of variable). Left–Right voting is modestly stronger among individual's with close party ties ($r = .69$) than among nonpartisans (.51). But again, the level of party system polarization emerges as important. In polarized party systems, all levels of partisanship display stronger Left–Right voting. Compared to political knowledge, the effects of partisanship are more similar between low and high polarization party systems. In both categories, the strength of Left–Right voting increases modestly as partisan closeness increases.

Multilevel analyses

Our findings to this point led us to model Left–Right voting as a hierarchical process affected by individual characteristics, contextual factors, and the inter-actions between the two.[20] The multilevel analysis estimates the fixed effects coefficient for each variable. The variance components estimate whether the effects of the micro-level predictors vary significantly across countries. If the variance component for the model intercept is statistically significant, this indicates that there is systematic cross-national variance in Left–Right voting. If a variance component for a micro-level coefficient is significant, it indicates the predictors' effect varies systematically across countries.

We conduct these analyses in three steps (Table 5.4). The first step links individual level characteristics to Left–Right legislative vote choice. We begin with the respondent's own Left–Right position as a predictor of vote, and then we add several standard demographic variables.[21] Social class, union membership, and education represent the socioeconomic cleavage. Age is included as a possible indicator of partisan aging. We considered other possible demographic predictors, but none rose to the level of substantive significance.

The first model in Table 5.4 displays the base micro model. Left–Right orientations are a strong and highly significant predictor of vote choice. Since the unstandardized coefficients are difficult to interpret, we also conducted a separate OLS regression (not shown) in which Left–Right attitudes produce a very large standardized coefficient ($ß = .58$) that overshadows the other variables in

Table 5.4 Multilevel analyses of Left–Right voting choice

Predictor	Base model	Micro interactions	Multilevel
Individual-level effects			
Left–Right orientations	.401* (.046)	.354* (.048)	−.223* (.057)
Social class	.072* (.017)	.071* (.025)	.071* (.025)
Union member	−.119* (.013)	−.117* (.024)	−.119* (.012)
Education	−.021 (.012)	−.021 (.012)	−.021 (.011)
Age	.003 (.001)	.000 (.001)	.000 (.001)
Knowledge	.052 (.020)	−.104* (.036)	−.100* (.035)
Strength PID	.001 (.007)	.013 (.012)	.013 (.012)
Knowledge*LR		.029* (.005)	.029* (.005)
PID*LR		−.002 (.002)	−.002 (.001)
Left–Right*Polarize			.178* (.016)
Intercept	2.766* (.280)	3.018* (.289)	6.437* (.344)
Macro-level effects			
Polarize			−1.049* (.094)
Variance components			
Left–Right orientations	.055*	.056*	.009*
Social class	.005	.005	.005
Union	.006	.006	.004
Education	.002	.002	.002
Age	.000	.000	.000
Knowledge	.004	.005	.004
Strength PID	.001	.001	.001
Intercept	1.815*	1.826*	.231*
−2xLog likelihood	46599.24	46587.07	46510.32

Notes: Table entries are the results of a multilevel regression model predicting legislative vote choice (parties coded by their Left–Right score). An asterisk denotes coefficients significant at the .01 level.

Source: CSES, module II.

the model. Social class and union membership have statistically significant effects, with the middle class leaning toward right parties and union members leaning toward the Left. The significant variance component for Left–Right attitudes indicates that there are significant cross-national differences in the impact of this variable, while none of the other individual-level predictors has a statistically significant variance component.

The second model in Table 5.4 examines the interactions between Left–Right voting and the two individual-level variables we discussed above: political knowledge and partisan attachment. We add two interaction terms to see if these characteristics strengthen Left–Right voting. Political knowledge has a statistically significant effect in strengthening Left–Right voting, but partisan closeness is not statistically significant. The significant variance component for Left–Right orientations in the lower panel of the table implies that significant cross-national differences are still not fully estimated in this model.

The third model in Table 5.4 adds the polarization of the party system as a *direct contextual effect* and as a *contingent effect* on the strength of Left–Right voting. Party system polarization has a very strong multiplier effect on Left–Right voting. The interaction effect (.178) is so large that the direct effect of Left–Right orientations becomes slightly negative (presumably because of colinearity). Polarization also appears to have a *direct contextual effect* on Left–Right voting, with more polarized systems being more leftist. These contextual effects substantially reduce the variance component for Left–Right orientations, which is now barely statistically significant. The variance component for the intercept is also much smaller, indicating we are better modeling the cross-national patterns in these surveys. In summary, our multilevel multivariate models show that the polarization of the party system does strongly affect the ability of citizens to cast a vote based on their own Left–Right attitudes.

A refinement on the multilevel model focuses on the political knowledge that voters bring to their decisions. Table 5.3 shows that voters' political knowledge strengthens the Left–Right voting relations, but primarily in low information contexts where party positions are less dispersed (lower party system polarization). We can extend our earlier bivariate analyses by testing for these effects in a multivariate analysis. To avoid the complication of a three-way interaction term (Left–Right position by political knowledge by party system polarization), we chose the more direct course of dividing our set of nations into those with a Polarization Index above or below the cross-national average.[22]

Table 5.5 presents several significant results. In both low and high polarized party systems, Left–Right positions are the strongest predictor of vote – but the effects are much smaller in low polarization systems (b = .122) than in high polarization systems (b = .525). Furthermore, there is a clear interaction of political knowledge and context. Political knowledge is much more important in

Table 5.5 Left–Right voting choice in low and high polarization contexts

Predictor	Low polarization party systems		High polarization party systems	
	Unst. b	ß	Unst. b	ß
Left–Right orientations	.122	.23	.525	.59
	(.011)		(.014)	
Social class	.068	.04	.171	.05
	(.020)		(.024)	
Union	.043	.03	−.126	−.05
	(.015)		(.017)	
Education	−.010	−.02	−.012	−.01
	(.007)		(.010)	
Religiosity	−.010	−.01	.143	.06
	(.013)		(.016)	
Age	.005	.06	−.002	−.01
	(.001)		(.001)	
Knowledge Index	.121	.09	−.041	−.02
	(.013)		(.016)	
PID closeness	.008	.02	.010	.02
	(.004)		(.004)	
Knowledge * LR	.031	.11	.004	.01
	(.005)		(.006)	
PID * LR	.037	.05	.086	.08
	(.011)		(.013)	
Constant	4.041		2.236	
	(.100)		(.121)	
Multiple R	.394		.680	

Note: Table entries are the results of OLS regressions predicting legislative vote choice (parties coded by their Left–Right score).

Source: CSES, module II.

facilitating Left–Right voting in low polarization systems. The unstandardized regression coefficient for the interaction term in low polarization systems (b = .031) is several times larger than in high polarization systems (b = .004).

In addition, party system polarization generally facilitates voting choice based on other variables in the model. The interaction term for party closeness shows that partisanship has a stronger effect in highly polarized systems. Social class, union membership, and religiosity all have stronger relationships in the theorized direction in highly polarized systems. This model explains a substantially greater percentage of the vote in highly polarized party systems (*R* = .680) than in less polarized systems ($R = .394$). Highly polarized party systems are where Left–Right voting works most effectively.

Political choice and democratic politics

The rationale for elections is the presumption that they allow people to make choices about competing programs of government by voting for a political party that shares their political views (Katz 1995; Blondel and Cotta 2001). We examined this assumption through the mechanism of Left–Right voting. Do voters use their Left–Right orientations as a major basis of voting choice, finding a party that closely represents their own political viewpoints as represented in the Left–Right scale?

As many other studies have demonstrated, Left–Right orientations are a strong predictor of vote choice in most elections in most nations. One might question whether this relationship is overstated because we have not controlled for other predictors of vote such as candidate image or party identification. However, in terms of policy-based voting, the direct relationship between Left–Right orientations and vote is the essential measure, even if part of this relationship is mediated by factors such as candidate image or partisanship. Our analyses show that policy voting is a substantial part of the electoral calculus for most individual citizens.

We have attempted to go beyond the simple question of whether policy voting is significant by identifying the conditions that facilitate or impede Left–Right voting. The lesson from these analyses is clear: context matters. The clarity of party choice strongly conditions whether people can translate their Left–Right orientations into choices for a party that shares their values. Moreover, the clarity of party choice is not primarily a function of the nature of the electoral system or the effective number of political parties in the election. Rather, choice is largely synonymous with the degree of Left–Right polarization among competing parties. In addition, established democracies with longer histories of electoral competition and presumably more stable party systems also facilitate Left–Right voting. The conclusion is simple yet important: in order for voters to make clear policy choices, they must have clear options among the available parties.

We also explored the variability in Left–Right voting within the electorate. As expected, Left–Right voting was stronger among citizens that are more knowledgeable and those with a partisan attachment. However, there is an ongoing debate on whether these effects are mediated by the political context. In contrast to earlier research (Ensley 2007; Lachat 2008), we found that the stratification of Left–Right voting by political knowledge is greater in low polarization party systems. When information on party positions from the political context is lacking (party system polarization), knowledge becomes more valuable in identifying party positions and linking one's preferences to party choice. When such information in more readily available in highly polarized systems, the voting differences between high and low knowledge individuals is narrower. In contrast, highly polarized systems show a slight tendency for partisanship to stimulate Left–Right voting, presumably because the stakes of the election are higher.

In summary, elements of the political context do have a significant influence in defining the framework for electoral choice, and maximizing the ability of voters to translate their preferences into a vote decision. A doubling or tripling of the relationship between orientations and vote is a significant improvement in the representativeness of elections, and hence the functioning of the democratic electoral process. If democracy means the empowerment of voters to make policy choices, then offering clear choices is essential to this process.

Appendix

CSES survey variables

Variable	Question wording	Coding
Left–Right self-placement	B3045: "In politics people sometimes talk of left and right. Where would you place yourself on a scale from 0 to 10, where 0 means the left and 10 means the right?"	0 = Left to 10 = Right
Party Left–Right placement	B3038: "In politics people sometimes talk of left and right. Where would you place Party A on a scale from 0 to 10 where 0 means the left and 10 means the right?"	0 = Left to 10 = Right
Political knowledge	This is a count of the three political knowledge variables in each nation (B3047). Respondents who are coded as refused or not ascertained on any one measure are coded as missing data.	0 = No item correctly identified to 3 = All items correctly identified.
Strength of partisanship	B3036. "[IF Respondent was close to any political party] Do you feel very close to this [party], somewhat close, or not very close?" We added nonpartisans as a fourth category	0 = Nonpartisan, 2 = Not very close, 3 = Somewhat close, and 4 = Very close.
Social class	B2012: Recoded from the occupation of the respondent, deleting farmers.	1 = Working class, 2 = White-collar employee, 3 = Self-employed
Union member	Combines whether the respondent or a member of household is a member of a trade union (B2005 and B2006). Where only one of these variables is available, it is used alone.	1 = Respondent union member, 2 = Other member of household union member, 3 = No union member

Variable	Question wording	Coding
Education	B2003: Education of the respondent	1 = None, 2 = Incomplete primary, 3 = Complete primary, 4 = Incomplete secondary, 5 = Complete secondary, 6 = Postsecondary vocational, 7 = Incomplete university, 8 = Completed undergrad university
Religiosity	B2024 Religiosity.	1 = No religious beliefs, 2 = Not very religious, 3 = Somewhat religious, 4 = Very religious
Age	B2001 Age	Coded in discrete years, 18+

Notes

* I would like to thank Chris Anderson, Willy Jou, and the contributors to this volume for their comments on this chapter. I also want to thank Rein Taagepera and Aiji Tanaka for their advice and assistance in developing the Polarization Index.

1. For example, *The American Voter* declared that the electorate "is almost completely unable to judge the rationality of government actions; knowing little of the particular policies and what has led to them, the mass electorate is not able either to appraise its goals or the appropriateness of the means chosen to secure these goals" (Campbell et al. 1960: 543). Also see Delli Carpini and Keeter (1996) and Lewis-Beck, Jacoby, et al. (2008).

2. The CSES planning group discussed including an issue battery in the questionnaire for the third module. Several of the European researchers proposed a typical battery of questions about the welfare state, social-cultural issues, environmental quality, and cultural diversity. At this point, the member from Namibia said he could include these questions in his survey if the Europeans asked a question on elephants in theirs (what should be done to limit elephants from eating farmers' crops). He said this issue was as relevant to Europe as the European questions on the welfare state were relevant to Namibia. In stark terms, this illustrates the complexity of issue comparisons across nations. CSES III did not include a standardized issue battery because of these considerations.

3. Many public opinion researchers question whether ordinary people can understand and utilize abstract political concepts like "Left" and "Right" (Converse 1964; Lewis-Beck, Jacoby, et al. 2008, ch. 10). We agree that abstract ideological thinking as meant by political theorists is largely confined to a small stratum of the public; we use the Left–Right scale as a surrogate for political identities and positions on contemporary issues.

4. We acquired these data from the CSES website (www.cses.org). There are some inconsistencies in the CSES that required adjustments. Japan and Taiwan used the Progressive–Conservative scale as an equivalent to Left–Right. The Japanese survey is based on the upper house election, while other nations are for the lower house. The French CSES survey was conducted before the 2002 legislative elections so legislative vote intention was not included in the CSES release. We acquired the original French survey to analyze legislative vote intention for 2002. We also corrected the respondent Left–Right self-placement for Chile and the Left–Right placement of the Italian parties to correct for errors in the data release.

122

5. There might be questions about the public's ability to accurately identify the Left–Right position of political parties (see discussion in Chapter 4). In other analyses we have compared the public's placement of the parties with other measures of party positions (see Dalton, Farrell, and McAllister forthcoming 2011: ch. 4). For example, there is a .88 correlation ($N = 168$) between citizens' Left–Right party placements from the CSES and the scores of party experts from the Laver and Benoit study (2006). Another project surveyed members of the national parliament and member of the European Parliament for several West European democracies (Katz and Wessels 1999). These elite self-placements are similarly correlated with citizen placement of the parties.

   Another issue involves the use of mean scores or interpolated medians. We explored both options, and found they generate essentially the same results in our analyses. Therefore, for the simplicity of calculation and to be comparable to other chapters (Chapters 4 and 9) we use mean scores on the Left–Right scale.

6. Overall, 91 percent of the cases from the basic nominal relationship are included in the Pearson r correlations. In a few cases of highly fragmented party systems (e.g., Brazil, the Czech Republic, and Israel), the percentage drops below 80 percent because Left–Right scores are not available for many smaller parties. The Philippines presents a special case because of the highly fragmented system and extensive nonpartisan voting in legislative elections; the included cases drop to 47 percent of the nominal relationship. The Belgian survey did not include the questions on the party placement of the parties; in this instance, we used the CSES principal investigator's estimates of party positions.

7. We use the Left–Right placement measure in the multivariate analyses that follow because this reflects our expectation of an ordered relationship between Left–Right attitudes and vote. Nevertheless, the two sets of correlations in the table are strongly related ($r = .85$).

8. For instance, when a voter sees two parties at similar distances from their own position, then this is not considered deterministic voting if they select one of the parties. And if there are small differences between two parties, and the voter decides because of other factors such as party competency or governing experience, this would not be counted as deterministic voting.

9. We did not do such analyses because they can also contain a degree of circularity, with individuals projecting a party position to be consistent with their own Left–Right self-placement.

10. To estimate this pattern, we calculated the distance between the respondent's own self-placement and their position of the first four parties rated on the Left–Right scale. We chose four parties because all but one nation (the United States) asked for the placement of at least four parties. We then counted the number of parties that were within one scale point of the respondent's own position. One fifth of the pooled sample did not have any party within one scale point, a third had a single party (thus a single Left–Right predicted vote choice), and the remaining two-fifths had two or more parties within a single scale point.

11. Van der Eijk, Schmitt, and Binder (2005: 178–80) measure the Left–Right dispersion of parties using the Comparative Manifesto data; Dalton (2008b) and Kroh (2009)

use citizen perceptions of party Left–Right positions based on CSES data; Wessels and Schmitt (2008) calculate the mean of absolute differences between party pairs.

12. Wessels and Schmitt (2008) suggest that the disproportionality of the vote-seats allocation should affect the degree of Left–Right voting. We use the Gallagher index of disproportionality, and find little relationship with either vote relationship as displayed in Table 5.2 (.01 in both cases).

13. Kroh (2009) maintains that the average clarity of party positions is another important trait of party systems. There is probably significant variance in the degree of Left–Right voting for specific parties as a function of their ideological distinctiveness; also see Wessels and Schmitt (2008).

14. We use a three-point scale: (*a*) proportional representation, (*b*) mixed electoral system, and (*c*) majoritarian electoral system. See appendix to this volume.

15. The values of the Polarization Index and its calculation is presented in the appendix to this volume. This relationship is comparable to Dalton's findings (2008*b*) with an earlier partial release of CSES Module II using another question on party preferences (B3024), which yielded a .63 correlation. In addition, we can replicate these analyses with the nations from the Module I dataset using the Cramer's V measure of Left–Right voting ($r = .69$, $N = 27$).

16. We entered the variables in Table 5.2 into a stepwise regression to determine which exerted significant independent effects. Only two variables entered the regression analysis (p $\langle$ .05): party system polarization ($\beta = .86$) and established/new democracy ($\beta = .28$). Combined they explained 74 percent of the overall variance in Left–Right voting across nations.

17. Education might serve as another measure of sophistication. We find a similar gradient in the strength of Left–Right voting with education level. The correlation is .45 for those with incomplete primary schooling and .65 among those with an undergraduate university degree.

18. There are several caveats in using this three-item knowledge index (see Elff 2008). The specific questions measuring political knowledge are not the same across nations. Often they request information on a political leader or a political institution, but the range of questions is quite varied. In addition, the distribution of knowledge is not directly comparable across countries. The three items did not produce comparably sized quartiles in each nation. The quartile approach also assumes an equivalency between quartiles in each nation. The wide social and political variation among CSES nations makes this assumption unlikely. We did calculate knowledge scores normalized by the national mean to control for the difficulty of the knowledge questions, but this yielded essentially similar results.

19. These different images reflect the current heterogeneity of the nonpartisan group. We expect that Left–Right and issue voting is stronger when nonpartisans are cognitively mobilized with high levels of political interest and political skills. See Dalton (2008*a*: chapter 10).

20. We used the MIXED model analyses of SPSS for these analyses (See Albright 2007). We also considered models with democratic development, but this had only weak effects.

21. See the chapter appendix for the coding of these variables. Because of missing data we did not include the religiosity variable as another potential predictor, but this is included in Table 5.5.

22. The mean Polarization Index for the nations in our study is 3.31. We divided the nations into those above and below this mean value. We removed interaction terms with the Polarization Index since we are physically controlling for polarization in the two separate regressions.

6

Follow the Party or Follow the Leader? Candidate Evaluations, Party Evaluations, and Macropolitical Context*

Yuliya V. Tverdova

Candidate-centered voting has been a somewhat elusive phenomenon. It is hard to find an informed electoral observer who would assert that leader personalities do not matter in present-day politics. Yet, academic research has failed to produce consistent evidence to establish an independent relationship between candidate evaluations and electoral outcome. The dominant theory of voting based on partisan identification is as powerful now as it was sixty years ago (Bartels 2000; Hetherington 2001; Green, Palmquist, and Schickler 2002; McCarty, Poole, and Rosenthal 2006; Bafumi and Shapiro 2009). None of the modern social and political trends, including cognitive mobilization and partisan dealignment, seem to have undermined the basic idea that party identifications largely structure political attitudes and voting choices. In fact, the strength of the party voting model may even make the quest for other voting predictors seem meaningless.

Fortunately, however, many electoral behavior scholars continue to search for alternative explanations of voting, fine-tuning, and refining the existing ones. The reason for this seemingly irrational academic behavior is simple: voting is about winning elections. And many elections are won due to short-term factors, such as economic performance, salient issues, and candidate personalities. This chapter looks at a wide cross-national range of elections to determine whether there is an independent candidate effect in predicting voting behavior and whether this effect is modified by the political context. Conceptually, I offer a model that tests two competing voting hypotheses: partisan and candidate-centered voting. I posit that individuals who feel represented by a political party should be highly likely to cast a vote for this party. Alternatively, I hypothesize that citizens who develop positive feelings of representation toward a political leader should be more likely to vote for this leader or the party this candidate represents. I then consider a wide variety of macropolitical conditions to predict the relative strength of both factors.

Methodologically, the analysis proceeds in two steps. First, I estimate the strength of party and candidate voting in thirty-five elections by country, including other potential correlates of voting choice. The second step tests system-level modifiers of the candidate and partisan-voting estimates from the first step. One of the methodological innovations of this study is the consideration of individual-level, party-level, and national-level factors in affecting vote choice.[1]

The next section briefly surveys past literature on the partisan model of voting. Then I discuss recent scholarly advancements in the study of the relationship between candidate evaluations and vote choice and develop a set of testable hypotheses. After presenting some descriptive evidence of candidate and party evaluations, I test the relative strength of partisan- and candidate-based voting using data from the Comparative Study of Electoral Systems (CSES). I conclude by considering the implications of political context on voters' rationality to prioritize the criteria that are most useful for the vote choice.

Partisan images, candidate images, and vote choice

Perhaps no other subject captivates electoral scholars more than the logic behind voting. After the provocative conclusion by economic modelers led by Anthony Downs (1957) that the very act of voting is irrational, researchers had to dive deep into the psyche of individual voters to understand the underpinnings of voting decisions.

The most powerful explanation of voting choice so far has been the Michigan model, which can be boiled down to the proposition that citizens vote primarily according to their party identification (Campbell et al. 1960). It implies that, over the course of their lives, citizens develop deep psychological attachments to political parties, which may have direct and/or indirect effects on voting behavior. At the end of the "funnel of causality," the model discusses three particular factors: party images, candidate images, and issue opinions. All of these are likely to be some function of party identification, yet are not perfectly correlated with it. Short-term factors like performance or political scandals may be one of the reasons for why these correlations are not perfect (see Chapter 7). Other reasons are certainly plausible as well: from voters' rational cost-benefit calculations regarding salient issues to purely affective feelings toward a candidate. Regardless of the reason, the three factors may differ from party identification, may be related to each other, and may feed back into party identification and modify it. This chapter focuses on two factors at the end of the funnel of causality, namely, party images and candidate images, and assesses their relative strength for individual voting choice.

The determining role of party identification has been challenged since the 1960s, when social transformations disrupted the well-predictable pattern of party-based voting (Nie, Verba, and Petrocik 1979). These years are known as the period of party dealignment. Postwar generations, increasingly mistrustful of the government and other political institutions, became more detached from political parties. With this loss of loyalty, the question of what goes into the vote function sparked a new interest. Supporters of the cognitive mobilization thesis maintained that technological advances coupled with growing levels of education should lead to more sophisticated forms of voting, namely, issue voting and performance-based voting (Dalton, Flanagan, and Beck 1984). Instead of relying on political parties for cues, voters were better equipped to make their own evaluations of parties' issue positions and performance, and thereby cast their votes accordingly. This would shift the basis for voting decisions from party ideologies to more rational, perhaps nonpartisan, calculations. Contrary to the expectation of the diminishing role of political parties, Bafumi and Shapiro (2009) find that voters are still strongly aligned along party lines.

Systematic research on the effects of political personalities on electoral outcomes – personalization – is quite diverse. This research stresses the increasing role of individual politicians in the political process. Ian McAllister (2007) defines personalization as a fundamental change in the operation of democratic systems without concomitant change in institutional structures. For Thomas Poguntke and Paul Webb (2005), personalization entails the increasing power resources of political elites, autonomy within party and government, as well as the shift in electoral campaigns toward individual candidates. Similarly, Gideon Rahat and Tamir Sheafer (2007) conceptualize personalization as the increasing weight of individual political actors concomitant with a decreasing weight of political parties. Rahat and Sheafer also consider institutional changes as part of the personalization thesis, which involves a modification of electoral rules and candidate selection methods to place more emphasis on individual candidates.

The above definitions of personalization imply a change over time. However, many studies of candidate effects on voting are either single-election or cross-sectional studies. The primary goal of these studies, including this one, is to investigate how much effect individual candidates have on election outcomes and whether institutional structures affect this relationship.

Most electoral scholars agree that party identification strongly influences more specific images of the parties and candidates of each election campaign. Thus, candidate variables are not especially impressive predictors of the vote once a party affiliation variable is introduced into the equation (Curtice and Blais 2001; Bartle and Crewe 2002; Bartle 2003; Bean 2003; Curtice and Hunjan 2006).

However, other researchers contend that leader images can have an impact separate from party images, which are also conditioned by party identification (Andersen and Evans 2003; Evans and Andersen 2005). The personal characteristics of leaders, such as "reasonable," "caring," "principled," "strong," and "effective" consistently prove to be important for individual vote choice (Bean and Mughan 1989; Bartels 2002; Bartle 2003). Many voters appear more preoccupied with personal attributes of political leaders than with issue stances or party platforms (Brown et al. 1988). Alternatively, the bond between voters and leaders is closer than between voters and parties (Campus 2002).

In spite of these controversial findings, the balance of research commonly favors the skeptics. Graetz and McAllister (1987) agree that opinions of political leaders have a marginal impact on election outcomes (see also Karvonen 2007). Anthony King (2002a, b) similarly contends that "it is unusual for leaders' and candidates' personalities and other personal traits to determine election outcomes" (216). Bartels (2002) also notes that direct candidate effects are modest, and candidate evaluations themselves are strongly affected by partisan and ideological biases. Dinas (2005), when writing about the 2004 Greek election, eloquently summarizes the argument: "[D]espite the fact that leadership evaluations appear to be strong predictors of individual voting behaviour, they cannot determine electoral outcomes" (29).

Critical for the final election outcome or not, candidate effects on voting behavior are hard to deny. Election campaigns in many nations have become more and more candidate-oriented and less focused on parties (Arian and Shamir 2001). Numerous nations display an increased media attention to political personalities, and this has grown over time as well (Langer 2007; McAllister 2007; Rahat and Sheafer 2007).

As with so many other facets of individual attitudes and behaviors, declaring a unidirectional causal relationship between party identification and candidate evaluations would constitute a bold statement. Perhaps more realistic is the assumption of a reciprocal relationship where candidate evaluations are biased toward partisan preferences, and party allegiance is affected by leadership personalities. Naturally, partisans rate their own leaders more highly, and prime ministerial candidates are more identified with their political parties than presidential ones (Bean and Mughan 1989). According to Bartle (2003), "the relative importance of leader and party images [for voting behavior] depend on precise assumptions about causal order" (339). In other words, when both leader evaluations and party preferences are used to predict voting choice, party identification usually overpowers the candidate effect (Anderson and Brettschneider 2003). The common inference researchers make after observing the weak coefficient of the candidate variable is that leaders have a limited, if any, impact on voting behavior. Yet this conclusion may be flawed if party preferences are also affected by leadership evaluations. In fact, empirical findings suggest that disliking the leader of one's own party is a significant predictor of vote defection (Graetz and McAllister 1987). In this case, the insignificant coefficient may indicate the absence of a direct relationship between candidates and the vote, but signal an indirect connection through party identification. Moreover, if the candidate effect is significant, its magnitude may be underestimated, because we can only observe the independent effect. The total effect, then, is the sum of the direct and indirect effects.

Following the primary debate about the relative importance of party identification and candidate evaluations for voting behavior, I propose to test these competing hypotheses directly. In line with the partisan model, I posit that feeling represented by a political party makes it more likely to stay loyal to the party. Alternatively, feeling represented by a leader should increase the probability of voting for this candidate or the candidate's party. I also control for a number of socio-demographic characteristics, such as education, age, gender, and income, as well as a more traditional measure of party identification.

Candidates and political context

As noted in this volume, institutional factors can often condition political behavior. Particular features of electoral systems may promote either party-based or leader-based evaluations as an influence on voting. Past literature, for instance, has repeatedly emphasized the connection between electoral formula and party strategies. In proportional representation systems, parties tend to rely more on their core constituency and build bonding strategies based on a narrow ideology. In majoritarian systems, parties use bridging strategies to connect with as many voters as they can – that is, they tend to move toward the median voter (Downs 1957). If parties converge near the median voter position, voters may use other factors, including candidate evaluations, to make a voting choice.

John Curtice and Sarinder Hunjan (2006) explored whether institutional rules and the political environment moderate the impact of leadership evaluations on voting behavior. They found no evidence in support of the personalization thesis in parliamentary democracies, but leader assessments in majoritarian parliamentary systems are more important than in proportional representation systems. In a similar vein, McAllister (1996) found only indirect leader effects in parliamentary systems, where voters are more focused on party policies than individual candidates. He also showed that leader evaluations carry more weight in countries with polarized politics, weak party identification, and are more important for larger parties. Klingemann and Wessels (2009) find that in electoral systems based on party voting, the primary focus is on party-liking, whereas in candidate-based or presidential election systems, the focus shifts to candidate-liking.

Other research has considered party-level factors. First, parties at the far ends of the ideological continuum commonly have a more devoted constituency – and thus stronger party-based voting – than parties in the center. Some research shows that left-wing parties may be more ideologically driven, whereas right-wing parties may benefit from the populist rhetoric of their leaders (Lobo 2006, 2008). Second, a number of studies found a direct association between party size and leadership effects (Schmitt and Ohr 2000; Curtice and Blais 2001; Johnston 2002). The underlying logic is that leaders of bigger parties have a higher probability to play a significant role in government, for example, to become prime minister, and are more likely to be visible during the campaign. Finally, candidate effects are more pronounced in newer democracies where party systems are still not fully institutionalized (Colton 2002; Liddle and Mujani 2007) and regimes often face crises (Merolla and Zechmeister 2006). In these nations politics revolves around prominent personality figures making them more recognizable to voters. Moreover, parties lack well-defined political platforms or performance history upon which voters could make their judgments. Individuals' voting decisions in new democracies, therefore, may be more strongly linked to evaluations of party leaders. Moreover, younger democracies with developing party systems tend to have more fluid party identities among their citizens than older democracies with well-established party systems (Norris 2004; Dalton and Weldon 2007).

This research leads to the following testable propositions. We should expect to see a higher level of partisan voting in party-centered elections than in candidate-centered ones. Furthermore, the number and the variety of party choices are commonly associated with stronger partisan voting. Similarly, more proportional systems have traditionally been linked to stronger party discipline and predominantly party-based politics.

Party characteristics also may determine whether voters use their feelings toward parties or leaders as a major criterion for electoral choice. I hypothesize a party's ideology and size will influence the correlates of voting behavior. While right-wing parties may benefit more from the popularity of their leaders, left-wing parties have traditionally relied on a stronger ideological doctrine, such as socialism, to attract voters. Larger parties also apparently profit from popular leaders, because voters see them as potential government leaders. In addition, the average age of parties in the political system as well as the level of democratic development should lead to more partisan voting due to party longevity and stability on one hand, and voters' familiarity with the party system on the other.

Data and measures

The CSES serves as a useful ground to test partisan- and candidate-centered voting in a cross-national environment. As noted elsewhere in this volume, the uniqueness of the study stems from the combination of multiple and comparable units of analysis in one dataset.

At the individual level, the country surveys included two questions pertaining to respondents' feelings of representation by political parties and leaders (see chapter appendix for question wording and Chapter 10).[2] The first question asks whether there is a party the respondent feels represented by, and then which party. The second question repeats this query, asking if there is a political leader that represents the individual. The fact that both of these questions have the same wording makes it a potentially more consistent comparison of the two potential influences on voting. According to the partisan hypothesis, respondents should vote for the party they feel represents them. Alternatively, candidate-centered voting assumes a strong impact of political personalities on voting. In addition, these feelings of being represented provide a different perspective on G. Bingham Powell's study of representation (Chapter 9) through the Left–Right agreement between voters and government.

Due to the originality of the questions about party and leader representation in the CSES surveys, few studies have used these two measures of party and candidate images (see Wessels 2009). It is not entirely clear whether these questions tap into the affective, evaluative, or cognitive dimensions of individuals' allegiances to political parties and leaders. People may feel represented because of their ideological proximity to a certain party or leader or because they simply like them. However, feeling represented by a party or candidate is a reasonable way to assess the overall efficacy of the electoral process, which seeks to represent the public through competitive elections. In addition, I used the traditional party identification variable to control for the impact of partisanship on both party images and candidate images.

The major contextual variables approximate the likely focus of the election. For example, presidential elections are by nature candidate-centered, whereas closed-list parliamentary elections are less likely to focus on individual candidates. Three variables account for election focus (see volume appendix). First is a dichotomous variable: (1) for a presidential election and (0) otherwise. The second variable measures the structure of the electoral choice and is a continuum from most party-oriented to most candidate-oriented ballot system (Farrell and McAllister 2006).[3] Finally, I used a variable measuring the structure of the executive (parliamentary, semi-presidential, and presidential).[4]

In addition, an important innovation of this research is the consideration of party-specific factors that may affect how feelings toward both parties and leaders affect voting. To cover the effect of ideology, I included two dummy variables for extreme left and right parties as well as a continuous measure of Left–Right party ideology. Further, I included parties' vote shares in the parliamentary elections and candidates' vote shares in the presidential elections to measure party size. Finally, to account for the consistent relationship between party age and the strength of party identification, I used a party age variable.

For control purposes, I included a measure of a country's democratic development as the age of democracy. Regime durability may have an important moderating effect on other contextual variables in the model. As a rule, political institutions, including electoral and party systems, in newer democracies are less developed and may not be fully accepted by the population. Consequently, features like the electoral formula or party ideology may not produce the same impact on voting behavior as in well-established democracies. For example, in contrast to expectations, the introduction of new electoral systems in the postcommunist countries of East Central Europe, the majoritarian formula yielded a larger number of parties and a higher fragmentation of legislature than the PR formula (Lewis 2000; Birch 2004). I model these possible differences by splitting the sample into new and old democracies in another step of the analysis.

Descriptive evidence

I begin by looking at the frequency distribution of variables. Table 6.1 presents the distribution of our two key independent variables: feelings that one is represented by a party or a political leader. Somewhat more than half of the population across these thirty-three democracies feel represented by political parties and/or by political leaders.[5] These are surprisingly low numbers, since many of those who do not feel represented by a party still cast a ballot for a party (or a candidate) in the election.

Furthermore, there is a wide cross-national variation in the respondents' feelings. In newer democracies fewer citizens feel represented by either parties or leaders. With the exception of Hungary, Albania, and the Czech Republic, less than half of the populations in new and developing democracies feel represented by a political party. This number varies from about 25 percent in Korea to a little over 48 percent in Mexico. Italy is the only nation in the developed group in which less than a majority of the citizens feel represented by a party, and this may reflect the continuing turbulence in the Italian party system.

Feelings of representation by a leader are relatively low in the newly established democracies as well. However, in Brazil and Chile the number who feel allegiance with a leader are substantially higher than the proportion of those feeling represented by a party (with more modest differences in Peru and Taiwan). Whereas 40 percent of Brazilians feel represented by a party, more than 63 percent feel close to a leader. In Chile, these numbers are 43 percent and 70 percent, respectively. All four of these countries had a presidential election in the CSES survey. On the other hand, Mexico and the Czech Republic are two recent democracies where fewer people feel represented by a leader than by a party. In a number of established democracies, over 80 percent of the public feel

Table 6.1 Feelings of representation and partisan identification

Country	Is there a party that represents your views?	Is there a leader that represents your views?	Partisan identification
Albania	62.8	72.4	60.1
Australia	83.1	79.3	83.9
Brazil	40.1	63.7	49.4
Bulgaria	46.0	43.6	42.4
Canada	68.9	67.9	38.5
Chile	43.6	70.1	35.1
Czech Republic	77.9	55.7	63.7
Denmark	83.9	73.4	50.0
Finland	64.5	51.2	46.6
France	57.5	59.6	55.8
Germany	68.9	57.9	41.6
Great Britain	73.4	66.7	35.4
Hungary	73.2	81.1	52.6
Iceland	64.3	55.5	54.2
Ireland	78.1	77.8	28.9
Israel	68.2	56.9	62.4
Italy	42.6	40.9	43.3
Japan	57.3	57.3	60.2
Korea	24.9	22.2	40.0
Mexico	48.3	38.2	51.9
New Zealand	79.7	82.7	55.0
Norway	81.8	71.8	41.3
Peru	33.9	46.2	39.5
Philippines	28.7	30.5	16.0
Poland	40.0	39.2	41.8
Portugal 2002	55.8	59.0	51.9
Portugal 2005	48.1	51.8	44.9
Romania	45.0	48.1	99.9
Slovenia	28.9	35.3	21.3
Spain	74.1	72.8	61.3
Sweden	77.7	63.7	48.8
Switzerland	86.6	79.6	44.9
Taiwan 2001	37.4	45.7	42.8
Taiwan 2004	36.9	46.5	48.9
United States	74.1	77.4	56.8

Source: Comparative Study of Electoral Systems, Module II.

represented by a political party, while the proportion who feels represented by a leader averages a little lower.

A more striking finding comes from the comparison between what one might initially think are very similar variables – feeling represented by party and party identification. In fact, in only a handful of countries are these two partisan variables on par with each other. In most nations, attachments to a political party are much lower than feelings of party representation. In a quarter of the CSES countries, this difference is 30 percent or more. In Ireland it is a staggering 50 percent. This evidence attests to my initial assumption that the two party variables tap into different dimensions of voters' feelings. While identification with a political party has been associated with more affective or psychological orientation, answers to the representation question may be of evaluative and cognitive nature, based on a party's performance or issue positions.

The next question is whether people feel represented by a party and leader from the same party.[6] Table 6.2 displays the proportions for three sets of variables: (a) whether the respondent feels represented by a party and a leader from the same party, (b) whether the respondent feels represented by the same party as the party identification, and (c) whether the respondent feels represented by a leader from the same party as the party identification. First, it is notable that the proportions of the matched cases are quite high in all three comparisons. Perhaps not surprising, they are the highest for the comparison of whether the party the respondent feels represented by is the same as the party identification. The only stunning exception is Hungary, where this match exists only for a slight majority of the population (52.9%).

Although the match between the party and leader cited as representative is generally quite close (over 80%), in some nations this match hovers near 50 percent. At a first glance, this is a surprising result, because there is no clear pattern in the countries' where we see the largest mismatches. Chile, the Philippines, Hungary, and Romania are new or developing democracies, for example, whereas Germany and New Zealand are both highly advanced. There are no immediate similarities among the electoral institutions in these six countries or their party systems either. With regard to the match between feeling represented by a leader and party identification, the discrepancies are not as eminent.

Education or political sophistication is often a significant moderating factor in party-based and candidate-centered voting (Glass 1985; Mughan 2000). Education is treated as a proxy for people's cognitive abilities to process political information. Compared to the least educated group, the most educated are almost 10 percent more likely to feel represented by a party as well as 8 percent more likely to feel represented by a leader. However, they are also less likely to pick a leader from the same party they feel represented by (the gap is only about 5%).[7]

Table 6.2 Consistency in voters' feelings of representation and partisan identification

Country	Party and leader from the same party	Party represents and PID – the same party	Leader represents and PID – the same party
Albania	87.2	91.7	81.9
Australia	83.3	84.0	80.3
Brazil	70.1	89.4	61.7
Bulgaria	86.1	73.6	85.0
Canada	92.6	97.7	95.2
Chile	41.2	94.8	41.9
Czech Republic	84.5	85.0	76.9
Denmark	80.9	95.9	83.8
Finland	68.2	93.9	74.3
France	77.5	91.5	77.9
Germany	50.8	89.7	51.0
Great Britain	89.8	95.3	90.2
Hungary	49.8	52.9	48.3
Iceland	85.2	96.6	84.1
Ireland	84.7	93.2	84.3
Israel	68.9	88.0	69.5
Italy	88.1	92.8	75.6
Japan	88.8	91.9	88.0
Korea	91.5	91.6	90.3
Mexico	65.7	89.6	59.7
New Zealand	47.9	77.0	73.3
Norway	73.9	92.5	72.4
Peru	82.3	79.4	74.2
Philippines	54.3	69.7	56.8
Poland	80.9	82.7	60.3
Portugal 2002	87.7	91.9	84.1
Portugal 2005	76.6	84.3	77.9
Romania	56.0	85.7	56.3
Slovenia	80.7	90.5	70.7
Spain	97.6	97.8	97.0
Sweden	86.6	95.6	78.2
Switzerland	66.0	76.6	56.9
Taiwan 2001	75.7	91.4	76.8
Taiwan 2004	79.7	90.0	82.3
United States	91.8	95.3	92.8

Source: Comparative Study of Electoral Systems, Module II.

Table 6.3 Feelings of representation by polity characteristics

	Is there a party that represents your views?	Is there a leader that represents your views?	Party and leader from the same party
Executive structure			
Parliamentary	72.6	67.5	66.5
Semi-presidential	44.2	47.9	76.9
Presidential	41.0	49.7	73.0
Systems with presidential elections			
Presidential elections	44.0	57.8	48.0
Only parliamentary elections	60.7	60.9	74.8
Electoral formula			
PR	58.6	58.5	77.7
Mixed	54.7	55.2	64.0
Majoritarian	65.9	65.0	86.1
Regime Durability			
Established democracy	69.6	65.4	77.6
New or developing democracy	43.0	48.9	70.8
Party system polarization			
Low	47.1	52.2	79.8
High	49.2	57.7	58.7

Source: Comparative Study of Electoral Systems, Module II.

I now turn to the system-level factors that might predict cross-national variation in partisan- and candidate-centered feelings of representation (see Table 6.3). First, presidential systems are considered to be more candidate-oriented; thus, we expect a relatively higher proportion of the public feels represented by leaders, while more people feel represented by parties in parliamentary systems. Contrary to this expectation, feelings of representation by both parties and leaders are much stronger in parliamentary systems than presidential ones. It may be a function of a spurious relationship with the age of democracy (regime durability in Table 6.3). Most of the presidential systems in the sample are new or developing democracies, which have much lower perceptions of representation than established democracies.

In addition, presidential elections do not seem to affect feelings of representation by a leader. However, they decrease the proportion of those reporting being represented by a party significantly compared to legislative only elections. Interestingly, the match between the party and the leader is much higher in the systems with elections in parliament only (74.8% versus 48% in the systems with either presidential and legislative elections held simultaneously or exclusively presidential elections). This suggests that in presidential elections, voters are more likely to choose a candidate from a party they do not necessarily feel closest to because of the personal attractiveness of the candidate.

My simple frequency analysis is a bit at odds with Anderson's view (Chapter 10), since I find that majoritarian systems are more conducive to stronger feelings of representation with regard to both parties and leaders.[8] Moreover, voters are also more consistent in their political preferences in majoritarian systems – over 86 percent of them report feeling represented by a party and a leader from the same party.

Finally, the polarization of the party system plays a minor role in determining the share of the population who feel represented by either a party or a leader. It is nevertheless very important in determining whether there is a match between the two. In more polarized systems, people more often pick a party and a leader from different parties, whereas in less polarized systems, there is much more consistency. This result seems somewhat odd since party switching is relatively easier between parties with close ideologies. However, more polarized systems are also associated with a larger number of distinguishable political choices, which may motivate some citizens to split their preferences or even votes.

To summarize, there is an impressive degree of variability in the feelings of representation in democracies. Many people may split these feelings between multiple parties. In other words, they may develop positive feelings toward one party and a leader from a different party. Moreover, this analysis indicates that feelings of representation are systematically conditioned by macropolitical factors.

Multivariate analysis

Karen Jusko and W. Philips Shively (2005) developed a two-step estimation strategy that I use in this study. Unlike standard hierarchical linear models, this approach estimates individual-level processes separately for each country in the first step. In these analyses we use the two representation variables – and a set of other individual-level variables – in multivariate models predicting vote choice separately for each significant party in the CSES elections. In a second step we use contextual variables to predict the coefficients for party-representation and candidate-representation variables that were estimated in the first step.

This last point requires further explanation. Individual vote choice in the CSES nations is coded as a choice of a party or candidate in a certain election. To use a traditional hierarchical model, we would need a common dependent variable combining the information about country-specific voting choices in a unified way. This, however, is not feasible for our analyses. Because the two-step strategy gives the flexibility of modeling each individual-level process separately, I can preserve all the original information about the vote choice instead of creating one common dependent variable.

Thus, the dependent variable in the first step is a binary choice of voting for a particular party (or presidential candidate) in a particular election and country. I identified 189 parties across all the CSES elections that had at least twenty-five voters as the bases of these analyses.[9] I also constructed dichotomous party-representation and candidate-representation variables (for presidential elections) for each of the parties in the first-step analyses. For example, one model predicts support for the French Communist party (PCF) as the dependent variable, and for this analysis I also created two variables for whether the respondent mentioned the PCF in the party-representation question or in the leader-representation question. I then included the major independent variables (feeling represented by a party, feeling represented by a leader, and partisan identification) and several basic socio-demographic control factors (age, gender, education, and income) in individual regressions for each of the 189 party vote choices.

The first step produced individual-level coefficients from 189 separate regressions, which I will not present here for reasons of space.[10] However, I summarize the outcomes of the first step in Figure 6.1. The figure displays the strength of the coefficients for party-based voting and candidate-based voting for these

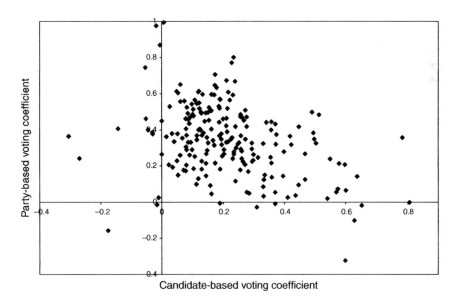

Figure 6.1 The relationship between candidate- and party-based voting

Note: Figure entries are the unstandardized regression coefficients predicting vote for 189 parties.
Source: Comparative Study of Electoral Systems, Module II.

189 parties. The x-axis shows the unstandardized regression coefficients for feeling represented by a party and the y-axis displays the coefficients for the feeling represented by a leader.[11]

On average, the mean coefficient for party-based voting (.34) is somewhat stronger than that for candidate-based voting (.21), which reaffirms the primacy of partisanship in voting choice. However, the figure also shows an understandable inverse relationship between party-based and candidate-based voting. The correlation between the two variables is −.32 and highly significant.[12] This means that when candidate representation has a stronger effect on vote choice, we are likely to see a diminished effect of party representation. For instance, party-based voting is strong (b = .61) for the Swedish Social Democrats, while candidate-based voting is weak for the party (b = .11). In contrast, candidate voting is relatively more important for the Le Pen's support in the 2002 French presidential elections (.40), while party-based voting for Le Pen is weaker (.28).

The second step of the two-step strategy uses the coefficients obtained in the first step as the dependent variables in another set of multivariate analyses. In other words, I predict the strength of the party-based and candidate-based voting coefficients in Figure 6.1 for the 189 parties. The reader may find it helpful to think about the second step as a series of interaction hypotheses in which the relationships in Figure 6.1 are predicted by contextual factors.

I proposed that the strength of the candidate-centered and party-centered voting should depend on both institutional characteristics of the polity and the characteristics of each individual political party. The overall model in the second step, therefore, includes both polity and party specific factors to explain the strength of partisan versus candidate-centered voting. Although the second step of the analysis contains units measured at different levels (party-level and polity-level), I estimated the model with OLS, which seems to be the most reliable way given the novelty of the procedure.[13]

Table 6.4 presents the results of two regression models – one estimating the strength of candidate-centered voting and the other the strength of party-centered voting. The R-squareds suggest that the model predicts the strength of the candidate-centered voting better than partisan voting. Although many system-level variables do not achieve statistical significance, it is not entirely surprising.[14] The major portion of the variation in survey data comes from differences among individuals, and this variation is commonly better explained by individual predictors rather than system-level factors.

Nevertheless, several party-level and polity-level variables significantly affect the strength of candidate-centered and party-centered voting. First, respondents are more likely to use their feelings of representation by party in their vote choice in proportional representation systems. In majoritarian systems, voters tend to rely more on their feelings of representation by political leaders. Other polity-level variables do not exert a statistically significant power over the

Table 6.4 Predicting coefficients for candidate-centered and partisan voting

	Coefficient for leader represents	Coefficient for party represents
National variables		
Nature of executive	.018	.014
	(.033)	(.039)
Presidential election	.366***	−.084
	(.069)	(.084)
Candidate-oriented system	−.006	.0004
	(.007)	(.009)
PR/Majoritarian system	−.068*	.114**
	(.029)	(.035)
Polarization Index	.016	.001
	(.016)	(.019)
Effective # of parties	−.012	−.004
	(.013)	(.015)
Durability of democracy	.011	.050
	(.052)	(.062)
Party variables		
Party size	.001	−.001
	(.001)	(.001)
Party ideology	.002	−.005
	(.013)	(.015)
Extreme Left party	.031	−.120
	(.054)	(.065)
Extreme Right party	−.046	−.010
	(.054)	(.066)
Party age	−.001*	−.0004
	(.0004)	(.0005)
Constant	.27**	.232**
	(.096)	(.114)
N	189	189
Adjusted R-squared	.284	.104

Notes: The dependent variables are the coefficients for party and candidate effects from the first stage model (see Figure 6.1). Table entries are unstandardized coefficients with standard errors in parentheses.
* $p \langle .05$; ** $p \langle .01$; *** $p \langle .001$.
Source: Comparative Study of Electoral Systems, Module II.

strength of either partisan or candidate-centered voting. In particular, this means that candidate voting is not systematically linked to party system polarization or the presidential/parliamentary structure of government. The latter finding should be interpreted carefully, however. Because I include both the parliamentary/presidential nature of the election and the general executive structure of the polity, the former may have overpowered the latter variable.

The executive structure in general does not matter, but the nature of the election itself determines the strength of these relationships.[15] The same logic may explain why the party/candidate-oriented electoral system fails to achieve statistical significance. In presidential elections, voters are much more likely to rely on their feelings of representation by political leaders than in parliamentary elections. Interestingly, there does not seem to be a similar effect of presidential elections on partisan voting.

Party characteristics are another set of contextual factors. The strength of candidate-based voting depends on the age of the political party for which the respondent voted. Specifically, feeling represented by a candidate matters more when choosing to vote for a younger party than a more established party. Younger parties may be more leader-driven than ideology-driven; thus feeling allegiance to the leader plays a greater role when considering a younger party rather than an older party. None of the other party characteristics is significantly related to the strength of candidate-based voting.

The strength of partisan voting also is not much affected by these party characteristics, except for extreme left ideology. The coefficient for the extreme left variable, however, only achieves statistical significance at the 0.07 level. Perhaps unexpectedly, the negative coefficient indicates that extreme left parties may suffer more from partisan dealignment than other parties. The same effect of extreme ideology is not at all present on the other end of the political spectrum, which conflicts with Lobo's finding (2006) that right-wing parties enjoy stronger leadership effects.

The effects of electoral institutions and party features may not be universal across countries. In well-established democracies, the effects of electoral and party systems may be more predictable, but newer democracies may exhibit more variable patterns. To account for the potential interaction effect between political institutions and the age of democracy, I performed a split-sample regression analysis. The results in Table 6.5 show the difference between the two sets of countries. In older democracies, partisan voting is more powerful in PR electoral systems than in majoritarian ones. The effect of the electoral formula is reversed for candidate-centered voting, although it is only significant at the 0.1 level. Interestingly, extreme left parties in established democracies enjoy a certain electoral advantage if people feel represented by their leaders. The link between feeling represented by a candidate and vote choice is more powerful when the leader is from an extreme left party. Finally, the nature of the election itself, whether legislative or presidential, plays a major role in determining the strength of candidate-centered voting.

In newly established or developing democracies, the patterns of both party-based and candidate-based voting are perhaps less intuitive. The most surprising finding is that candidate-centered voting is not stronger in presidential elections.

Table 6.5 Predicting coefficients for candidate-centered and partisan voting in old and new democracies

	Old democracies		New democracies	
	Leader represents	Party represents	Leader represents	Party represents
National variables				
Nature of executive	.023	.037	−.014	.04
	(.061)	(.09)	(.054)	(.054)
Presidential election	.454**	.047	.204	−.074
	(.141)	(.206)	(.191)	(.184)
Cand.-oriented	−.015	−.006	.008	.005
	(.009)	(.013)	(.026)	(.025)
PR/majoritarian system	−.072	.172**	.186	−.0007
	(.042)	(.061)	(.101)	(.098)
Polarization Index	−.031	−.058	−.002	.015
	(.042)	(.061)	(.025)	(.025)
Eff. number of parties	−.014	−.005	−.073**	.027
	(.02)	(.029)	(.032)	(.031)
Party variables				
Party size	−.0004	.002	.004**	−.004**
	(.001)	(.002)	(.002)	(.002)
Party ideology	.029	.006	−.022	−.012
	(.017)	(.025)	(.019)	(.019)
Extreme Left party	.126	−.052	−.065	−.149
	(.069)	(.101)	(.096)	(.093)
Extreme Right party	−.08	−.055	.052	.0003
	(.064)	(.093)	(.098)	(.10)
Party age	−.0003	−.0007	−.002	−.0001
	(.0005)	(.0007)	(.001)	(.001)
Constant	.313	.261	.284	.28
	(.189)	(.275)	(.159)	(.158)
N	111	111	78	78
Adj. R-squared	.381	.113	.225	.225

Notes: The dependent variables are the coefficients for party and candidate effects from the first stage model (see Figure 6.1). Entries are unstandardized coefficients with standard errors in parentheses.
* $p \langle .05$; ** $p \langle .01$; *** $p \langle .001$.
Source: Comparative Study of Electoral Systems, Module II.

Similarly, PR-systems do not have a strengthening effect on partisan voting. Some other variables, however, became significant in the interaction model. Larger parties benefit from the popularity of their leaders, whereas smaller parties seem to do better in the partisan model. Also, having a greater number of parties in the system appears to work against candidate-based voting in developing democracies.

Overall, both the results of the pooled analysis and the split-sample regression in new and old democracies concur with the proposition that the relative strength of candidate-centered and partisan voting for individual parties fluctuates slightly with the political environment where elections take place.

Discussion

In the voting literature, the Michigan model still stands strong almost half a century after it was developed. However, party identification has been losing power as the core predictor of voting because of social and political dealignment. Modern electorates, no longer aligned according to the socioeconomic status, have gained cognitive skills and wider access to information enabling them to make more independent political decisions. Yet, many voters still develop deep psychological attachments to political parties and some never change them through the course of their lives. Other voters take a more critical approach to politics and carefully evaluate parties' issue positions, past performance, and leadership choices. Put differently, they develop party and candidate images that, although originally fueled by party identification, may motivate them to rethink their political affiliation or switch their vote between parties.

The scholarly community remains divided about candidate effects on voting behavior and election outcomes, but I argue that leader personalities matter and provide empirical evidence to support this claim. I expected to find independent effects of party and candidate evaluations on individual vote choice. I first hypothesized that those who feel represented by a leader would be more likely to vote for this leader or their party. As a competing hypothesis, I maintained that individuals who feel represented by a particular party should also be more inclined to vote for this party. The results revealed a strong connection between vote choice and both party and leader sentiments. This holds both in simple bivariate relationships and in multivariate analyses controlling for each other, and other potential predictors such as party identification.

Voting, however, does not happen in a political vacuum. The institutionalist approach claims that voting behavior is constrained by systemic factors, such as electoral formula, the structure of the government, the nature of party competition, and so on. This project was to identify contextual characteristics that predict the strength of candidate effects relative to partisan voting.

I found that candidate-centered voting becomes more powerful when the focus of elections shifts toward individual leaders, such as in presidential elections. However, presidential systems and a candidate-oriented ballot structure do not seem to exert an independent effect on the strength of candidate-centered voting. Moreover, less proportional systems make it more likely that voters would rely on their feelings about candidates to guide their voting behavior. More proportional systems, in contrast, play to the advantage of the partisan model.

The evidence also indicates that both the age and ideological positions of parties are at least marginally important for candidate-driven and partisan voting. The voting impact of political leaders appears to be weaker in older parties, and partisan voting is weaker in extreme left parties. Finally, after separating newer democracies from the older ones, I found significant differences between the two groups of countries in the conditions under which either voting model prevails.

Several recent studies find that the most sophisticated and interested voters pay closer attention to leader personalities.[16] How irrational is this? Given a powerful role of the chief executive in the government formation and consequently policymaking, candidate-centered voting does not seem irrational at all. The historical significance of individual leaders for party politics and setting the national agenda is hard to underestimate either. Recall, for example, the change in the Labour policies under Tony Blair. Thus, it should not come as a surprise that the most politically alert build leader personalities in to their voting calculations. That is, of course, if such calculations are based on politically relevant aspects rather than the color of the politician's suit or the name of his dog. The rationality of building leader personalities into voter calculations becomes even more evident when considered under different political conditions. In presidential systems and presidential elections, where the chief executive exercises substantial individual powers, paying closer attention to candidate personalities perhaps makes more sense than in parliamentary closed-list systems, in which the chief executive is highly constrained by the party. As Klingemann and Wessels (2009) conclude in their study of candidate effects, voters rely on information that seems most useful under particular macropolitical conditions, which falls into the very definition of rationality. Of course, the danger of blindly following the elites is the loss of government accountability to the public and a potential for power abuse. Is this a plausible scenario? It certainly is, in the absence of independent media, viable political opposition, and active civic groups. If these elements of a healthy democratic society are present and working, either candidate voting or partisan voting does not strike me as particularly dangerous.

Appendix

Variables used in the study

Individual-level variables

Variable	Question wording	Coding
Vote choice	B3005: This variable reports the presidential candidate or party affiliation of the presidential candidate for whom the respondent voted B3006: This variable reports the vote(s) cast by the respondent in lower house elections B3007: This variable reports the vote(s) cast by the respondent in upper house elections	Country and party-specific: coding 1 = Voted for the candidate or party, 0 = Otherwise
Party representation	B3024: [If there is a party that represents your views], which party represents your views best?	Country and party-specific coding: 1 = Represented by the party, 0 = Otherwise
Leader representation	B3026: [If there is a leader that represents your views], which leader represents your views best?	Country and party-specific coding: 1 = Represented by the leader, 0 = Otherwise
Party identification	B3029_1: [If you feel close to any political party], what party is that?	Country and party-specific coding: 1 = Feel close to the party, 0 = Otherwise
Income	B2020. Household income quintile	1 = Lowest quintile to 5 = Highest quintile
Gender	B2002. Gender of respondent	1 = Female; 0 = Male
Education	B2003: Education of the respondent	1 = None, 2 = Incomplete primary, 3 = Complete primary, 4 = Incomplete secondary, 5 = Complete secondary, 6 = Postsecondary vocational, 7 = Incomplete university, 8 = Complete undergrad university
Age	B2001 Age	Coded in discrete years, 18+

Party-level variables

Party age	B5011 and author's sources	Coded in discrete years since the founding year
Party size	B5001, B5003, B5005, and author's sources	Share of the votes received in the current election
Party ideology	B3038. Averaged responses of the party's ideological placement by country	
Extreme left	B5012. Parties that are classified in the CSES dataset as communist, ecology, or socialist parties	1 = Communist, ecology or socialist parties, 0 = Otherwise
Extreme right	B5012. Parties that are classified in the CSES dataset as right liberal, conservative, or nationalist	1 = Right liberal, conservative, or nationalist parties, 0 = Otherwise

Notes

* I would like to thank Ryan Sirah for his assistance in the empirical analyses in this chapter.

1. For the details on this particular methodology of estimating multilevel models, please refer to a special issue of *Political Analysis* (2005). Karen Jusko and W. Phillips Shively (2005) and Christopher Achen (2005) specifically discuss this two-step strategy.

2. I excluded a few countries from the original dataset. Belgium and the Netherlands have missing data on the key variables. In addition, the results of the Russian 2004 presidential election were influenced by the so-called enormous "Putin" effect. Vladimir Putin, who won the election in the first round with over 70 percent of the popular vote did not belong to any political party.

3. It is based on several attributes of a country's electoral system, including the formula, district magnitude, and the ballot structure (see volume appendix). Because Farrell and McAllister (2006) adapted the candidate-orientation measure for legislative elections, and my analysis includes several presidential elections, I assigned all presidential elections a maximum score of 10 on the index. The only other polity that has a score of 10 is Ireland, which uses a Single Transferable Vote system.

4. The inclusion of several variables accounting for the executive structure and the focus of elections may raise concerns of multicollinearity. To address this concern, I estimated my models using different combinations of these variables. In the end, accounting for the nature of the election (the presidential variable) reduces the effects of the executive structure variable and the candidate-orientation variable virtually to zero and highly increases the predictability of the models. In turn, failure to include the presidential variable significantly reduces the fit of the models. This leads me to believe that the exclusion of the presidential dummy is likely to produce biased estimates. The inclusion or exclusion of the other two variables (with the presidential dummy in the model), in contrast, does not affect any other coefficient estimates or the fit of the models in any noticeable way. Because previous studies used both the executive structure and the candidate-orientation variables in their analyses, I decided to keep both of them for these analyses.

5. Although there are thirty-three countries in my dataset, there are thirty-five election studies. Portugal and Taiwan fielded two election studies in the second CSES module.

6. If a person lacked a response on any of these questions, s/he was coded as missing.

7. These results are not presented in a table, but are available from the author upon request.

8. Anderson (Chapter 10) found that more proportional systems enhance the feelings of representation by a party, but have no direct effect on the representation perceptions by a leader.

9. In fact, the number of party-choice and candidate-choice variables could have been higher except for missing data in the independent variables. The initial threshold for the inclusion of a party/candidate into the analysis was if at least twenty-five respondents had voted for them.

10. Routinely with dichotomous choice variables, researchers use estimation procedures such as binary logit or probit. In this case, however, the estimates from the first step

are not directly transferable to the second step and would require additional transformation, say, into probability statements before entering into the second step. Given
the robustness and consistency of OLS with binary dependent variables, I decided to
estimate the first-step regressions by OLS (see also Jusko and Shively 2005).

11. In a vast number of regressions, feeling represented by a party and party identification
have strong independent effects on vote choice. This means that the party representation variable and party identification tap into different dimensions of party allegiances. Moreover, despite the two party variables, the candidate effect, measured by
voters' feelings of representation by a leader, directly affects vote choice as well.

12. As one might expect, both party-representation and candidate-representation variables have strong positive bivariate relationships with vote.

13. I also analyzed the contextual (party-level and polity-level) factors sequentially. That
is, I only included party-specific variables and controlled for polity-specific characteristics with country dummies. However, under this scenario party-level estimates
become overpowered by the country dummies. I do not report these results in the
chapter, but they are available upon request.

14. To determine whether these results are sensitive to the inclusion of the party identification variable, I repeated the first step analysis without it. It turns out that none of
the contextual estimates (party-level and country-level) are affected by this modification. The only coefficient that changes significantly is for the representation by party
variable, which picks up the effect of the party identification variable.

15. Bean (1993), based on the Australian and New Zealand data combined with earlier
research, found broad similarities in voters' responses to political leaders in parliamentary and presidential systems.

16. Brader and Tucker (2008) argue that partisans are also more sophisticated than their
fellow citizens.

7

Context, Political Information, and Performance Voting*

Timothy Hellwig

In recent years, students of democracy have paid much attention to the relationship between government performance and the vote. This is for good reason: if elections are to work as instruments of democracy, then voters ought to be able to control politicians' actions by giving them incentives for implementing good policies.[1] When governments perform well, they are rewarded with continued support of the electorate, and when they fail to live up to expectations they are removed from office. Disagreement persists, however, on the prevalence of this accountability relationship in the real world. Do voters hold governments to accounts, in the sense of supporting them during times of peace and prosperity and abandoning them during hard times? What factors unique to particular electoral settings affect whether performance evaluations serve as instruments of accountability? Further, what types of citizens choose their representatives according to the government's performance in office and who discounts such evaluations in favor of other criteria?

This chapter addresses these questions. It aims to advance current understandings of electoral accountability in cross-national perspective. It does so in three ways: by examining how macro-contexts work in conjunction with individual-level factors to influence the salience of the performance-based vote; by placing performance voting alongside other components of the voter's calculus; and by utilizing a broader indicator of performance evaluations more suitable for making comparisons across national contexts.

Current scholarship examines performance voting by exploring how individuals obtain and use information – either information about performance and policy responsibility or information about how the macro-environment structures the voting decision. Investigations have for the most part been limited to one or the other of these factors – either individual-level attributes or macro-level contextual factors – in order to better understand voter propensity to hold politicians to account in democratic elections. Those taking the first approach make use of large-N surveys of single electorates while those seeking cross-national variation draw on country-level indicators of election returns and performance indicators.

This chapter first and foremost examines how macro-political contexts shape electoral accountability. In doing so, it falls squarely in the cross-national camp. The increased availability of comparable cross-national surveys, however, means we no longer are limited to inferring the voter's calculus from aggregate-level data. Country-level variation, we suspect, does much to explain why the performance–vote relationship may be stronger in Britain, for example, than Belgium. But individual-level heterogeneity ought to matter as well, perhaps in ways that work in conjunction with context. This chapter uses data from Module II of the Comparative Study of Electoral Systems (CSES) from thirty-five national-level elections to examine how political context and individual differences matter for how governments are held to accounts. A consideration of both macro as well as micro factors, *and connections between them*, offers a more realistic picture of how voters incorporate performance evaluations into their decision.

Although there are many studies on performance voting, the relationship between system performance and the vote is generally studied in isolation, with little attention to the many other factors that scholars have identified as important for understanding how people vote. The reason for this neglect arises, no doubt, from the use of aggregate-level research designs. At the country level, measures of performance are readily available, particularly of economic conditions. But measures for other relevant sociological or psychological factors are generally lacking. It is not enough, however, to understand how context influences one element of the vote in isolation. Not considering how context affects the range of voting criteria runs the risk of producing biased estimates of the relationship. As Raymond Duch and Randolph Stevenson ask in their recent book, "How is the *vote calculus* conditioned by context? [H]ow does context condition the importance that voters accord their evaluations of government performance or their issue positions or maybe candidate personality when they make a vote decision?" (2008, 358 emphasis in original). Questions such as these motivate the research presented here. With the CSES data we can now better match a "unified" micro model of vote choice from theory with a statistical model, and do so across macro contexts.

These two objectives – to consider *how contextual and individual attributes jointly shape performance voting* and to consider their effects on voter choice *within the overall calculus of voting* – are facilitated by the measurement of the key independent variable. Past assessments of accountability relationships have arguably been compromised by operationalizing retrospective "performance" more narrowly than democratic theory would imply. Sometimes by choice but more often by convenience, this operationalization is usually in the form of the economy. A common rationale is that the economy is easily understood, transparent, and salient to the majority of the electorate the majority of the time. Claims that "the economy is always an important issue to voters" may well be true (Wlezien 2005, 556). It is not clear, however, whether the economy is always the *most* important issue to most of the voters in any given election or in any given democracy. Matthew Singer's (forthcoming, 2011) examines the CSES data and finds that in only a third of surveys do that a majority of respondents say the economy is the most important issue. This means we must ask whether the lack of an "economic vote" in a given election is due to institutional barriers to clear assignment of policy responsibility or to the low salience of the economy relative to other issues. The use of the economy for gauging retrospective voting in cross-national perspective arguably is also compromised given that all governments do not have equal control over economic policy (Hellwig 2010). Focusing on overall performance evaluations rather than evaluations of economic conditions provides for a more consistent and cross-nationally comparable estimate of the accountability relationship.

The next section presents a theoretical framework for how context affects the voter's calculus and, by implication, performance voting. I then develop a set of hypotheses linking performance voting to political context and, at the individual level, to incentives for voters to acquire information about politics. These claims are then assessed with data from the CSES in the following two sections. The final section concludes.

Context and performance voting in comparative perspective: toward a third phase of scholarship

It is no stretch to say that the cross-national study of performance voting (or, most frequently, *economic* voting) has received more sustained attention than many other topics addressed in this volume. We can identify three phases to this evolving research agenda. Early cross-national works of performance voting, such as Martin Paldam's seventeen-country study (1991) at the macro level and Michael Lewis-Beck's five-country analyses (1988) at the micro level, called attention to variation in the strength of economic voting across countries.[2] This heterogeneity was readily apparent even though advanced industrial countries shared many qualities in terms of democratic stability and parliamentary forms of government.

Motivated by such observations, a second generation of work explicitly incorporated information about the political context into empirical models. Powell and Whitten (1993), for example, identified institutional factors that bear on the extent to which incumbents can diffuse responsibility for economic conditions.[3] Their ideas about the "clarity of responsibility" have subsequently been applied and adapted by several scholars, particularly in cross-national opinion studies (e.g., Anderson 2000; Anderson 2006; van der Brug et al. 2007 Duch and Stevenson 2008; Tillman 2008).

Incorporating "context," variously defined, into analyses of election returns and of vote choice has done much to minimize – but by no means eliminate – the instability dilemma identified by Paldam (1991). However, in detailing how institutions help office holders refract blame, the research on context and economic voting had little to say about the individual voter's decision process. So even though this "second generation" of studies on (economic) performance outcomes and the vote better specified the macro-level effects that impeded or facilitated the (economic) performance–vote connection, it did little to advance our knowledge of the micro mechanisms behind the process. Just how do voters incorporate information about political context? How does that information affect the voter's decision to base her choice on performance evaluations? And, more broadly, how does context give incentives to emphasize certain components of the vote function and discount others?

Students of comparative economic voting are only beginning to confront these issues. For example, Mark Kayser and Christopher Wlezien (forthcoming) present a voting model in which the strength of economic voting varies inversely with partisanship. They argue that low information voters, if unanchored by partisan attachments, are more sensitive to short-term swings in economic conditions than those with high information (also see Zaller 2004). Duch and Stevenson (2008) study how context shapes the economic vote based on how retrospective voters use information about the economy. Their model specifies how voters assess the influence of actors, like political parties, whose status derives from election outcomes compared to the influence of exogenous, nonelectorally chosen actors. Contributions such as these highlight the individual "microfoundations" underlying observed relationships.

Research on political information and performance voting, however, typically has little to say about macro contexts.[4] Tackling the questions posed above requires a model that combines political context, voter information about politics, and the individual voter's calculus. Doing so is consistent with the general framework for voter choice advanced in this volume. This relationship between institutions and citizen incentives to become informed about politics in turn affects the sets of choices in voters' minds. Such a framework is also consistent with the notion that performance (economic) voting is conditioned by individual and contextual factors alike (Anderson 2007*b*). While few would disagree with such claims, empirical studies rarely combine these two contingencies.

Finally, the framework advanced here is consistent with recent arguments about context and the calculus of voting (Chapter 1; Wessels and Schmitt 2008; Klingemann and Wessels 2009). To think seriously about context, we must consider how it matters for the voter's acquisition of information and how it shapes not just one determinant of the vote but the entire vote function.

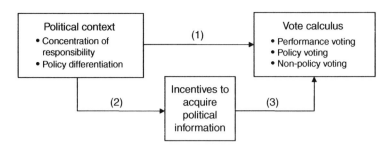

Figure 7.1 Theoretical framework of how context and information condition vote choice

Context should affect not just the performance vote but also the relevance of the various criteria voters use to evaluate the available choices. The vote function, note Bernhard Wessels and Hermann Schmitt (2008, 21), is not one but many, and "varies in response to the specifics of the institutional settings."

Figure 7.1 displays the theoretical framework in general terms, providing linkages from context to information to the vote calculus. It depicts three causal paths. The first (1) shows context directly affecting the choices voters have in elections. The second (2) charts how context affects information about politics. And the third (3) examines how information matters for the vote decision. The next section identifies key contexts and lays out a set of hypotheses linking them to the voter's calculus and, within it, to performance voting.

Political context, political information, and performance voting: hypotheses

I begin with the voter's calculus. Research on the determinants of vote choice generally focuses on three factors: performance evaluations, the policy proposals of competing parties, and non-policy factors (such as partisanship, candidate images, scandals, and the like). Scholars have recently taken these approaches in two directions. One is to examine how context conditions each of these factors (e.g., Huber, Kernell, and Leoni 2005; Duch and Stevenson 2008;). The second extension is emphasized in the spatial modeling literature and investigates the relative importance these components on the vote (Blais et al. 2004; Adams et al. 2005). The approach advanced here is informed by both of these extensions.

If g represents the incumbent government, then we can express the utility of voter i for g as:

$$U_{ig} = \beta_1 y_i - \beta_2 |v_i - p_g| + \beta_3 t_{ig} \tag{1}$$

The first term on the right-hand side represents a simple sanctioning mechanism: y_i is i's evaluation of government performance. The second term, $|v_i - p_g|$, represents policy voting as the absolute difference between the ideal point of voter i and the position of governing executive g. The third term, t_{ig}, captures the non-policy-based affinity of i for g. And the β s are unknown constants measuring the respective salience to the voter of performance evaluations, policy positions, and non-policy attachments.[5] This model, however, must allow for the possibility that macro-political contexts condition the influence of performance evaluations and other components of the vote. Thus it can be re-expressed as

$$U_{igk} = \beta_1 y_i Z_k - \beta_2 |v_i - p_g| Z_k + \beta_3 t_{ig} Z_k \qquad (2)$$

where Z_k is a particular contextual arrangement in country k. While the focus of this chapter is on the first term on the right-hand side, performance evaluations, the general expression of Equation (2) allows contextual factors to affect the voter's utility through different components of the vote function.[6]

We now consider context. I identify two types of macro-political contexts expected to influence how performance assessments (and other factors) on the utility for voting for an incumbent party. The first pertains to the concentration of decision making. When the levers of policy are controlled by just one elected official, then the accountability relationship should be strong. In such a scenario voters evaluate policy outcomes, perfunctorily identify the actor most likely responsible, and select accordingly. But as responsibility for policy outcomes spreads over more and more actors, power sharing induces uncertainty in the minds of the electorate about how to use the vote to punish or reward any particular candidate or party in the next election. Hence, when responsibility is diffuse, rational voters ought to discount their retrospective performance evaluations as determinant of vote choice and lean more heavily on other components of the vote function.[7]

Expectations regarding the effects of arrangement of policy responsibility assume a backward-looking electorate: the voter decides based on his or her assessment of decisions previously made and carried out by the sitting government. But opportunities for new policy directions should matter as well. This point was noted by Downs some years ago:

[E]very election is a judgment passed upon the record of the incumbent party. But the standards used to judge its record are of two types. When the opposition's policies in period t have differed from those of the incumbents, the judgment expresses the voters' choice between the future projections of those two policy sets. But if the opposition's policies have been identical with those of the incumbents (*sic*), mere projection provides the voters with no real choice. (Downs 1957, 41–2)

The salience of performance evaluations in the overall vote calculus thus depends on whether the election outcome is expected to yield a new set of policies. For example, consider the case where a citizen is dissatisfied with policy results as they have evolved over the sitting government's tenure. Retrospective reward–punishment models predict that this individual will vote against the incumbent party in the next election. However, this is more likely if the voter had reason to think that placing a different set of actors in office would produce a different set of policies. If the voter perceives little or no policy differences among party competitors, she has less reason to expect a reversal in policy outcomes even if a new government takes office. The same logic applies to the case in which the voter evaluates past government performance in a positive light: the incumbent may reap little from a solid record (aside from gains in reputation) in the event that opposition candidates advocate identical policies. The effects of past performance should thus be contingent on the concentration of responsibility but also on the range of policy alternatives (Lewis-Beck 1988; Anderson 1995b, 2000; see also Anderson 2007; Wlezien 2004).

Arguments about the distribution of responsibility and the range of policy options suggest two testable "contingency" hypotheses for the first causal path in Figure 7.1:

Hypothesis 1a: *The influence of government performance evaluations on incumbent support is greater when administrative responsibility for policy is concentrated.*

Hypothesis 1b: *The influence of government performance evaluations on incumbent support is greater when alternatives over policy are large.*

Hypotheses 1a and 1b provide us with two testable claims. However, they do little to suggest how political context influences performance voting *indirectly*, by way of the voter's acquisition of political information. To what extent does political context affect citizens' incentives to become informed about politics? When policy responsibility is limited to a few actors, assigning credit or blame is a simple task requiring little knowledge of the intricacies of government portfolio allocations or power-sharing arrangements. The voter need not engage in a comparative assessment of party policy preferences or contributions to policy outcomes. All that matters in order for the voter to reelect or reject incumbents is whether observed outcomes surpasses or falls short of some predetermined performance threshold. Or, as put by Morris Fiorina, "in order to ascertain whether the incumbents have performed poorly or well, citizens need only calculate the changes in their own welfare."[8] In this situation, institutions provide little incentive for voters to acquire detailed information about politics. All that is required is to know which actors are in government and which are in opposition.

Party policy differentiation, however, is a different matter. As noted, the distinctiveness of party policy offerings should facilitate performance-based voting. A broad range of offerings signals to voters that their choice could have consequences for whether the next government adopts policies different from or similar to the incumbent. This assertion, however, assumes a level of sophistication on the part of the electorate. In order for the range of policy alternatives affect the voter's calculus, the voter must first be *aware* of the diversity of policy appeals present among competing parties. As Robin Best and Michael McDonald argue (Chapter 4), in order to have popular control of the direction of policy, voters must recognize the meaning of policy packages on offer. This requires a certain degree of information about national politics. And the more diverse the party system – in terms of policy packages on offer, the more knowledgeable a voter must be to make an informed choice.

The result is that our two contexts work at cross purposes: incentives for voters to acquire information about politics increase as (*a*) policy responsibility becomes more diffuse and (*b*) the range of policy alternatives becomes greater. Two hypotheses for the direct relationship between political context and political information which we can test using the CSES data are:

Hypothesis 2a: *Voter levels of political information are greater in contexts where the concentration of responsibility is low.*
Hypothesis 2b: *Voter levels of political information are greater in contexts where the range of party policy alternatives is large.*

We finally consider how political information affects the voter's calculus (causal path 3 in Figure 7.1). It is hypothesized that high information are disproportionally found in certain kinds of contexts. But the story does not end here. The politically sophisticated may, after all, vote on different bases than uninformed voters. As Martin Kroh (2009, 221) notes, "individual processes leading to vote choice do not apply to all voters" (see also Rivers 1988). As regards performance voting, Brad Gomez and Matthew Wilson (2001) argue that political sophistication conditions the individual's ability to attribute responsibility for policy outcomes to government actors, which, in turn, affects the connection between economic perceptions and vote choice. Voters with higher levels of political knowledge should be able to link information across levels of abstraction necessary for connecting the government policy to their own personal financial situation. Less sophisticated individuals vote differently, by taking cues not from their own circumstances but from general conditions characterizing the national economy. John Zaller (2004) also draws connections between knowledge about politics and vote choice, suggesting that more sophisticated voters make electoral decisions on the basis of ideology where the less informed rely more on short-term factors like the performance of the economy.

I advance an argument similar to Zaller's. The task of voting retrospectively in terms of performance evaluations is relatively simple. Thus for low information voters we should observe a particularly strong connection between performance evaluations and the vote. However, the task of voting prospectively, in terms of the policy positions of alternative future governments, places a greater burden on the voter. So with reference to Equation (1) we assume that politically informed voters are more likely to base the vote decision on policy distance, $|v_i - p_g|$, and less likely to be swayed by general performance evaluations, y_i, when judging their utility for incumbent government g. That high information voters are less likely to emphasize general performance evaluations is consistent with Gomez and Wilson's argument (2001) about the weak link between evaluations of the national economy and the vote among high sophisticates. This leads to a third pair of testable hypotheses:

Hypothesis 3a: *High information voters place less emphasis on performance-based voting relative to low information voters.*
Hypothesis 3b: *High information voters place greater emphasis on government policy-based voting relative to low information voters.*

Data and measures

As with other contributors to this volume, this chapter combines micro-level data from the CSES Module II (2001–6) with macro-level data on political institutions. For sake of comparability, I omit surveys that do not report vote choice for legislative elections or that otherwise lack data on key measures.[9] This leaves us with thirty-five electoral contexts, incorporating a far greater range of cases than typically found in individual-level studies of voting behavior (see appendix to volume). The dependent variable is *Government Party Vote*, coded 1 if the respondent reported voting for a party having belonged in government prior to the election and 0 otherwise (see chapter appendix for information on the individual-level variables).

As shown in Equation (1), the model of incumbent vote choice has three key independent variables.[10] The first of these, *Government Performance*, is constructed using responses to the item "Thinking about the performance of the government in [capital] in general, how good or bad a job do you think the government in [capital] has done over the past {...} years?" The text in {...} is specific to the particular election study and pertains to the number of years since the last election or, if more recent, since the last change in government.[11] This measure has two attributes that make it preferable to the perceptions of economic conditions items typically used in studies of individual performance voting. First, it explicitly connects evaluations of performance *of the government* over its *term in office*. Second, it asks for evaluations of performance in *general* terms. Both of these characteristics may minimize the individual-level instability, or "noise," that has characterized studies of performance voting in terms of economic voting due to uncertainty about the voter's time horizon and to uncertainty about the salience of the economy vis-à-vis other issues.[12]

The second predictor, *Government Policy Distance*, is a measure of the linear difference between the policy preferences of the voter and the government.

Policy preferences are summarized using the Left–Right scale. As many have argued, the Left–Right scale adequately summarizes the issues and cleavages that structure political competition in a given country, even though the content of the scale may vary across space and time (see Chapter 5). For the voter's preferences I use the respondent's self-placement on the Left–Right scale. For the government's policy preference I use a composite measure which combines the Left–Right position of governing parties weighted by each party's share of cabinet portfolios (see volume appendix). *Government Policy Distance* is the absolute difference between these two scores.[13]

The third individual-level predictor taps whether the respondent holds any form of non-policy-based affinity for a political party. The CSES module asks a question on the closeness to a preferred party.[14] *Government Partisanship* is coded 1 if the respondent self-identified as being close to a party in government prior to the election, -1 if reported being close to a party not in government, and 0 otherwise.

Testing hypotheses requires indicators for the two contexts discussed above. Measures for the first of these, the distribution of administrative responsibility, are now commonplace in studies of comparative economic voting. Many researchers employ a variant of the number and size of parties included in the governing coalition on grounds that control over policy is more diffuse as the number of parties with cabinet portfolios increases. In their recent study, Duch and Stevenson (2008) propose a summary measure for the distribution of responsibility. Their measure compares the actual distribution of cabinet portfolios among parties in a given legislature to the hypothetical case where portfolios are distributed evenly across all parties represented in the legislature. This measure can be expressed as $\sqrt{\sum_{j=1}(\lambda_{jk}^c - \delta_k)^2}$ where λ^c is the actual share of cabinet portfolios held by party j just before the election in country k, and δ is the share of portfolios held by each party if the policy responsibility were spread evenly over all n parties with seats in the legislature (such that $\delta = 1/n$).

A limitation of this measure is that responsibility is gauged exclusively by the distribution of cabinet portfolios. For instance, the majority/minority status of the government ought to affect the concentration of responsibility insomuch as opposition parties may be more empowered when the government does not control a majority of seats in parliament. To account for this possibility, I modify the contextual measure using information on party seat shares. First, I create a measure as above but which uses party seat shares in the legislature, λ^s, in place of party cabinet portfolio shares, λ^c. This seat-based dispersion measure, $\sqrt{\sum_{j=1}(\lambda_{jk}^s - \delta_k)^2}$, is then used to discount the importance of the portfolio-based index. Thus, the measure used, Concentration of Responsibility, equals $(1 - \varphi)\sqrt{\sum_{j=1}(\lambda_{jk}^c - \delta_k)^2} + \varphi\sqrt{\sum_{j=1}(\lambda_{jk}^s - \delta_k)^2}$, where φ is equal to 0 for majority governments and for minority governments. This means that for cases where the government held a majority of seats prior to the election, *Concentration of*

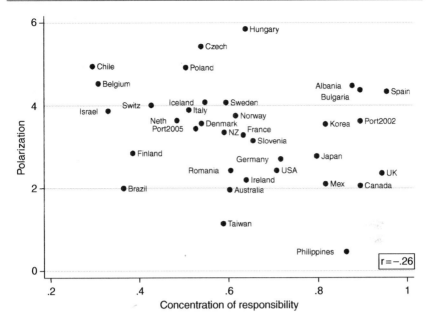

Figure 7.2 The concentration of administrative responsibility and party system polarization
Source: CSES, module II and calculations as described in text.

Responsibility is based only on cabinet portfolios, and the measure is discounted by seat allocations in cases of minority governments.[15]

The second contextual measure gauges the range of policy alternatives. Researchers have recently begun to investigate how countries differ in terms of the diversity – as opposed to simply the number – of policy alternatives available to the voter (Wessels and Schmitt 2008; Klingemann and Wessels 2009). The diversity of party policy appeals, as argued above, is used by the prospectively oriented voter to assess the range of possible policy offerings resulting from the election outcome. As a measure of policy diversity I use the party system polarization index as described in Chapter 5 (see also Dalton 2008b).[16]

Figure 7.2 shows how the thirty-five election cases are located on these two measures of political context. The horizontal axis charts country locations on the *Concentration of Responsibility*. Single-party majoritarian democracies with single-party governments such as the United Kingdom, Canada, and Spain score high on this measure while highly fragmented coalition and/or minority governments like Belgium, Israel, and Chile score low. The vertical axis separates cases in terms of the diversity of party messages. This dimension, *Party System Polarization*, appears orthogonal to the concentration of administrative responsibility (the correlation between the two measures is −.26 and not statistically significant). For example, where Spain and Canada are nearly identical in terms of responsibility concentration, the former provides a far greater set of policy choice options to the voter than the latter (see Dalton 2008, 918–19).

Of course, it is likely that other country-level factors account for cross-national differences in the voter's calculus. The model below thus includes two contextual control variables. Since the model of voter utility advanced above derives mainly from the study of established democracies, it is necessary to model components of the vote conditioned on the length of time the country has been democratic. Thus, I include a measure equal to the number of years since 1955 the country scored at +6 or above on Polity IV's democracy scale. Since the measure is skewed, I take the natural log prior to analysis. Also, the sample pools countries with presidential and parliamentary regimes, a context found to affect electoral accountability (Hellwig and Samuels 2008; Nishizawa 2009). The analyses therefore include an indicator variable scored 1 for presidential regimes and 0 otherwise.[17]

Analysis 1: How context conditions the performance vote

Since models combine data at the individual (micro) and country (macro) levels, I assesss hypotheses with multilevel modeling techniques. Failure to recognize the multilevel nature of the data risks several statistical problems, including clustering, nonconstant variance, and underestimation of standard errors (Raudenbush and Bryk 2002; Gelman and Hill 2007). The statistical model can be expressed as a series of equations. The first models the respondent's decision to support a government party as a function of performance evaluations, policy distance, and partisanship. The slopes associated with each of these components of the vote function (as well as the intercept) are then specified as contingent on the macro-level predictors measuring the concentration of responsibility, party system polarization, country experience with democracy, and presidential regime type. Combining these equations we estimate a hierarchical nonlinear model with a logit link function. The model is estimated with random slopes as well as random intercepts to account for unobserved country-level variance.

Table 7.1 presents the results of two models.[18] Model 1 is a baseline specification that excludes the contextual measures (see Equation (1)). All components of voter calculus are statistically significant and signed in the expected directions. The probability of voting for an incumbent party is greater for those with positive evaluations of government performance, policy preferences close to those of the sitting government, and who identify as feeling close to a government party.[19]

Model 2 models these predictors as contingent on political context (as depicted in Equation (2)), with results displayed in five blocks. The first block

Table 7.1 Multilevel model of effect of political context on incumbent vote choice

	Model 1		Model 2	
Individual level				
Intercept	−.670**	(.089)	−.684**	(.083)
Government performance	.589**	(.066)	.587**	(.073)
Government policy distance	−.209**	(.039)	−.199**	(.033)
Government partisanship	1.890**	(.102)	1.947**	(.091)
Contextual level				
Concentration of responsibility			.120	(.426)
Party System Polarization			.224**	(.053)
Years democratic (Ln)			.002	(.094)
Presidential regime			−.035	(.118)
Cross-level: government performance				
Performance x Conc. Of responsibility			.675**	(.322)
Performance x Polarization			.134**	(.058)
Performance x Years democratic (Ln)			.107	(.088)
Performance x Presidential regime			−.106	(.141)
Cross-level: government policy distance				
Policy Distance x Conc. of resp.			−.346*	(.193)
Policy Distance x Polarization			−.115**	(.021)
Policy Distance x Years democratic (Ln)			.004	(.033)
Policy Distance x Presidential regime			.021	(.049)
Cross-level: government partisanship				
Partisanship x Conc. Of responsibility			.664*	(.370)
Partisanship x Polarization			.226**	(.067)
Partisanship x Years democratic (Ln)			.353**	(.133)
Partisanship x Presidential regime			−.499**	(.176)
Variance components				
Intercept	.252**		.202**	
Performance slope	.146**		.124**	
Policy distance slope	.047**		.031**	
Partisanship slope	.346**		.199**	
-2*LogLikelihood	138724.12		138843.86	
N obs contextual level	35		35	
N obs individual level	46569		46569	

Notes: Dependent variable is *Government Party Vote*. Cells report coefficients from a hierarchical nonlinear model with binary logit link function. Robust standard errors in parentheses. Cases weighted prior to estimation. Estimation performed using HLM 6.2 using restricted PQL.

* $p < .10$, ** $p < .05$, two-tailed test.

Source: CSES, module II and calculations as described in text. Nonindicator contextual variables are entered as deviations from their mean.

of coefficients is nearly identical to those reported in Model 1.[20] Reading down the column, the next set of coefficients estimates the direct influence of contextual variables on *Government Party Vote*. The coefficient on *Party System Polarization* is positive and statistically significant, suggesting that incumbents do better when voters can tell parties from one another in terms of Left and Right.

Our chief interest, however, pertains to the third set of estimates regarding how context conditions performance voting. These coefficients model the slope on *Government Performance* conditional on the four macro measures. As expected, *Concentration of Responsibility* has a positive and statistically significant conditioning influence on *Government Performance*. Evaluations of the incumbent government's job matter more for vote decisions when administrative responsibility is concentrated in the hands of fewer actors. The coefficient on the *Performance x Polarization* interaction is also positive and precisely estimated. Voters are more likely to channel positive assessments of government performance into support for the incumbent – and negative assessments into support for opposition parties – when provided with a wider menu of options to choose from among competing parties. Put differently, a clearly distinguished set of policy alternatives, as gauged by Left–Right polarization, facilitates retrospective voting.

These results can be expressed more substantively as predicted probabilities. Figures 7.3*a* and 7.3*b* use Table 7.1 Model 2 estimates to chart the probability a given respondent votes for a government party based on its performance evaluations conditioned across values of political context. In Figure 7.3*a* the conditioning context is *Concentration of Responsibility*.[21] It shows that respondents with negative performance evaluations (*Government Performance* = −1) are less likely to vote for an incumbent party in contexts where policy responsibility is more concentrated. Put differently, the effect on vote choice of a swing from good to poor performance evaluations – a measure of what we might call the "performance vote," as shown by the vertical arrow – is greater when responsibility is concentrated than when diffuse.[22] Figure 7.3*b* performs the same exercise but ranges the conditioning *Party System Polarization* across its in-sample values holding all other contextual-level variables fixed. Confirming expectations, the effects of performance evaluations are considerably greater for countries where voters have a wide range of choice (in terms of the dispersion of Left–Right policy offerings) than when competing parties converge in the policy space.

The fourth and fifth blocks of coefficients in Model 2 of Table 7.1 assess the conditional influence of context on policy-based voting and on partisan-based voting, respectively. While not the central focus of this chapter, the results warrant some discussion. Policy distance matters more for the voter (is more negative) when concentration of responsibility is high and, especially, when

(a)   Probability of vote incumbent conditioned on concentration of responsibility

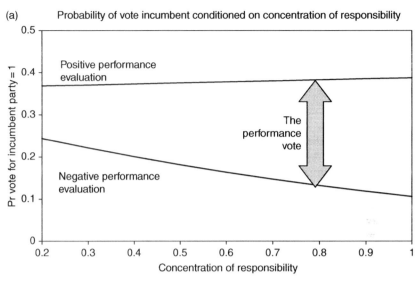

(b)   Probability of vote incumbent conditioned on party system polarization

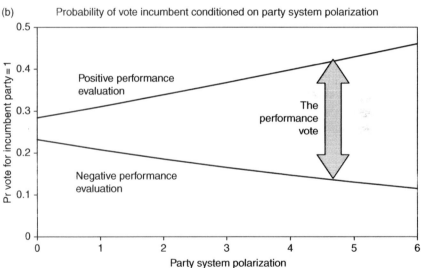

Figure 7.3 Conditional effects of political context on performance voting

Note: Figures report the predicted probability that an individual with *Policy Distance* set to its median value and no partisan attachment and residing in a non-presidential regime with mean sample values on *Concentration of Responsibility, Party System Polarization*, and *Ln Years of Democracy* votes for an incumbent party.

Source: Estimates from Table 7.1 Model 2.

parties are polarized. The latter, in particular, squares with intuitions: the voter should place a premium on parties' policy appeals if the system is polarized to the extent that an alternative future government could well locate policies far away from his or her preferred location (for a similar findings, see Kroh 2009; Lachat 2008).[23] The last block shows that context also shapes partisan voting. Notably, partisan-based voting is stronger in older democracies and weaker under presidentialism. Both these results make sense: party attachments should be less durable in new democracies, and the candidate-centered voting prevalent in presidential systems should weaken the bond between party sentiment and the vote (see Chapter 6).

Returning to performance voting, we can conclude from Table 7.1 and Figure 7.3 that the data offer support for Hypotheses 1a and 1b. The distribution of administrative responsibility matters. However, the *range of policy choice* also influences the degree to which voters emphasize their assessments of retrospective performance as a component of their vote calculus.[24] Moreover, as Figure 7.2 showed, the range of policy choice cannot simply be derived from the number of actors having a hand in policymaking. This has consequences for how context matters for electoral accountability. Accountability is strongest when responsibility is concentrated. However, probabilities displayed in Figure 7.3b suggests that all is not lost for accountability even if responsibility is diffused, *as long as party policy offerings are large enough to choose among a set of policy alternatives*. The flip side is also true, of course, that concentrated responsibility does not guarantee the presence of performance-based voting: even if responsibility is the jurisdiction of a single actor, the utility of the election as instrument of accountability will be compromised if voters judge there to be no real policy alternative.

Table 7.2 highlights this joint effect of context on performance voting. It displays the size of the performance vote in four different macro contexts. The macro contexts are produced by taking combinations of diffuse versus

Table 7.2 The size of the performance vote in four political contexts

		Concentration of responsibility	
		Low (10th ptile)	High (90th ptile)
Party System Polarization	High (90th ptile)	.25 e.g., Belgium, Chile	.33 e.g., Albania, Bulgaria
	Low (10th ptile)	.09 e.g., Brazil, Finland	.20 e.g., Canada, Mexico

Notes: Cells use estimates from Table 7.1 Model 1 to display the difference in the predicted probability of voting for the incumbent if the respondent evaluated government performance positively relative to negatively under particular values of *Concentration of Responsibility* and *Party System Polarization*. Countries displayed in cells are representative of these four contexts (see Figure 7.2).

concentrated administrative responsibility and low versus high levels of polarization. These levels are set at the 10th and 90th percentiles in the sample of countries considered here. The performance vote is strongest, accounting for a one-third swing in predicted probabilities, when both *Concentration of Responsibility* and *Party System Polarization* are large (upper right corner of Table 7.2). And the estimated performance vote is weakest when responsibility is diffuse and polarization is low (.09, lower left corner). The magnitude of the performance vote lies between these extremes for the "off-diagonal" cases. It seems clear, then, that we must consider not one but at minimum two dimensions of macro-political context in order to understand variation in the performance vote.

Analysis 2: the intervening influence of political information on the performance vote

The previous section showed how performance voting is contingent on political context. I now probe the context–performance vote nexus further by considering how the macro-political environment affects how informed voters are and, in turn, how this information figures into the overall vote calculus. Do political contexts found to affect the performance vote provide voters reason to become more or less informed about politics? And does the use of this information affect whether cross-pressured voters choose representatives based on performance evaluations as opposed to other components of the vote function? I pose these questions to come closer to our goal of incorporating both the contextual and individual-level contingencies of the performance/economic vote into a single analytic framework (see Figure 7.1, causal paths 2 and 3).

This investigation requires a measure of political information. One approach is to compare survey responses on a battery of objective information items. This technique has been shown to produce reliable information scales for discerning high from low information individuals within a single country survey (e.g., Delli Carpini and Keeter 1996). Module II of the CSES includes a three-item knowledge battery. Respondents in each country received a set of objective knowledge questions of varying difficulty pertaining to politics in their country which, it is intended, capture variation in citizen knowledge levels. I use these indicators to construct a four-point *Political Knowledge Index* such that low information individuals are scored 0 and high information respondents are scored 3 (see chapter appendix for details).

But factual knowledge indices, however well-designed, may be of limited use for comparing information levels cross-nationally. The specific questions are not the same across all countries. Moreover, a look at the data reveals that quartiles in the four-point index are of varying sizes across countries. Given such shortcomings, I supplement analyses using the political knowledge index with an alternative measure for political sophistication. We can be more confident in our findings if analyses using the different measures produce similar results. The alternative measure is based on the respondent's ability to place the two largest political parties in the country on the Left–Right scale. I create a variable *Left–Right Party Placement* coded 1 for respondents who place respondents in the correct order on the Left–Right dimension and 0 otherwise, where the "correct" order is provided by the mean placement of parties in a given survey.[25] The measure correlates positively, albeit modestly, with the political knowledge index ($r = .17$, $p < .001$).[26]

Our expectations are that voter propensities to become politically informed decline as policy responsibility becomes more concentrated (Hypothesis 2a) and as the range of policy alternatives narrows (Hypothesis 2b). Mass publics should be less politically informed when the concentration of administrative responsibility is high and when the range of party policy alternatives is low. These claims are tested in Table 7.3. In the first model the four-point *Political Knowledge Index* is the dependent variable and the model is specified as a hierarchical linear model with an identity link function. The second model dichotomizes the index into low and high knowledge respondents and estimates a hierarchical nonlinear model with a logit link.[27] In Model 3 the dependent variable is the dichotomous *Left–Right Party Placement* measure, estimated with logit link function. In all models the contextual predictors are the same as given in the preceding text, to which I add a set of individual-level controls for gender, age, education, and income (see chapter appendix for measurement details).

In all cases coefficients on the individual-level controls are signed in their expected directions. Our interest, however, pertains to context. In Models 1 and 2 – with political information measured using the knowledge index – the coefficient on *Concentration of Responsibility* is negative and precisely estimated. It is easier for individuals to discern "who's in charge" when policy responsibility is concentrated in a small number of parties. This ease is such that, all else being equal, voters have fewer incentives to take on the costs of becoming informed in the politics of their country. This result supports Hypothesis 2a: voter levels of political information are lower in contexts where the concentration of responsibility is high. Models 1 and 2 also show that individual knowledge scores are higher in younger democracies and in presidential regimes.[28] *Party System Polarization*, however, is estimated to have no effect on responses to the objective knowledge items. Thus, the claim that information levels are positively correlated with the range of policy alternatives is not supported in Models 1 or 2 (Hypothesis 2b).

Model 3 employs *Left–Right Party Placement* as the measure for political information. Unlike above, the concentration of responsibility has no affect on the voter's ability to correctly place the two largest parties on the Left–Right scale. Yet the coefficient on polarization is now positively signed and statistically significant.[29] This provides support for Hypothesis 2b: Voter levels of political

Table 7.3 Multilevel model of effect of political context on political information

	Model 1 DV: Political Knowledge Index identity link		Model 2 DV: Political Knowledge Index logit link		Model 3 DV: Left–Right Party Placement logit link	
Individual level variables						
Constant	2.339**	(.096)	−.428	(.027)	.368**	(.144)
Female	−.295**	(.020)	−.650**	(.040)	−.299**	(.040)
Age	.007**	(.001)	.014**	(.002)	.008**	(.002)
Education low	−.387**	(.031)	−.846**	(.072)	−.544**	(.054)
Education high	.281**	(.030)	.637**	(.060)	.511**	(.067)
Income low	−.112**	(.020)	−.249**	(.051)	−.038	(.034)
Income high	.142**	(.020)	.281**	(.048)	.396**	(.052)
Contextual level variables						
Conc. of resp.	−.759**	(.344)	−1.835**	(.833)	.087	(.521)
Party Sys. Polarization	−.004	(.061)	−.057	(.163)	.704**	(.067)
Years democratic (Ln)	−.179**	(.087)	−.526*	(.294)	.270**	(.116)
Presidential regime	.336*	(.196)	.846*	(.450)	.147	(.164)
Variance components						
Level 1	.760					
Level 2	.193		2.054		.314	
-2*LogLikelihood	133710.12		132623.28		147318.52	
N obs contextual level	32		32		34	
N obs individual level	49061		49061		52695	

Notes: Dependent variables are *Political Knowledge Index* (Models 1 and 2) and *Left–Right Party Placement* (Model 3). Cells report coefficients from a hierarchical linear model (Model 1) or nonlinear model with logit link function (Models 2 and 3). Robust standard errors are in parentheses. Cases weighted prior to estimation. Estimation performed using HLM 6.2 using restricted PQL.

* $p < .10$, ** $p < .05$, two-tailed test.

Source: CSES, module II and calculations as described in text. Nonindicator contextual variables are entered as deviations from their mean. Models 1 and 2 have missing values on the dependent variable for Bulgaria, Denmark, and Iceland. Model 3 has missing values for Belgium.

information are lower in when the range of Left–Right alternatives provided by competing parties is low. The implication is that a *wider* range of policies on offer motivates citizens to become *more* informed.

Inferences drawn from Table 7.3 appear to depend on how political information is measured.[30] In one case expectations for the effects of the concentration of responsibility are borne out, while for the other we find support for expectations regarding the dispersion of party policy positions. Both sets of results, however, are consistent with the logic of the argument: Controlling for individual-level factors, context – notably, those *identified as conditioning the performance vote* – matters for individual levels of political information. Citizens become more informed where the complexity of political environments require it, that is, where policy responsibility is spread over many actors and where differences in the policy packages on offer from competing political parties are significant.

We now turn to our last pair of causal claims. Hypothesis 3 addresses how political information affects performance voting, stating that politically informed individuals discount performance voting (3a) and place more weight on policy-based voting (3b) relative to those with low levels of information. I test this claim by estimating a model of individual vote choice as in Table 7.1, this time specifying the performance, policy, and non-policy components of the voter's calculus contingent not on context but on level of political information.

Table 7.4 presents the results. Model 1 measures political information with the knowledge index and Model 2 measures it by placing parties on the Left–Right

Table 7.4 Multilevel model of effect of political information on incumbent vote choice

	Model 1		Model 2	
Individual-level variables				
Intercept	−.946**	(.108)	−1.009**	(.077)
Government performance	.597**	(.078)	.465**	(.080)
Government policy distance	−.192**	(.042)	−.082**	(.032)
Government partisanship	1.977**	(.108)	1.742**	(.144)
Knowledge Index	.157**	(.051)		
Performance x Knowledge Index	−.050*	(.030)		
Policy Distance x Knowledge Index	.015	(.017)		
Partisanship x Knowledge Index	−.047	(.039)		
Left–Right party placement			.445**	(.091)
Performance x LR placement			.093	(.075)
Policy distance x LR placement			−.148**	(.040)
Partisanship x LR placement			.233**	(.113)
Variance components				
Level 2 intercept	.150		.141	
-2*LogLikelihood	121384.62		130849.94	
N obs contextual level	32		34	
N obs individual level	41419		44563	

Notes: Dependent variable is *Government Party Vote*. Cells report coefficients from a hierarchical nonlinear model with logit link function. Robust standard errors are in parentheses. Cases weighted prior to estimation. Estimation performed using HLM 6.2 using restricted PQL.

* $p < .10$, ** $p < .05$, two-tailed test.

Source: CSES, module II. Models 1 and 2 have missing values on the dependent variable for Bulgaria, Denmark, and Iceland. Model 3 has missing values for Belgium.

scale. Coefficients on *Government Performance, Government Policy Distance,* and *Government Partisanship* are again in the expected directions in both models. As regards the conditioning influence of political information, Model 1 results show that political information moderates the relationship between government performance evaluations and incumbent party vote choice (the coefficient on *Performance x Knowledge Index* is $-.05$, statistically significant at $p < .10$). This is consistent with Hypothesis 3a, that high information voters put less weight on performance-based voting. None of the other interaction terms with the knowledge index achieves statistical significance, however. Model 2 results shows that high information voters – as measured by their ability to correctly place parties on the Left–Right scale – give greater weight to the policy distance component of the vote function than do low information respondents (the coefficient on *Policy Distance x LR Placement* is $-.15$, statistically significant at $p < .05$). This is consistent with Hypothesis 3b, that high information voters are more likely to vote in terms of policy agreement.

Given the nature of the nonlinear interactive model, the conditioning effects of political information on performance-based relative to policy-based voting is better illustrated by considering how voters decide when they are cross-pressured. Consider, for example, the case where a voter identifies herself as holding policy preferences identical to the incumbent governments' (*Policy Distance* = 0) but at the same time has negative evaluations of the government's performance in office (*Performance* = -1).[31] If this voter were informed about politics, Model 1 estimates predict he or she would vote for an incumbent party with probability .28. Faced with the identical set of evaluative criteria, however, Model 1 predicts a voter with low information would select an incumbent with probability of .18.[32] The implication from this example is that high information respondents still support the government with some probability, even with a poor performance record, as long as they are agree with its positions over policy. This is consistent with Zaller's work (2004) on the United States in showing that low information voters "float" on the basis of short-term outcomes while high information voters are anchored by policy appeals. With reference to Figure 7.1, this study's contribution is to demonstrate that the likelihood of becoming politically informed may, in the first place, be affected by political context.

Conclusion

In a recent assessment of the field, Christopher Anderson (2007) observes that empirical research is very successful in demonstrating how the strength of economic voting depends on two moderating factors: the attributes of individual voters and the political context. Yet few of these studies have combined, either implicitly or explicitly, these micro- and macro-level contingencies to advance a single unified framework for understanding the economic/performance-based voting.

This chapter takes a first step toward such a unified framework by considering both contextual- and individual-level factors conditioning the performance vote. In addition to combining the "levels of analysis," I argue that our theoretical approaches and empirical designs must recognize that voting as control of political incumbents is but one element of the voter's calculus. And certain contexts may well condition other components of the voter's decision calculus to a greater extent than it does her retrospective performance evaluations. The contingencies affecting policy- and partisan-based voting in Table 7.1 are examples. Third, I suggest that retrospective evaluations should be measured in general rather than specific terms to best gauge the salience of performance voting – and the effect of context therein – compared to the other components of the voter's calculus. Achieving these three objectives would put scholarship onto a much needed "third phase" for the cross-national study of economic/performance voting.

The empirical analyses in this chapter attempt to fulfill these objectives. Results reveal that performance assessments matter more for the vote when responsibility for policy is concentrated and when the party system provides for many policy options. In addition, context matters for whether individuals invest in information about politics. While constructing a definitive, cross-nationally reliable indicator of political information remains a challenge, our results suggest that the same sorts of contexts shown to *condition* the performance vote *directly* affect individual political information levels. The upshot is that low information voters incorporate context mainly to condition performance evaluations while high information voters do so mainly to affect the policy-component of the vote function. Future efforts in theorizing, data collection, and concept measurement should strive to improve on the theoretical framework and empirical model presented here. By doing so we can improve our understanding of just whether and how elections encourage the public welfare by providing politicians with incentives – via the threat of sanction – to implement good policies.

Appendix

Micro-level measures

This appendix describes the survey items and coding practices used for constructing the individual-level variables used in the analysis. The source for all variables is the CSES Module II. For information on the macro-level variables, see the appendix to this volume.

Variable	Question wording	Coding
Government party vote	B3006_1, vote choice in lower house. Exceptions are for Japan, where B3007_1, vote choice for upper house, is used instead, and for France, where vote intentions for first round legislative election are used instead.	1 if the respondent reported voting for a party having belonged in government prior to the election and 0 otherwise
Government performance	B3011. "Thinking about the performance of the government in [capital] in general, how good or bad a job do you think the government in [capital] has done over the past {...} years?" The text in {...} is specific to the particular election study and pertains to the number of years since the last election or, if more recent, since the last change in government.	"good" or "very good" are coded +1, those saying "bad" or "very bad" are coded −1, and those responding otherwise are coded 0
Government policy distance	Constructed by taking the absolute distance between the respondent's self-identified position on the Left–Right scale and the government's Left–Right position. The respondent's position is taken from item B3045, "In politics people sometimes talk of Left and Right. Where would you place yourself on a scale from 0 to 10, where 0 means Left and 10 means Right?" This question was not asked in the Japan module; for the Japanese case I substituted responses from item B3046. For the government's policy preference I use a composite measure which combines the Left–Right position of governing parties weighted by each parties' share of cabinet portfolios before the election (see volume appendix).	
Government partisanship	Constructed from B3028 and B3029_1: "Do you usually think of yourself as close to any particular political party?" If the answer is yes, then they receive the follow-up "What party is that?"	+1 if the respondent self-identified as being close to a party in government prior to the election, −1 if reported being close to a party not in government, and 0 otherwise
Political knowledge	This is a count of the three political knowledge variables in each nation (B3047). Respondents who are coded as refused or not ascertained on any one measure were coded as missing data.	0 = No item correctly identified to 3 = All items correctly identified
Left–Right party placement	Constructed from items B3038_A through B3038_I: Variable coded 1 if respondent correctly places two largest political parties on the Left–Right scale and 0 otherwise. "Largest" parties are designated based on vote shares. Correct placement refers to party's mean placement by all respondents in the survey.	1, correctly place both parties; 0 otherwise

(*continued*)

Micro-level measures (Continued)

Variable	Question wording	Coding
Female	B2002	1 for female, 0 for male
Age	B2001	Respondent age in years
Education low	B2003	1 for respondents with only primary levels of education or less, 0 otherwise
Education high	B2003	Coded 1 for respondents with secondary degrees or greater, 0 otherwise
Income low	B2020	1 for respondents with household incomes in lowest two quintiles, 0 otherwise.
Income high	B2020.	Coded 1 for respondents with household incomes in highest two quintiles, 0 otherwise

Notes

* For helpful comments and suggestions, I thank Chris Anderson, Russell Dalton, and participants at the "Citizens, Context, and Choice" workshop at Cornell University, June 2009

1. The complement to this accountability view of democracy as citizen control of politicians is the notion of representation, generally expressed as the programmatic congruence between voters and politicians (see Chapter 9).

2. See also contributors to the volume edited by Norpoth, Lewis-Beck, and Lafay (1991).

3. These factors include coalition and minority governments, "strong" bicameralism, opposition power sharing through legislative committee system, and party cohesion.

4. As Kroh (2003, 24) concludes from his review of voters' reasoning, "contextual accounts for individual voters' reasoning are less common than individual-level explanations." In addition, studies that combine context and voter knowledge have focused on other components of the vote function, such as partisanship (Huber, Kernell, and Leoni 2005) and ideology (Kroh 2003).

5. Equation (1) differs from most utility functions in that it pertains to i's utility for government g, rather than for a given party (which may or may not be a member of the incumbent governing coalition). This set-up facilitates comparisons of the effect of government performance on voter support across a wide range of democracies. However, in the case of multiparty governments, work on economic voting in advanced industrial democracies demonstrates that retrospective performance does not always affect members of the governing coalition equally (van der Brug et al. 2007; Duch and Stevenson 2008). I address this issue in the analyses below (see note 24).

6. That is, it shows how context might condition policy- or partisan-based voting. For alternative perspectives on policy and partisan voting, see Chapters 5 and 6.

7. This intuition is consistent with Powell and Whitten's clarity (1993) of responsibility perspective. An alternative perspective – though with similar empirical implications – is found in Duch and Stevenson (2008, ch. 8). Other studies show a connection between the diffusion of responsibility and the voter's calculus (van der Brug et al. 2007; Hellwig 2008).

8. Indeed, this simplicity is what makes the simple reward–punishment model such an attractive feature of representative democracy (Key 1966; Fiorina 1981).

9. The 2004 Russian and 2004 Taiwanese studies are excluded because they are presidential elections. The 2006 Peruvian election is excluded due to missing data for the government performance measure. The French survey included in CSES Module II took place after the 2002 presidential vote but before the National Assembly election. I therefore use vote intentions for the first round of the legislative elections in France. For all other surveys I analyze the respondents' reported vote choice.

10. Details on individual-level measures are found in the appendix to this chapter. Details on macro-level measures are in the appendix to this volume.

11. Respondents who say "good" or "very good" are coded +1, those saying "bad" or "very bad" are coded −1, and those responding otherwise are coded 0. Respondents in some countries were provided with a different set of response categories. The Danish and Dutch surveys, for example, included an intermediate category, and examination of the data and questionnaires revealed some variation in the allowance of "don't know" responses. For this reason, I employed the above three-category response set for this variable. Statistical analyses with a four-category response variable ("very good," "good," "bad," "very bad") produced similar results and are available upon request.

12. Space constraints prevent further discussion of these issues here. For an illuminating discussion of the issue of the voter's time horizon, see Peltzman (1990). Singer (forthcoming, 2011) discusses the role of salience for economic voting.

13. Specifically, government Left–Right positions are calculated using the formula Σ(cabinet portfolio share$_j$)*(party Left–Right score$_j$) where j indexes parties. Party Left–Right scores are taken from country mean citizen evaluations of party positions from the CSES, supplemented with expert survey data from Benoit and Laver (2006) for the Belgian case, where the CSES data are missing.

14. The question wording is in the chapter appendix. There are some differences in question wording across the country surveys (see questionnaires at http://cses.org/download/module2/module2.htm). Such differences, however, are not likely to be of great consequence given the straightforward nature of the question.

15. Duch and Stevenson (2008, 278–82) make a similar adjustment using information on minority governments and on institutional strength of the opposition. Not surprisingly, in our sample it correlates highly with other macro contexts used in previous studies of cross-national economic voting, including the effective number of governing parties ($r = -.64$), effective number of parliamentary parties ($r = -.72$), and the Gallagher (1991) index of electoral system disproportionality ($r = +.46$).

16. Party system polarization is equal to where $\sqrt{\sum_{j=1} VS_j[(P_{jk} - \bar{P}_k)/5]^2}$ $\bar{P}_k$ is the weighted mean of all the parties' positions in country k, P_{jk} is the position of party j in country k, and VS_j is vote share for party j. The index has a value of 0 when all parties are located at the same Left–Right policy position and 10 when all parties are split

between the two extremes. The index is identical to Ezrow's measure (2007) of party policy dispersion with the exception that the 5 in the divisor normalizes the value with a theoretical maximum of 10. I rescale *Party System Polarization* from 0 to 1 so as to place it on the same units as *Concentration of Responsibility*.

17. A pure presidential regime is one in which both the executive and legislative branches enjoy separation of origin and survival (Shugart and Carey 1992). These cases include Brazil, Chile, South Korea, Mexico, the Philippines, and the United States.

18. I estimated models by penalized quasi-likelihood using HLM 6.2. Estimation by full maximum likelihood does not substantively affect model estimates.

19. Two issues warrant discussion regarding the baseline specification reported in Model 1. The first of pertains to endogeneity. Recent work has debated whether subjective economic perceptions are endogenous to the vote and, therefore, overestimate the strength of the economic vote (Evans and Andersen 2006). The common response to such concerns is to exogenize the right-hand-side variable of interest using instrumental variables regression. It is not clear, however, whether the CSES data provide adequate measures to use as instruments. The presence of exogenously determined variables – such as SES and demographic items – is collected unevenly across the country modules. This concern aside, I performed two-stage ordered probit by regressing *Government Performance* on gender, age, education, income, a full set of country dummies, and, following Lewis-Beck, Nadeau, and Elias (2008), political interest. Replacing *Government Performance* in Model 1 with the instrument produced in the first-stage regression yields a coefficient of .35 ($p < .05$). (The magnitude of the coefficient rises to 2.64 when the country dummies are excluded from the stage 1 ordered probit model.)

The second issue pertains to modeling the dependent variable dichotomously as for/against a governing party. This is a common approach to studying voting behavior across diverse contexts (Anderson 2000; Anderson 2006; see also Tillman 2008). However, in cases of coalition government it is likely the voter's decision to vote for a party that holds the office of chief executive may be informed by different components of the vote function than the decision to select a junior coalition partner. For this reason I re-estimate all models with the dependent variable equal to 1 if the respondent selected the party of the chief executive; that is, the prime minister's party for parliamentary and hybrid ("semi-presidential") regimes and the president's party for presidential regimes. Models using this measure, which I label *Chief Executive Vote*, also include measures for *Policy Distance* and *Partisanship* on the right-hand-side based solely on information from the party of the chief executive. Unless otherwise noted, results with this alternative measure do not differ from what are reported below. But since the independent variable of central interest, *Government Performance*, refers in the CSES questionnaire to "the performance of the government," not simply the prime minister. Therefore, it is most appropriate to relate the performance measure to support for the government as a whole rather than one of its components.

20. This is not surprising because contextual predictors are mean-centered prior to estimation.

21. The figure charts the probability of *Government Party Vote* = 1 for an individual with *Government Policy Distance* set to its median values and no partisan attachment and residing in a non-presidential regime with mean sample values on *Party System*

Polarization, and *Ln Years of Democracy*. Though the theoretical range for *Concentration of Responsibility* is between 0 and 1, no case in our data has a value of 0 (meaning responsibility for policy is distributed perfectly equally across parties). Figure 7.3*a* thus charts the context across values ranging from .2 to 1.

22. Specifically, the difference in probabilities when *Concentration of Responsibility* equals .2 is (performance good – performance bad = .37 −.24 = .12. When *Concentration of Responsibility* is high (1.0), the difference in probabilities is .39 −.11 = .28.

23. The negative coefficient on *Government Policy Distance x Concentration of Responsibility* implies that policy distance plays a greater role in when responsibility is concentrated, or clear. Voters in such "representational" systems may weigh policy more heavily. This effect, however, is weak ($p = .082$) and is not robust to a model with *Chief Executive Vote* as the dependent variable.

24. For more on the different consequences of polarization and the number of parties, see Chapters 10, 5, and 2.

25. The two largest parties are identified using vote shares in the election. This method is also used in Elff (2008). Gordon and Segura's cross-national study (1997) of political sophistication also employs a measure based on how close the respondent can locate each of the parties in the system to its country sample mean location in terms of the Left–Right scale.

26. Election studies for Bulgaria, Denmark, and Iceland in the CSES did not include the objective information items, and the Belgian study did not include respondent assessment of party Left–Right positions. Consequently, the number of nations in the models below differs depending on the dependent variable. I re-estimated the models with a common set of thirty-one country cases (omitting the four above); doing so has no effect on results of interest.

27. In Model 2 the dependent variable is dichotomized such that respondents correctly answering two or more of information items are coded 1 and all others are coded 0.

28. The negative coefficient on *Years Democratic (Ln)* appears anomalous. The finding that voters in presidential systems are "more knowledgeable" is likely due to the prevalence of items asking for information on a political leader, a task that is arguably easier in more personalized presidential systems.

29. Model 3 results also show, as we might expect, that experience with democracy increases political information levels.

30. Clearly, decisions on how "political information" is measured play a role here. Information in terms of objective knowledge scales is not the same as information culled from placing parties in Left–Right space. Future research is required to discover how best to produce valid and reliable knowledge scales for use in cross-national analyses.

31. For this example, we assume the voter has no partisan attachments (*Government Partisanship* = 0).

32. The respective probabilities predicted from Table 7.3 Model 2 estimates are .24 and .19.

8

Strategic Defection Across Elections, Parties, and Voters[*]

André Blais and Thomas Gschwend

This chapter examines how the propensity to strategically defect from one's preferred party depends on characteristics of voters, parties, and elections. Looking at the amount and sources of strategic defection is important for at least two reasons. First, electoral outcomes are often interpreted as mandates (see Fowler and Smirnov 2007), which implies that voters are expressing their sincere preferences when they decide which party or candidate to support. That interpretation has to be revisited if vote choice is substantially strategic. This is implied in studies of policy voting or Left–Right voting, for example, see Chapters 4, 5, and 7. Second, looking at strategic defection allows us to better understand how electoral rules do or do not affect voter's behavior. Arguably, one of the best established laws in political science is Duverger's law, according to which the plurality rule leads to a two-party system because supporters of weak parties desert them for more viable parties (Duverger 1954; Riker 1982). Hopefully, our study will contribute to the debate about the merits and limits of Duverger's law (see Grofman, Blais, and Bowler 2009).

We define a strategic voter as someone who decides how to vote on the basis of preferences *and* expectations about the outcome of the election (Blais et al. 2001). The strategic voter can be contrasted with the sincere voter, who votes solely on the basis of her preferences, and the momentum voter, who considers solely the outcome of the election (the bandwagon voter goes with the momentum while the underdog voter goes against it).[1] We define a defector as someone who votes for a party other than the preferred one.

We adopt a two-step approach. We first identify the set of voters who desert their preferred party. We then screen out among those deserters those who did so for nonstrategic reasons – that is, they voted for a different party because they preferred the leader of another party. The remaining deserters are assumed to be strategically motivated.

The approach is relatively straightforward with regards to the measurement of defection. We are looking at people who vote for a party that is not their preferred one. The only issue concerns the measurement of preferences, which is discussed below. Note that the point of reference is the voter's preference in a specific election, not one's traditional party loyalty. A number of studies, in the United States in particular, have looked at the sources of partisan defection, that is, voting for a party other than one identifies with (see Kernell 1977; Beck 2002). In this study, we are interested in desertion from one's short-term (sincere) preference.

The approach is more indirect when it comes to ascertaining the strategic component of defection voting. Strictly speaking, we would need to tap voters' perceptions about the likely outcome of the election in the district, in the legislature, or with respect to the composition of the government (see Blais, Dostie-Goulet, and Bodet 2009). Such data are not available in the Comparative Study of Electoral Systems (CSES). We thus proceed indirectly. People may decide to desert their preferred party for all kinds of reasons, some strategic and some nonstrategic. We extract the most important nonstrategic consideration, and then we assume that what is left is mostly strategic.

The most important nonstrategic reason for deserting one's preferred party is simply that one prefers the leader of another party and puts greater weight on leaders than on parties. As Tverdova mentions in Chapter 6, election campaigns can be highly candidate-oriented, and there is growing evidence that a substantial number of voters vote on the basis of their views about party leaders (see Poguntke and Webb 2005; Aarts et al. forthcoming). When the best-liked leader does not belong to the best-liked party, there is an incentive to desert the preferred party, and this may have nothing to do with strategic motivations. As indicated below, we can identify those deserters who support the party of the preferred leader, and we construe them *not* to be strategic deserters.

We consider all deserters whose desertion is not leader-induced to be strategic. There are other nonstrategic reasons for deserting one's preferred party, the most obvious being the willingness to cast a personal vote (Cain, Ferejohn, and Fiorina 1987). There is some evidence that a number of voters focus on local candidates when deciding how to vote (see Blais et al. 2003; Marsh et al. 2008, chapter 8) and some of them may end up defecting from the preferred party because they just like a local candidate from another party. Unfortunately, the CSES data do not allow us to screen out such a local candidate vote. There are good reasons to assume, however, that the local candidate vote is much smaller than the party leader vote (Blais et al. 2002) while at the same time more likely to be idiosyncratic rather than systematic, and thus that non-leader-induced desertion is mostly strategic.

While we focus on strategic defection, we do not assume that non-defection – that is, voting for one's preferred party – is necessarily nonstrategic. It is indeed possible for a strategic voter to vote for her preferred party, if she does so in part

177

because she believes that this party is a viable option (Abramson et al. forthcoming).

We wish to relate the propensity to strategically desert one's preferred party to characteristics of elections, parties, and voters. There is strong evidence for each in the existing literature.

Electoral system

We first consider characteristics of elections. While the conventional wisdom is that strategic voting is most prevalent in single-member plurality systems, in a comparative study Gschwend (2009) shows that the frequency of strategic voting in an electoral district is negatively correlated with district magnitude. As a consequence, most studies focus on strategic voting in the United States (Abramson et al. 1992; Burden 2005), Britain (Cain 1978; Alvarez, Boehmke, and Nagler 2006), and Canada (Black 1978; Blais and Nadeau 1996; Merolla and Stephenson 2007). More recently, however, studies have documented the existence of strategic voting in countries such as France (Blais 2004; Gschwend and Leuffen 2005), Germany (Gschwend 2004, 2007a), Spain (Lago 2008), Portugal (Gschwend 2007b), New Zealand (Blais et al. 2004), and Israel (Aldrich et al. 2005). A comparative study of elections in the United States, Britain, the Netherlands, and Israel even comes to the provocative conclusion that there may be no difference in the overall magnitude of strategic voting between first-past-the-post, runoff, and PR elections (Abramson et al. forthcoming).

Three observations can be made about the contrast between first-past-the-post and PR elections. First, no voting system is immune from strategic considerations (Gibbard 1973; Satterthwaite 1975). Second, strategic voting seems to be easier in single-member district plurality elections. All that voters need to know is who the top two candidates are in their local constituency. In a large PR district, it becomes more difficult to determine which six or seven parties are viable among the twelve that are running (Cox and Shugart 1996). This has led Cox (1997, 122) to suggest that "strategic voting fades out in multimember districts when the district magnitude gets above five." Gschwend (2007b) and Lago (2008) show, however, that even in large districts voters can use a simple shortcut to ascertain party viability – that is, whether the party won at least one seat in the previous election. Third, there may be more options for strategic voting in a PR system. There are likely to be more parties, and so there is a greater likelihood for voters to find another party (besides the most preferred one) that is deemed to be "acceptable," a necessary condition for agreeing to desert one's first preference (Blais 2002). Furthermore, there are a greater variety of strategic considerations in a PR system because voters may be concerned not only with the outcome of the election in their local district but also with the formation of the (coalition) government after the election (Blais et al. 2006). On the one hand, voters might anticipate the impact of their vote on policy and engage in some sort of policy balancing by voting for parties that take more extreme positions than their most preferred one (Kedar 2005; Bargsted and Kedar 2009). On the other hand, there is evidence of at least three different types of strategic behavior in Austria and Germany. First, is a "rental vote." Major party supporters might cast their vote strategically in favor of a preferred junior coalition partner if this party is perceived as uncertain to pass a minimum vote threshold. Second, small party supporters might avoid wasting their vote for the preferred party if it is not expected to pass the minimum vote threshold, and, thirdly, there is explicit strategic coalition voting to influence the composition of the next coalition government (Gschwend 2007a; Meffert and Gschwend 2009). The upshot is that the link between the electoral system and strategic voting is not obvious. Still, we test the standard hypothesis according to which there is less desertion of the preferred party in PR elections.

The above hypothesis posits a simple contrast between PR and non-PR elections. But that dichotomy may be too crude. On the one hand, there are some mixed systems (Massicotte and Blais 1999). On the other hand, some PR systems are less proportional than others, especially because of low district magnitude or high thresholds (Taagepera and Shugart 1989; Lijphart 1994). We therefore distinguish electoral systems on the basis of their degree of disproportionality.

Party characteristics

We consider not only the electoral system but also the potential impact of the electoral supply side. We first look at the number of parties contesting the election. The assumption is that the greater the number of available options the more likely voters ought to feel that there is at least one other party that is "good enough" to support. Secondly, we consider the degree to which the party system is polarized (Dalton 2008b). It is not clear, however, how polarization could affect strategic desertion. If more polarization means more choice we should observe more desertion; but if this means greater ideological differentiation among the parties, this could reduce the incentive to defect from one's first choice.

We assume that the temptation to desert one's preferred party also depends on the nature of that party. The most important characteristic is the party's relative strength – that is, the percentage of the vote obtained – at the constituency level. The most common incentive for casting a strategic vote is probably the desire not to waste one's vote on a party that has no chance of winning. The literature has referred to forms of « inverse » strategic voting, at the expense of strong parties (see Cox 1997; Blais 2004; Blais et al. 2004; Gschwend 2004, 2007a), but the most frequent pattern must be desertion of the weak. We test the hypothesis that, everything else being equal, weak parties are more likely to be deserted.

179

Voter characteristics

We finally examine voters' characteristics that may foster the propensity to vote strategically. We focus on two characteristics: level of information and strength of party attachment. We test the hypothesis that better-informed citizens are more inclined to vote strategically (Duch and Palmer 2002; Gschwend 2007a), presumably because it is easier for them to assemble information about the possible outcomes of the election. The second characteristic is party attachment. It is one of the most robust findings in the strategic voting literature that strong partisans are less likely to behave strategically than weak- or nonpartisans (e.g., Karp et al. 2002; Gschwend 2007a). We therefore expect strategic defection to be most frequent among nonpartisans and most rare among strong partisans.

The data

Our analyses examine legislative (lower house) elections in module II of the Comparative Study of Electoral Systems (CSES). Table 8.1 lists the twenty-four countries and the twenty-five elections that are covered by the study.[2] The pooled data set includes 24,080 respondents who reported having voted in the election and with no missing data on any of the variables included in the analysis.

As indicated above, the dependent variable is whether the person strategically deserts her preferred party. For a person to be construed as a strategic defector, two conditions must be met. First, the person must vote for a party other than the preferred party. Second, the defection should not be due to the fact that the person votes for her preferred leader.

To determine a respondent's preferred party, we rely mostly on her ratings of the various parties on a 0 to 10 scale (see chapter appendix for information on this variable). The party that receives the highest rating is deemed to be the preferred party. This is relatively straightforward. There are two problems with this approach, however. First, respondents were typically invited to rate up to six of the more popular parties (in terms of vote share) in the country. The implication is that some of the smaller parties were not rated, and so those who prefer a small party were not allowed to rate that party. This is a particular concern for us since we expect supporters of small parties to be more prone to defect. To correct for this problem, we consider whether the respondent indicates that there is a (small, unrated) party that she feels closest to. For these individuals, the preferred party is defined as the party to which they feel closest.

The second problem concerns ties in party ratings. Seventeen percent of the respondents give their highest ratings to two parties or more. In those cases, again, we consider whether they indicate that they feel closest to any party. The party that the person feels closest to is then construed to be the preferred party.

Table 8.1 Defection levels across nations

	N	% Defection	% Strategic defection
Albania (2005) (PR)	725	40	36
Australia (2004)	1414	17	12
Brazil	711	71	68
Canada (2004)	1206	19	16
Chile (2005)	617	47	40
Finland (2003)	716	17	14
Germany (2002) (PR)	1554	25	21
Germany (2002)(SMD)	1522	27	24
Ireland (2002)	1312	27	24
Israel (2003)	648	23	19
Italy (2006)	356	38	37
Mexico (2003)	978	33	27
New Zealand (2002)(PR)	1123	21	14
New Zealand (2002)(SMD)	1101	36	28
Norway (2001)	1279	12	9
Peru (2006)	1216	43	36
Poland (2001)	536	37	35
Portugal (2002)	617	16	9
Portugal (2005)	1399	14	10
Romania (2004)	480	51	25
Slovenia (2004)	276	14	13
Spain (2004)	793	10	6
Sweden (2002)	762	11	10
Switzerland (2003)	650	20	16
Taiwan (2001)	981	40	37
United Kingdom (2005)	517	11	8
United States (2004)	591	15	14
Total N	24080		

See the Appendix for the construction of variables.

Source: Comparative Study of Electoral Systems, module II.

In short, for the great majority (82%) of respondents, the preferred party is the one that receives the highest rating. For a minority, that is, those with ties on highest party ratings and those who feel closer to a small party that is not rated, the preferred party is the party they feel closest to. According to the first condition, 26 percent of the respondents vote for a party that is not the preferred one.

The second condition for being construed as a strategic defector is that the defection ought not to be due to preferences among the party leaders. As a consequence, all defectors who vote for the party whose leader they evaluate the most positively are defined as not strategic. This leaves us with 22 percent strategic defectors.[3]

There are alternative ways of measuring strategic defection, and more specifically party preference. Our approach relies mainly on responses to questions where people are asked to tell how much they like or dislike the various parties. The party that is liked the best is construed to be the preferred party. We believe that this is the most direct and adequate indicator of voters' preference. There are problems with such ratings, the most important being that different people use the scales in different ways (see Brady 1985). The problem is not as serious in this case since we are not comparing party ratings across individuals.

Still, it is useful to determine if the findings are sensitive to the way the dependent variable is measured. We have explored one alternative, in which the preferred party is defined as the party that is perceived by the individual as closest to her position on the Left–Right scale.[4] The assumption here is that the preferred party is the party that is perceived to be most proximate on the overall Left–Right dimension. It seems to us more logical to infer preferences on the basis of questions about likes and dislikes than on the basis of questions about ideological orientations but we acknowledge that perceived ideological proximity to a party can be used as an indirect indicator of preference. When preference is measured in terms of ideological proximity, we get higher figures for "defection" (37% instead of 26%) and "strategic desertion" (25% instead of 22%). This suggests that preference is measured less adequately. Because the ideological measure of preference is noisier (see Chapter 4), there are more people whose vote choice does not appear to coincide with their sincere preference, thus yielding higher numbers of defectors. We determine how similar or different the patterns are with this alternative measure.

Table 8.1 indicates the proportion of strategic desertion in each election. It is extremely high in Brazil and particularly low in Spain. The finding regarding Brazil is consistent with Ames, Baker, and Renno results (2009), which show an exceptionally high level (70%) of ticket-splitting in that country. Ames, Baker, and Renno (2009, 18) conclude that this is so because "Brazil's elections for the national legislature are localized affairs, with voters choosing native sons and daughters attractive because of their presumed ability to deliver local-level public goods." There is clearly a lot of defection in Brazil but defection seems to be induced by local candidates rather than being strategically oriented.[5] Because we are unable to take into account such local candidate vote, the Brazilian estimate of strategic defection is problematic.

Among these twenty-five elections, sixteen were held under PR, four under plurality (Canada, United States, United Kingdom) or majority (Australia), and five were mixed systems. Among the latter, voters have two votes in Albania, Germany, and New Zealand, while they have only one vote in Taiwan and Mexico. Mexico is classified as PR because it has a corrective component while Taiwan is coded as non-PR because it is a parallel system (Massicotte and Blais 1999). As for the countries with two votes, we consider each vote separately.[6]

Note that we can examine only the (national) PR vote in Albania because of lack of information about respondents' single-member district.

Table 8.2 compares the proportion of strategic desertion in PR and non-PR systems. Contrary to conventional wisdom, there appears to be as much strategic defection in PR as in non-PR elections.[7] We also wish to distinguish elections on the basis of how proportional or disproportional their outcomes are. To that effect, we use the Gallagher disproportionality index (see the volume appendix). Table 8.2 suggests that there may be no relation between frequency of strategic desertion and level of disproportionality.[8]

Table 8.2 Bivariate relationships with strategic defection

Electoral system	Strategic defection	
	%	Freq
PR	22	16748
Non-PR	21	7332
Disproportionality		
Low	22	8297
Medium	20	8097
High	23	7686
Effective number of electoral parties		
Low	16	7437
Medium	23	7028
High	26	9615
Party system polarization		
Low	28	8691
Medium	20	7363
High	17	8026
Strength of preferred party		
Low	34	8240
Medium	20	8075
High	11	7765
Partisanship		
None	27	10039
Low	22	2778
Medium	19	7315
High	15	3948
Information		
Low	21	7926
Medium	23	8547
High	22	7607

See the Appendix for the construction of variables.

Source: Comparative Study of Electoral Systems, module II; *N* = 24,080.

In order to characterize the political supply side we consider two different dimensions: the number of parties contesting the election and the overall polarization of the party system. The number of parties is an indicator of the opportunity structure: the more parties are contesting the election, the easier it is to desert the most preferred party. We use the effective number of electoral parties (see the volume appendix). Table 8.2 indicates that the likelihood of strategically defecting from the preferred party is modestly correlated with the effective number of parties. The second factor characterizing the political supply side is party system polarization (see the volume appendix). Table 8.2 suggests that strategic defection is somewhat more frequent when there is less polarization.

We also take into account the preferred party's electoral strength. As indicated above, the temptation to desert one's preferred party should be stronger when that party is weak. Our measure of party strength is the proportion of the vote received by the preferred party in the respondent's constituency. Table 8.2 confirms that strategic defection is negatively correlated with popular support for the preferred party.

Finally, we consider two characteristics of voters: strength of partisanship and political information. Our indicator is whether the respondent feels closer to any party and how strongly she feels. There are four categories: very strong identification, somewhat strong identification, not very strong identification, and no identification. Table 8.2 shows that the propensity to cast a strategic vote declines with party attachment.

The final variable is the respondent's level of information. CSES collaborators were invited to include three factual questions (one relatively easy, one relatively difficult, and one "medium") to tap people's level of information about politics; the specific questions vary across countries. We have centered and standardized the variable, and so we are tapping people's level of information, relative to their country's mean and variance.[9] As can be seen in Table 8.2, the amount of strategic defection seems to be similar across information groups.

Multivariate analyses

We wish to determine whether and to what degree the propensity to strategically defect from one's preferred party depends on characteristics of voters, parties, and elections. Given that our dependent variable is dichotomous, we estimate a logit model predicting the propensity to strategically defect depending on the seven factors discussed above.

Table 8.3 presents the estimation results of a model incorporating our three individual-level and four contextual-level variables, and a dummy for Brazil, where the estimated amount of strategic desertion is exceptionally high and problematic, as explained above. To account for nonindependence in the structure of the CSES data we report standard errors that are clustered by election.

Table 8.3 Robust cluster logit estimations of strategic defection

	No interaction		Interaction	
Individual level				
Information	.139	(.128)	−.151	(.266)
Partisanship	− .719**	(.108)	−.748**	(.104)
Strength of preferred party	−3.698**	(.478)	−1.256	(.720)
Contextual level				
PR electoral system	−.160	(.280)	−.155	(.260)
Number of electoral parties	.705	(.702)	.611	(.650)
Disproportionality	.307	(.447)	.936	(.543)
Party sytem polarization	−1.441	(.851)	−1.398	(.856)
Brazil	1.580**	(.477)	1.733**	(.456)
Interaction				
Information*Disproportionality			.630	(.502)
Strength*Disproportionality			−5.099**	(1.529)
Constant	.106	(.563)	−.189	(.563)
N	24080		24080	
Clusters	25		25	

See the Appendix for the construction of variables.
*P ⟨ .05 **P ⟨ .001
Source: Comparative Study of Electoral Systems, module II.

The results are rather clear-cut. Two of the three individual-level variables, party identification and strength of the preferred party, are significant while the four contextual variables (the electoral system, the degree of disproportionality, party system polarization, and the effective number of parties) are not.[10] Not surprisingly, the Brazilian dummy variable is also highly significant. The hypotheses that nonpartisans and supporters of weak parties are more prone to cast a strategic vote are confirmed, but there is no support for the expectation that the better informed are more prone to strategically desert their preferred party.

The nil findings regarding the direct impact of contextual factors are consistent with the weak bivariate relationships observed in Table 8.2 and are not due to collinearity. The correlations between contextual factors are modest, and in no case does a significant effect emerge if one of them is omitted. This nil finding may be the most important result of this study. The conventional wisdom according to which there is less strategic voting in PR or less disproportional systems is not supported by the data. The verdict is similar to the one reached by Abramson et al. (forthcoming) on a smaller set of nations.

Even though contextual factors do not have a direct effect on strategic voting they may well interact with individual-level variables (see the introduction). We formulate two hypotheses in this regard.

The first hypothesis is that information has a smaller effect in more dispro-portional systems such as first-past-the-post. Presumably, all that is required in such a system is to determine whether a given party is one of the two strongest competitors in the constituency, something that may be easy to ascertain in most circumstances. In more proportional systems with large districts, it is more complicated to know which parties do or not have a chance to win a seat (but see Gschwend 2007b, 2009 and Lago 2008) and, perhaps more importantly, the focus of attention is likely to shift to potential government coalitions, about which information may not be easily available.

The second hypothesis is that the propensity to desert weak parties is stronger in more disproportional systems. The assumption is that in disproportional systems those who vote strategically abandon their weak first choice in order to support a more viable alternative while there are more varieties of strategic considerations in more proportional systems and as a consequence weak parties are not as systematically disadvantaged.

The second column of Table 8.3 tests these two hypotheses. The first hypoth-esis is not supported. There appears to be no relationship between information and strategic defection, in very disproportional as well as in very proportional systems. However, the second hypothesis is clearly confirmed. As expected, the propensity to desert weak parties is considerably stronger in more dispropor-tional systems. This nicely squares with the reported negative correlation between frequency of strategic voting and district magnitude in Gschwend (2009).

We checked whether there were other interaction effects between our con-textual-level and individual-level variables. Not surprisingly, there is a positive interaction effect between the strength of the preferred party and PR, which means that the desertion of weak parties is less widespread under a PR system, which is the flip side of the negative interaction effect with disproportionality reported in Table 8.3. We also find that the impact of partisanship is weaker as the number of parties increases. More importantly, given the findings displayed in the other chapters, there is no evidence of any interaction effect between polarization and the three individual-level variables.

We can also determine how different our results are depending on whether we measure defection on the basis of party ratings or party proximity and whether we take out leader-induced defection or not. Table 8.4 tests the sensitivity of our findings to the operationalization of the dependent variable. As can be seen, the patterns are similar across the various specifications. In all estimations, partisan-ship has a strong negative impact and there is a powerful interaction effect between strength of preferred party and disproportionality. The only difference is that disproportionality is positively correlated with the general measure of defection but not with the specific indicator of *strategic* desertion.

The implications of our findings are illustrated in Figure 8.1, which shows how the predicted probability of strategic defection declines with the preferred

Table 8.4 Robust cluster sensitivity analysis using logit estimations with various measures of defection

	Strategic defection (Ratings)	Defection (Ratings)	Strategic defection (LR proximity)	Defection (LR proximity)
Individual level				
Information	.151 (.266)	−.271 (.228)	.200 (.358)	.566* (.243)
Partisanship	−.748** (.104)	−.623** (.131)	.299** (.105)	−.625** (.087)
Strength of preferred party	−1.256 (.720)	−1.389 (.821)	−1.398* (.559)	−1.003* (.327)
Contextual level				
PR electoral system	−.155 (.260)	.046 (.264)	−.065 (.212)	.012 (.130)
Number of electoral parties	.611 (.650)	−.285 (.614)	.714 (.516)	.164 (.324)
Disproportionality	.936 (.543)	1.414* (.449)	.636 (.571)	.923* (.447)
Party system polarization	−1.398 (.856)	−1.399 (.796)	−.553 (.728)	.039 (.440)
Brazil	1.733** (.456)	2.054** (.401)	1.713** (.348)	1.665** (.214)
Interaction				
Information*Disproportionality	.630 (.502)	.714 (.453)	.299 (.574)	.003 (.488)
Strength*Disproportionality	−5.099** (1.529)	−5.995** (1.562)	−1.963* (.914)	−1.719** (.437)
Constant	−.189 (.563)	.261 (.480)	−.696 (.601)	−.715 (.392)
N	24080	22618	20339	22618
Clusters	25	26	25	26

See the Appendix for the construction of variables
Source: Comparative Study of Electoral Systems, module II.

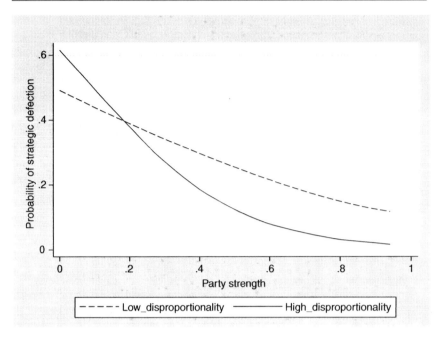

Figure 8.1 Impact of party strength by disproportionality

party's electoral strength in elections with relatively low or high degrees of disproportionality (one standard deviation below or above the mean). The propensity to defect is much more strongly dependent on party strength in more disproportional systems. Figure 8.1 indicates that, as we would expect, strategic desertion of weak parties is more frequent in more disproportional systems.[11] But the figure also shows that while there is hardly any strategic defection from strong parties in more disproportional elections, we observe some non-negligible desertion of these strong parties in more proportional elections. The pattern is reversed at the high end of party strength: desertion is more frequent in more proportional systems. This is why there is no difference overall, between PR and non-PR elections (Table 8.2 and Table 8.3, column 1).

The findings regarding the interaction between disproportionality and party strength are in line with our predictions. The downward sloping lines indicate that in all systems weak parties are more likely to be deserted than their stronger counterparts. The pattern, again, is much stronger in the most disproportional elections.

The preceding analysis is based on robust cluster logit estimations. One could argue that a hierarchical linear model (Raudenbush and Bryk 2002) would be more appropriate. But Arceneaux and Nickerson (2009) show that at least in some conditions there is no meaningful difference in the findings produced by these two methods. As an additional check on the robustness of our results, we performed a multilevel analysis with random intercepts as well as random slopes.

The findings are presented in Table 8.5. The results of the multilevel model are quite similar to those of the robust cluster logit estimations presented in Table 8.3. None of the contextual variables has a direct effect on strategic defection. Among the individual-level variables, partisanship is the most powerful variable. And there is a strong interaction effect between strength of preferred party and disproportionality. The only difference is that according to the multilevel model information has a main negative effect and a positive interaction effect with disproportionality[12] while the robust cluster logit estimation indicates that neither effect is significant. We infer that the results concerning the impact of information are not robust, and we conclude that information has no clear impact on the propensity to strategically desert one's preferred party.

Table 8.5 Multilevel logit model of strategic defection

Individual level		
Information	−.479*	(.226)
Partisanship	−.847**	(.048)
Strength of preferred party	−.993	(.709)
Contextual level		
PR electoral system	−.016	(.396)
Number of electoral parties	−1.398	(1.168)
Disproportionality	1.249	(.687)
Party sytem polarization	−.579	(.979)
Brazil	3.413**	(.993)
Interaction		
Information*Disproportionality	1.161*	(.412)
Strength*Disproportionality	−5.369**	(.706)
Constant	.126	(.661)
Country-Level Variance		
Information	.150	(.330)
Strength of preferred party	3.102	(.490)
Constant	.764	(.153)
Micro N	24080	
Macro N	25	
Deviance	21404.74	

Notes: Hierarchical nonlinear model with random intercepts and random slopes. Estimation performed using Stata 10, xtmlogit function.
See the *Appendix* for the construction of variables.
*P ⟨.05 **P ⟨.001

Source: Comparative Study of Electoral Systems, module II.

Conclusion

We have looked at the propensity to strategically defect from the preferred party across elections, parties, and voters. We have used the CSES module II data set to compare twenty-four countries, twenty-five elections, and 24,080 voters.

We find clear support for the effect of two individual-level characteristics. Strong partisans and supporters of strong parties are much less prone to desert their preferred party. Contrary to our expectations, however, the better informed are not more prone to strategically defect. There is no support for the view that only the most sophisticated citizens have the ability or the information required to think strategically. This indicates that voters might not need a PhD in political science to strategically defect their most preferred party. Rather the electoral environment is likely to provide voters with cues that facilitate strategic voting.

But perhaps the starkest results concern the nonimpact of contextual factors. Our findings are consistently negative. There is no support for the conventional wisdom that there is more strategic defection in more disproportional systems[13] or for the alternative hypothesis that it is easier to desert a preferred party when and where there are more alternative options. The only substantively important contextual effect is a conditional one. While strategic desertion is almost exclusively at the expense of the weakest parties in the most disproportional systems, the bias is more muted in the most proportional systems.

We hope to have shown that the CSES data set offers a great opportunity to study strategic defection in a comparative perspective. The most important advantage associated with the CSES is that it covers an a wide variety of elections with very different rules and party systems, which allows us to examine in a systematic fashion how contextual factors affect the propensity to desert one's preferred party.

CSES has some drawbacks. The most important disadvantage is that because it is a postelection study it is impossible to take into account voters' subjective expectations about the outcome of the election. Still, the survey questionnaire could be improved to allow us to better measure whether people do (or do not) vote for their preferred party. We would suggest two such improvements. First, it would help if there were a direct question asking respondents what party they like the most. The existing set of questions that tap how much people like or dislike the most important parties is extremely helpful but it has two shortcomings. The first is that the weakest parties are excluded, and so it becomes impossible to identify supporters of the smaller parties, which are precisely the most likely to vote strategically. The second is that the rating questions produce a number of ties. The solution, it seems to us, is very simple. CSES could just add the following question: "All in all, which party did you like the most in this election?" Secondly, it would be possible to include questions tapping how much respondents care about the outcome of the election, at the district level and with respect to government formation, and whether they thought that their vote might count, perceptions and attitudes that should be related to the propensity to vote strategically. We could also gauge expectations indirectly by better describing the electoral environment in that regard. For instance, it would be helpful to know how many seats a party actually won in each electoral district and whether parties issued positive or negative coalition signals before the election about which parties they are willing to form a governing coalition with (Meffert and Gschwend 2009).

The data presented here, as well as in the literature reviewed above, make it clear that it is incorrect to assume that vote choice merely reflects voters' preferences. They also indicate that strategic defection is *not* confined to the least permissive electoral systems or highly informed voters. Strategic voting is pervasive for all types of voters and it occurs in all kinds of contexts. If we want to understand what voters express in the ballot box, we need to determine how their sincere preferences interact with the rules of the game in affecting their final vote decision.

Appendix

CSES survey variables

Variable	Question wording	Coding
Desertion	Preferred party based on party ratings on a 0 to 10 scale (B3037) and Party Identification (B3033, B035, B3029_1). Vote: B3006_1, B3006_2. See text for full description.	1 if the person voted for a party other than the preferred party, 0 otherwise
Strategic Desertion	Preferred leader: B3026. See text for full description	1 if the person deserted her preferred party (see above) and did not vote for the preferred leader, 0 otherwise
Information	B3047. Three political knowledge questions in each country. Proportion of correct answers minus mean proportion in the country, divided by the standard deviation.	Scale from 0 to 1
Party ID	B3028 and B3036. "Do you usually think of yourself as close to any particular political party?" (If yes): "Do you feel very close to this party, somewhat close, or not very close?"	0 =No Party ID to 1 = Very strong Party ID

Notes

* We thank Pascal Doray-Demers for his excellent research assistance.
1. We leave aside a fourth possibility: the voter whose choice is unaffected by preferences or expectations.
2. We excluded election studies that do not provide information about respondents' district (Belgium, Bulgaria, Czech Republic, Denmark, Hungary) or that did not include questions about respondents' level of information (Iceland) or leader ratings (the Netherlands). Two other countries (South Korea and Philippines) could not be included because of lack of data on electoral outcomes at the district level.
3. This does not mean that only 4 percent of the electorate voted for a party leader. It rather means that 4 percent deserted their preferred party to support the party of their preferred leader. Many more voters may have decided to stick with their preferred party in good part because they liked the leader or may have deserted their preferred partly because they did not like the leader. See Chapter 6 for a more detailed examination of the role of leader evaluations.
4. Again, we use the party one feels closest to for those who identify with a party whose position of the Left–Right scale was not asked in the survey as well as for those with two or more parties equally proximate to their own positions.
5. Ames, Baker, and Renno (2009) show, for instance, that split ticket is not based on policy balancing.
6. We consequently assume that voters form independent decisions in every tier in mixed systems. If voters' decision in one tier depends on their decision in the other tier, there are contamination effects (Herron and Nishikawa 2001; Gschwend et al. 2003; Ferrara and Herron 2005; Gschwend 2007a). If contamination effects are present we expect more straight-tickets than otherwise. Thus we would underestimate the degree of strategic voting that has occurred if both tiers were independent. We did test whether strategic defection is more frequent in elections with mixed systems or with two votes, and we found no significant difference.
7. We use a simple PR/non-PR dichotomy instead of the three-category PR/mixed/majoritarian because we look separately at the two votes in mixed systems with two votes.
8. For the purpose of displaying bivariate relationships in Table 8.2, all the independent variables except the electoral system and party identification were divided into three categories of about equal size.
9. More precisely, the information variable was constructed in the following way. The respondent's number of correct answers to the factual questions was subtracted from the mean number of correct answers in the country. That relative score was divided by the country's standard deviation (to control for the fact that the variance varies across countries) and the normalized relative score was finally transformed into a 0 to 1 variable.
10. Note that strength of preferred party is not, strictly speaking, an individual-level variable; it is rather the combination of an individual characteristic, that is, the person's preferred party, and a contextual factor, that is, how much support that preferred party enjoys in that election.

11. The difference is relatively modest, however. The predicted probability of strategically deserting a party with 1 percent of the vote in the district is .6 in a more disproportional system, compared to .49 in a more proportional system. The difference would be twice as large if we were to contrast the most and least disproportional elections.
12. Note that these results more or less contradict our initial hypothesis that information has a smaller effect in more disproportional systems. This hypothesis would entail a positive main effect for information and a negative interaction effect; we observe exactly the opposite in Table 8.5.
13. There is more strategic desertion of weaker parties in more disproportional systems but this is counterbalanced by less desertion of stronger parties.

Part III

Electoral Choice and Representation

9

Party Polarization and the Ideological Congruence of Governments[*]

G. Bingham Powell, Jr.

The previous chapters have examined how political contexts shape citizens' behavior. This chapter turns to one of the principal consequences of electoral processes – the representation of citizens by their government. A consistent theme in this volume indicates that greater variety of partisan choice facilitates citizen participatory activities. Greater party system polarization seems to help voters to use ideology in making electoral choices, to encourage citizen mobilization, to facilitate the application of government performance assessments, and to diminish the alienation of voters with more extreme ideological positions (see Chapters 2, 5, and 7). Yet, there is good reason to think that such individual helpfulness may come at a collective cost. The polarization of the party system may make it more difficult to generate close congruence between citizens and policymakers. The Comparative Study of Electoral System (CSES) studies make it possible to examine these paradoxical connections in a systematic way.

Ideological congruence measures the fit between the preferences of the citizens and the committed policy positions of their representatives, an important feature of liberal democracy. Normative theorizing about democracy implies that competitive elections should systematically create a close connection between citizens and their policymakers (e.g., Dahl 1989). Because of its special normative status as the position that can defeat any other in a straight vote, the position of the median citizen has particular significance. Good ideological congruence implies minimizing this distance.

Thus far, most research on ideological congruence has focused on the effects of the election rules, primarily the distinction between single member district (SMD) and proportional representation (PR) electoral systems. Some studies have concentrated on legislative congruence (Powell and Vanberg 2000; McDonald and Budge 2005), while others have focused on government congruence (Huber and Powell 1994; McDonald, Mendes, and Budge 2004; Blais and Bodet 2006; Powell 2006; Golder and Stramski 2010). Recent research suggests that another primary democratic institution, the political party system, also has major effects on ideological congruence and that the effects of these two institutions – the election rules and the party systems – may be interactive (Kim, Powell, and Fording 2010).

Ideological congruence studies published before 2006 were based on either citizen-and-expert surveys or on the Comparative Manifesto Project (CMP), using elections before the late 1990s. They consistently found greater congruence in the PR parliamentary systems than in the SMD parliamentary systems. But two recent studies by Blais and Bodet (2006) and Golder and Stramski (2010), using the CSES data (1996–2004), find no significant difference in government congruence between the two types of electoral systems. Comparing the alternative methods and sources over the last three decades, Powell (2009) argues that changing levels of congruence, especially in the SMD systems, not the alternative measurement approaches, are responsible for the lesser difference between SMD and PR outcomes in more recent studies. As estimated from several different approaches, the most recent decade shows a sharp increase in congruence (decline in distance) in the SMD systems, whereas the congruence in the PR systems remains at about the same level. Powell (2008) suggests that the over-time differences are a consequence of changing levels of party system polarization.

This chapter uses the first two modules of the CSES project to replicate, extend, and explore the effects of party systems and election rules on government ideological congruence. The analysis builds on the literatures of government formation and party competition. The hypotheses assume that the effects of party systems and election rules are conditional, rather than additive.

Theoretical expectations

My theoretical analysis of government ideological congruence builds from the well-known literature on government formation in parliamentary systems. When a single party wins a majority in the legislature, it generally forms a majority government by itself (except in times of national emergency or when confronting unusual super-majority institutional rules). Such single-party majorities are rare in PR systems, although fairly common in SMD systems, primarily because of vote-seat distortion, as in the typical British election. In 2005, for example, the British Labour Party won a parliamentary majority (and formed a government) with only 35 percent of the vote. Thus, in SMD systems we are much more likely to encounter the direct election of government majority parties (Rae 1971). The plurality vote winner is the party most likely to win this majority (Powell 2000).

If no party receives a legislative majority, as is typical in PR parliamentary systems, then coalition bargaining either implementing preelection commitments, as discussed in Golder (2006) and Powell (2000, 2006), or in postelection negotiations is necessary to form a government. Such bargaining may result in either a minority government that draws support from "outside" parties, as in Sweden in 2002, or a multiparty majority government, as in Germany in 1998 and 2002. In either case the parties most likely to be involved are the plurality vote winner (which is likely to become the largest party in the legislature) and the median party in the legislature. The plurality party can most easily contribute toward the needed legislative majority and under the government formation rules in many countries has the right to make the first attempt to form a government (Martin and Stevenson 2001). The median legislative party has theoretical bargaining advantages in a unidimensional space (Laver and Schofield 1990; Martin and Stevenson 2001).

Thus, the literature on government formation in parliamentary systems points to two political parties, the plurality vote winner and the median legislative party, whose proximity or distance from the median citizen are particularly likely to contribute to the distance of the government from the citizens – its ideological congruence. According to Laver and Schofield (1990: 113), each of these parties is a member of about 80 percent of governments in parliamentary systems. For direct evidence of the role of these party distances in government ideological congruence, using several approaches to measuring congruence, see Powell (2009). We expect the distances of these two parties to constitute a critical causal mechanism in connections between the institutional conditions (election rules, party system) and ideological congruence.

We can draw on theory of institutions and party competition to link institutional conditions and distances between the median citizen and these two key political parties. Following Cox (1990, 1997: ch.12), we expect that in multiparty systems the parties will disperse as the voters are dispersed, and with more parties the niches between the parties will be smaller. Thus, unless there is two-party competition (Downs 1957) the larger the effective number of parties, the closer to the median citizen will be the median voted party. Up to some maximum set by the carrying capacity of the election rules, under PR the median voted party will generally become (or be close to) the median legislative party. Thus we expect a greater number of effective voted parties to be associated with legislative medians closer to the median citizen. The legislative median party, as mentioned above, should pull governments toward that median citizen. Under SMD, however, these expectations are less clear, as the carrying capacity of the system is more easily exceeded; geographic distributions may also cause vote-seat distortion, and two party competition may cause convergence toward the center.

*Hypothesis 1. Under PR a greater **effective number of electoral parties** decreases government distance from the median citizen (increases congruence) because party competition leads to smaller distances between the median voter and the median legislative party, which forms or joins most governments.*

*Hypothesis 1a. Under SMD a greater **effective number of electoral parties** has indeterminate effects on government congruence (limiting two-party Downsian convergence to the median and increasing vote-seat distortion, but also reducing niches between parties.)*

The second key property of the party system is its polarization – the degree the party system spreads out across the Left–Right spectrum, rather than being concentrated towards its center (see Sartori 1976; Warwick 1994; Dalton 2008b). There are several ways to conceptualize and measure party system polarization. Following the convention proposed by Dalton (2008b), also see Kim, Powell, and Fording (2010) and Warwick (1994), we assume that the spread of the parties should be weighted by the votes received by the parties. The polarization measure proposed by Dalton is correlated at .99 with the weighted standard deviation of the party positions, the polarization measure used in Kim, Powell, and Fording (2010). That is, these measures are linear transformations of each other.

In this conceptualization, we expect that the level of polarization is shaped above all by the distance of the largest (plurality vote winning) party. As already suggested, the critical role of that party in government formation is well known. Moreover, as polarization reflects weighted distances of all the parties, the effect of polarization on government distance may also operate through the legislative median party, and even other potential coalition partners, creating what should be relatively robust effects. If the parties are clustered close to the center of the party system, governments will be highly congruent, as long as that center itself is close to the median citizen. If they are dispersed, effects will be more variable, but incongruence can easily emerge. These effects may well be exaggerated under SMD election rules, where the plurality vote winner may be able to form a majority government by itself (Rae 1971; Taagepera and Shugart 1989; Lijphart 1994).

*Hypothesis 2. Under PR, greater **party system polarization** increases government distance from the median citizen (decreases congruence) because party polarization implies greater distances from the median voter for the plurality party and/or the median legislative party, which form or join most governments.*

*Hypothesis 2a. Under SMD greater **party system polarization** greatly increases government distance from the median citizen (decreases congruence) because party polarization implies greater distance between the median voter and the plurality vote winner, which often forms a single-party majority government.*

Our expectations about the effects of the election rules depend on the party system. If party system polarization is low, we expect low distance (high congruence) between the median citizen and the government, regardless of the election rules (Kim, Powell, and Fording 2010). However, Hypothesis 2 implies that polarization will have more impact in SMD systems. If polarization were substantial and roughly equal between the SMD and PR systems, the distance would be less under PR. In terms of the causal mechanisms of government formation in parliamentary systems, this lesser distance would be created by the way the median legislative party pulls parliamentary governments toward the median citizen in PR representation and government formation.

Hypothesis 3. *Effects of the **election rules** will depend on the polarization of the party system: Where polarization is low, we expect government distance to be low, regardless of the election rules. Where polarization is equally substantial, distances should be greater under SMD than under PR.*

Another feature of the institutional context, which has not been explored in previous work on ideological congruence, is the distinction between presidential and parliamentary (and mixed) political systems. In the strong presidential systems the chief executive is directly elected and has substantial political powers. Unfortunately, the features of the party system interact with the rules for electing the chief executive, especially the distinction between plurality and run-off elections (Colomer 2001, ch. 3). Moreover, the presence of independent candidates and the importance of candidate personality blur our expectations about the connection between party system and government congruence. Even the way to conceptualize the make-up of that government may be controversial, although I shall assume it is at the position of the president's party. In general, we still expect that where the party system is polarized, and thus the parties offer alternatives further from the center, the chief executive that emerges from the election will on average be further from the median citizen. However, these effects should be weaker and/or more variable under presidential systems than under parliamentary ones.

Hypothesis 4. *In **presidential systems**, greater party system polarization will increase government (executive) distance from the median voter (decrease congruence.)*
Hypothesis 4a. *However, the effects of polarization will be less than under presidential systems than under parliamentary systems.*

These hypotheses extend our concern with context and choice to the analysis of ideological congruence between the median citizen and the government that emerges after the election. They interactively link the institutional conditions of election rules and executive selection and the party system conditions of number and polarization of the party system. They suggest that these features of institutional and party system context will shape the representational out-comes of citizens' choices in the elections. If these hypotheses prove true, they will explicate the role of the institutional and party contexts in the workings of representative democracy.

Testing the hypotheses

The Comparative Study of Electoral Systems (CSES) project makes it possible to test our hypotheses about the implications of party systems across a much wider range of political systems than ever before. It is particularly interesting to be able to extend our analysis of ideological congruence outside the realm of established Western parliamentary democracies that have been the locus of previous studies. We can explore ideological congruence in more recently established political systems and even add a small number of strong presidential systems to the familiar parliamentary ones (and the United States.) Unfortunately, there are no legislatures elected only by SMD in the new political systems, so we shall not be able to greatly extend what has already been shown about the election rules. Moreover, the time frame is a relatively limited one, as the CSES Module 1 studies only begin in 1996 and CSES Module 2 continues only as late as 2006. For that reason the design is primarily cross-sectional.

The key to analyzing ideological congruence of governments is to estimate the positions of citizens and governments on the same scale, so as to correctly observe the distance. The CSES provides a powerful way to do this because citizens were asked to place themselves on a Left–Right scale (whose content is completely self-defined) and also to place the political parties in their country on that same scale. We can use the average citizen placement of each party as an estimate of its true position. It turns out that it makes little difference whether we use all the citizens or only the more educated (Golder and Stramski 2010). We can then estimate the position of the government by weighting the parties which are its members (either by their proportion of legislative seats or by the similar proportion of cabinet portfolios, as done here.)

Table 9.1 shows the level of ideological congruence, the distance between the median citizen and the government on the ten-point Left–Right scale, in the thirty-three democracies that were part of the CSES Module 2. The aver-age government is about one point away from the median citizen. The average distance is a little further in the twenty "old" democracies (1.24) than in the thirteen "new" democracies (1.08,) but there is lots of variability in each group. In the old democracies the citizen–government distances range from .07 in Canada in 2004 to 2.37 in Portugal in 2002. In the new democracies these distances range from .10 in Taiwan in 2004 to 3.29 in Poland in 2001.

Table 9.1 Ideological (in)congruence: distance between the median citizen and the government in old and new democracies

Old democracies		New democracies	
Australia 2004	1.96	Bulgaria 2001	.92
Belgium 2003	.59	Chile 2005	.80
Canada 2004	.07	Czech Rep. 2002	1.02
Denmark 2001	2.18	Hungary 2002	2.86
Finland 2003	.53	Japan 2004	2.30
France 2002	1.54	Korea 2004	1.30
Germany 2002	.73	Mexico 2003	.70
Great Britain 2005	.24	Peru 2006	.20
Iceland 2003	2.17	Poland 2001	3.29
Ireland 2002	1.42	Romania 2004	.20
Israel 2003	1.12	Russia 2004	.90
Italy 2006	1.67	Slovenia 2004	1.60
Netherlands 2002	1.87	Taiwan 2004	.10
New Zealand 2002	1.08		
Norway 2001	1.79		
Portugal 2002	2.37		
Spain 2004	.70		
Sweden 2002	1.48		
Switzerland 2003	.70		
United States 2004	1.68		

Source: Comparative Study of Electoral Systems, module 2.

As the median citizen is usually in the center of the scale, the maximum of ideological distance would be about 5. On one hand, the average distances of about a point suggest relatively successful democratic representation. On the other hand, the handful of cases where the government is two or three points from the median citizen, as in Poland and Hungary in the new democracies and in Denmark and Australia in the old democracies, show that even competitive elections and legitimate government formation procedures can sometimes result in rather low representative congruence.

This method of relying on citizen placements is not without flaws. It is subject to citizen error and ignorant guessing, which may pull estimates toward the center of the scale, as well as to projection and rationalization, which may reduce distances from favored parties. It assumes that average citizens' conceptions of distance are similar in different countries and across different elections. However, it avoids some of the strong assumptions necessary in other approaches, such as assuming that all voters make ideological choices or assuming that citizens and experts share common visions (see Powell 2009). It will, of course, be most reassuring for our confidence in the hypothesized relationships if similar results emerge from different methods.

As already suggested, both of the party system properties (the number of electoral parties and the polarization of the party system) take account of the support received by the parties, not the simple number and ideological placement of the parties.[1] The number of electoral parties (ENEP) is the effective numbers of votes received by the respective parties in the election, following the usual formula devised by Laakso and Taagepera (1979). The polarization of the party system is the measure devised by Dalton (2008*b*), which is similar to measures of the weighted standard deviation of the party distribution on the Left–Right scale.[2]

As our theoretical hypotheses argue that effects of both number and polarization of the party system may be different under SMD and PR election rules, Table 9.2 shows an interactive model. Reading down the independent variables, we see first the constant term, then the effective number of electoral parties

Table 9.2 Conditional regression analyses of government distance: election rules

		Old democracies	New democracies	All democracies
Independent variables	Manifesto	CSES	CSES	CSES
Constant	−.14	.38	−.09	.11
	(.21)	(.81)	(.87)	(.51)
ENEP	−.03	−.13	−.09	−.12
	(.03)	(.11)	(.17)	(.09)
ENEP SMD	−.03	−.28	—	−.29
	(.09)	(.35)	—	(.34)
Polarization of party	.32**	.42*	.51**	.48**
system	(.03)	(.20)	(.11)	(.09)
Polarization * SMD	.21**	.50	—	.44
	(.08)	(.56)	—	(.53)
SMD election rules	−.19	−.28	—	−.01
	(.34)	(1.68)	—	(1.54)
R-square	36%	25%	57%	41%
Number of cases	327	(37)	(19)	(56)

Notes: The dependent variable is the distance between median voter and government (low congruence). Entries are unstandardized coefficients; standard errors in parentheses (panel-corrected for the Manifesto data).
* = significant at .05 ** = significant at .01

The 100-point manifesto data scale has been translated into a ten-point scale for comparison to CSES, and the "Dalton" version of the polarization measure is used. The "old democracies" in CSES are Australia, Belgium, Canada, Denmark, Finland, France, Germany, Great Britain, Iceland, Ireland, Israel, Italy, Netherlands, New Zealand, Norway, Portugal, Spain, Sweden, Switzerland, and the United States. "New" democracies are Bulgaria, Chile, Czech Republic, Hungary, Japan, Korea, Mexico, Peru, Poland, Romania, Russia, Slovenia, and Taiwan. SMDs are Australia, Canada, Great Britain, France, and the United States.

Source: Comparative Study of Electoral Systems, Module 2 and Comparative Manifesto Project.

(ENEP), the effective number of parties multiplied by presence of SMD election rules, the polarization of the party system, the polarization multiplied by the presence of SMD election rules, the SMD election rule dummy. In reading such an interactive model, we recall that the unmultiplied terms are the party systems' effects under PR. To get the party system effects under SMD we add the unmultiplied and multiplied terms together. However, we cannot have great expectations of statistical significance under the SMD cases, because we have only nine elections held under SMD (in Australia, Canada, Great Britain, France, and the United States.)

The first data column reproduces ideological congruence analysis using a very different approach to estimating the positions of voters and governments – the party statements in their election manifesto and the support voters give to them.[3] This analysis involves twenty countries, primarily Western parliamentary democracies, and covers nearly a half century of elections, for a total of 327 cases. To facilitate comparison in the table, the dependent variable has been divided by ten, so that its 100-point scale corresponds to the ten-point CSES Left–Right scale. The second data column shows the similar twenty "old democracies" in the CSES data, with the same statistical model.[4]

The results for the "old" democracies in columns 1 and 2 show that increasing the effective number of electoral parties is helpful in reducing government distance, as predicted in Hypothesis 1. This negative relationship between number of parties and distance appears in both the Manifesto and CSES data, and is larger in the SMD settings. But the effects are very small and not statistically significant with either measure or set of cases. As in many of the chapters of this volume, expectations about the sheer (effective) number of electoral parties (ENEP) were not significantly realized.

Party system polarization, in contrast, increases the distance between government and median citizen substantially, even under PR, as predicted by Hypothesis 2. The relationship is about the same magnitude in both Manifesto and CSES data and is statistically significant, strongly so in the larger Manifesto data set, but at the usual .05 level even in the thirty-seven CSES cases. The party system polarization effects under SMD, adding the unmultiplied and multiplied coefficients, are even larger, significantly so in the Manifesto data set, just as predicted by Hypothesis 2a. In the CSES data the effect of polarization is about twice as great under SMD as under PR; although the difference is not statistically significant, the small number of SMD cases makes the large standard error unsurprising. The polarization results seem remarkably similar given the very different measurement approaches and quite different data sets in the two "old" democracy columns. Moreover, these polarization effects seem substantively important: an increase in party system polarization from 3 units (about the mean) to 4 (an increase of about a standard deviation) would increase government distance by nearly half a point in the PR settings, double that in the SMD settings. Recall that the average government distance is about one point in the CSES cases.

The third column shows the statistical analysis in the nineteen elections in thirteen newer CSES democracies. There are no SMD cases, so we see only the constant and the number and polarization of the party system. The effective number of parties has very little effect, but polarization is, again, strongly and significantly related to greater distance (less congruence). The fourth column combines all the fifty-six CSES cases in thirty-three countries. We see that more parties are helpful, but the effects are small and the coefficients about the same size as the standard errors. Polarization, however, is strongly and significantly related to greater distance, with size of the coefficients much larger under SMD, but the difference is not statistically significant.

The statistical results, then, are quite robust across both methods of analysis and the subsets of old and new democracies. As we expect from Hypothesis 1, a greater number of electoral parties is associated with more congruent (less distant) governments, but the effects are very small and fall short of statistical significance at the .05 level. The impact is greater, but still insignificant, in the (small number) of SMD systems. Much more powerfully and consistently, the polarization of the party system is associated with less congruent (more distant) governments, in line with Hypothesis 2. An additional unit of polarization is associated with governments about a half unit (on the ten-point scale) further from the median citizen, even in the PR systems. Effects in the SMD systems seem to be about twice as large, although the difference is not significant in the CSES data as it is in the much larger Manifesto data set.

Also in line with the reasoning of Hypothesis 2, systems with higher polarization show more variance in government distance, as well as on average greater distances. The twenty-six cases with polarization levels at or below 3.35 have an average distance from the median citizen of .80 (on the ten-point scale) and a standard deviation of .62; the thirty cases with higher levels of polarization are on average more than twice as far away at 1.67, but have a larger standard deviation also, of .85. Greater polarization facilitates greater distance, but does not determine the coalition building outcomes.

Figure 9.1 presents a scattergram of the relationship between party system polarization and government distance (incongruence). The nine SMD cases are shown by squares. The forty-seven PR cases are shown with circles. The dashed and more steeply sloped line is the relationship between polarization and government distance in the SMD settings. The solid, less steeply sloped line is the relationship in the PR settings. We can see that this is a strong and systematic relationship, although it still has a lot of variability.

We cannot be very sure about effects of either the election rules or presidential systems, because of the very small numbers of SMD and presidential cases in the CSES data set. However, the complementary results from the Manifesto data provide some reassurance about the robustness of the SMD results. As suggested by the coefficients in Table 9.2, if polarization is minimal, election rules seem to have no net effect on congruence. In the CSES data polarization is substantially

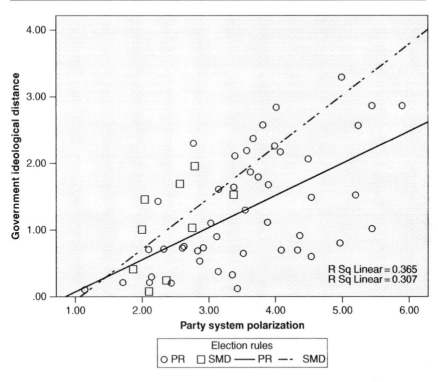

Figure 9.1 Party system polarization and government distance
Source: Comparative Study of Electoral Systems.

less in the SMD systems than in the PR systems (2.43 versus 3.46), which translates into rather similar levels of congruence. In the long period of the Manifesto data, polarization is nearly as large in the SMD systems as in the PR systems, 3.2 and 3.6. Its much greater effect on congruence in the former leads to a notable PR advantage in average congruence, as found in various studies with pre-1996 data (see Powell 2008, 2009). These results are consistent with Hypothesis 3.

Examining the nature of the chief executive yields results roughly consistent with Hypothesis 4, but because of the small number of cases, these results should be considered only suggestive. The mixed executive systems, having both a directly elected president and a significant prime minister, look very much like the parliamentary systems, with party system polarization associated with governments significantly further from the median citizen. Average government congruence levels are similar to those in the PR systems. The strong presidential systems (Chile, Israel 1996, South Korea, Mexico, Peru, Russia, the United States) also show more parties as helpful and party polarization as

Table 9.3 Conditional regression analyses of government distance: executive type

Independent Variables	Parliamentary	Presidential	All democracies
	CSES	CSES	CSES
Constant	−.02	1.24	−.02
	(.49)	(.54)	(.49)
ENEP	−.10	−.29*	−.10
	(.10)	(.10)	(.09)
ENEP* Presidential	—	—	−.19
			(.19)
Polarization of party system	.50**	.35*	.50**
	(.10)	(.15)	(.09)
Polarization * Presidential	—	—	−.16
			(.26)
Presidential executives	—	—	1.26
			(1.00)
R-square number of cases	39%	68%	41%
	(48)	(8)	(56)

Notes: The dependent variable is the distance between median voter and government (low congruence). Entries are unstandardized coefficients; standard errors in parentheses.
* = significant at .05 ** = significant at .01
 The "Dalton" version of the polarization measure is used. The presidential systems are Chile, Israel 1996, Korea, Mexico, Peru, Russia, and the United States. All other cases are considered parliamentary.
Source: Comparative Study of Electoral Systems, Module 2.

harmful to congruence. Each is close to significance at .05 within the subset of eight cases, as shown in the middle column of Table 9.3. As predicted in Hypothesis 4a, the polarization coefficient is smaller than in the parliamentary and mixed systems, as we can see by comparing the left and middle columns. But in an interactive specification, shown in the last column of Table 9.3, the difference is less than its standard error and thus not significant at .05. Average distances are slightly less (more congruent) than in the PR and mixed systems, as is the average level of polarization.

Exploring the causal mechanisms

Despite the pleasing robustness of the party system polarization results, aggregate effects of the sort shown in Table 9.2 are notorious for their ability to coexist with varying interpretations and misleading specifications. We can offer some reassurance by exploring the causal mechanisms of government formation that underlie our original hypotheses.

For example, Hypothesis 1 was founded largely on the expectation that in multiparty systems, more parties in competition would lead to smaller niches between the parties. These smaller niches, in turn, would lead the parties closest to the median voter to be more congruent. In PR systems, especially, these parties will usually become, or be very close to, the party commanding the legislative median, which is expected to be advantaged in (unidimensional) government formation. Hypothesis 2 was founded on the greater distance between the plurality vote winner and the government in more polarized systems, a prediction supported by the greater average distances of the other parties, including the legislative median party, as well. The tendency of plurality vote winners to become legislative single-party majorities under SMD was expected to enhance the polarization effects.

We can explore these causal mechanisms by looking directly at the distances between the legislative median party, the plurality vote winning party, and the average citizen. These should largely account for the effects of the number and polarization of the party system in parliamentary systems. Entering them into the same equation should eliminate or at least substantially reduce the party system effects.

The CSES data allow us to use citizen perceptions to estimate the positions of these critical linking parties, parties that previous theory has identified as playing major roles in government formation in parliamentary systems. Table 9.4 shows three successive models of party system effects on government distance from the median citizen in the parliamentary democracies in the CSES studies.[5] On the left side of the table we see these models estimated for the "old" democracies; on the right side we see the models when we add thirteen cases from seven newer democracies of Eastern Europe and Taiwan.

Model 1 shows just the two party system properties from Hypotheses 1 and 2: effective number of electoral parties and polarization. As we expect from the previous analysis in Table 9.2, a greater effective number of parties reduces distance (increases congruence). However, the effect is not large and only significant at about .09, slightly below usual significance standards. Polarization, on the other hand, has a large and significant effect increasing distance (decreasing congruence). Model 2 adds the distance of the median legislative party from the median citizen to the model. As we expect from our hypothesized causal mechanism, adding this variable cuts the small coefficient for number of parties in half; it is now smaller than the standard error. Polarization remains significant, although slightly diminished. The distance of the median legislative party is itself a strong and significant increaser of distance between government and median citizen.

Model 3 adds the distance between median citizen and plurality vote winning party. Not only is this variable strong and significant in its own right, and its addition increases the R-square, but its incorporation in the model greatly reduces the direct effect of party system polarization, with which it is strongly associated. In Model 3 both party system properties (ENEP and Polarization) are insignificant, now that the linking parties are included, which is what we would

Table 9.4 Exploring the causal mechanism of party system effects in parliamentary democracies

Independent variables	Old democracies			All democracies		
	Model 1	Model 2	Model 3	Model 1	Model 2	Model 3
Constant	.58	.07	.35	.06	−.19	.20
	(.63)	(.53)	(.47)	(.52)	(.51)	(.44)
ENEP	−.21	−.16	−.15	−.15	−.11	−.12
	(.12)	(.10)	(.09)	(.11)	(.11)	(.09)
Polarization of party system	.44**	.33**	.12	.52**	.44**	.15
	(.16)	(.13)	(.13)	(.09)	(.10)	(.11)
Distance: legislative median & med voter	—	.69**	.55**	—	.37*	.26
		(.17)	(.16)		(.18)	(.15)
Distance: plurality winner & med voter	—	—	.34**	—	—	.48**
			(.11)			(.11)
R-square	24%	51%	63%	42%	48%	64%
Number of cases	33	33	33	46	46	46

Notes: The dependent variable is the distance between median voter and government (low congruence). Entries are unstandardized coefficients; standard errors in parentheses (panel-corrected for the Manifesto data).
* = significant at .05 ** = significant at .01
The "old democracies" are Australia, Belgium, Canada, Denmark, Finland, France, Germany, Great Britain, Iceland, Ireland, Israel, Netherlands, New Zealand, Norway, Portugal, Spain, Sweden, and Switzerland. "New" democracies are Bulgaria, Czech Republic, Hungary, Poland, Romania, Slovenia, and Taiwan.
Source: Comparative Study of Electoral Systems, Module 2 and Comparative Manifesto Project.

expect if they constitute much of the causal mechanisms through which the party system works.

We have too few cases to be very confident about more fine-grained exploration of these mechanisms. As we can see from the right side of Table 9.4, the effect of the plurality party is especially strong in the new Eastern European democracies, whereas the legislative median party is somewhat stronger in the older democracies. This is true even if the SMD systems are excluded from the older democracies. Similarly, the plurality party effects seem somewhat stronger, relative to the legislative median party, in the mixed parliamentary–presidential systems than in the pure parliamentary systems, but we cannot disentangle this from age and regionalism.

Within the older democracies the SMD systems are, as we might expect, particularly notable for the nearly perfect correlations between the plurality vote winners, the legislative median parties, and the government. These are generally the same party. Under the SMD election rules the vote–seat distortion turns a plurality of votes into an absolute majority of seats, which includes, of course, the legislative median. That legislative majority party becomes the government. Occasionally in France and Australia things are slightly more complicated, but not in these elections.

In the PR systems, in contrast, the elections are followed by a government coalition formation process, in which the legislative median party and the plurality party each has a role to play.[6] The correlations between plurality vote winner distance and government distance is .63; between legislative median party distance and government distance it is .54. The correlation between the plurality distance and the legislative median distance is only .26, emphasizing the different nature of the parties in most PR elections in most countries. Thus, the causal process of government formation is, as we anticipated, both theoretically and from the interactions in Table 9.2, somewhat different under PR and SMD.

Concluding observations

Modern democratic government is representative government. Citizens exert their influence primarily through participation in competitive elections, directly or indirectly choosing those who make the policies. The discovery of the best electoral arrangements for representation, however, has proved difficult. In part it has proved difficult because we have conflicting goals for representation. We want to encourage thoughtful and supportive citizen participation, a process in which citizens choose representatives in whom they can have confidence. At the same time, we want to encourage the formation of governments who will be as close as possible to the citizens for whom they make policies. The single position that has the best claim to be as close as possible to everyone is the position of the median voter. But the arrangements that seem to work best for citizens' participation and party support do not seem to be the arrangements that are most successful at inducing the formation of governments at the most desirable position.

This familiar dilemma emerges again when we consider the findings of the earlier chapters in this volume, which examine how citizens respond to their political context, and contrast them to our findings on ideological congruence of governments and citizens in this chapter.

Our analysis of ideological congruence between median citizen and government confirms the important role that party system polarization plays in promoting greater distances (less congruence). In new democracies as well as older ones, the more polarized elections tend to be followed by less congruent governments. These results from the CSES-based analysis are consistent with previous and current research using different data based on the Manifesto approach, applied to the older democracies over a substantial time span. These polarization effects seem to emerge at least in part because polarization is fundamentally associated with the presence of plurality parties and legislative median parties more distant from the citizen median. These parties are the key building blocks of parliamentary government. Where they are more distant from the median citizen, the governments that emerge after elections are also likely to be more distant. Because polarization seems to have even stronger effects in SMD systems, it also plays an important conditioning role in the connection between election rules and congruence. In conditions of low polarization, both types of election rules seem to induce congruent governments.

Several chapters in this volume, analyzing the effects of the party polarization context on individual behavior, reveal the helpfulness of such polarization for individual citizens in a variety of ways (also see Dalton 2008*b*; Downs 1957). Greater party system polarization seems to help voters to use ideology in making electoral choices, to encourage citizen mobilization, to facilitate the application of government performance assessments, and to diminish the alienation of voters with more extreme views. From a normative point of view, our finding that greater party polarization tends to diminish ideological congruence stands in sharp contrast to these contextual effects on individual behavior. Polarization seems to facilitate the quality and quantity of citizen electoral involvement, yet to constrain the ideological congruence between the median citizen and the governments, whose formation is a critical outcome of the election. Interestingly enough, the polarization of the party systems seems more powerful at both levels than does the simple number of electoral political parties, with which it is only weakly associated, or the election rules, whose effects it conditions.

These contradictory effects invite us to explore further the complex and powerful implications of the party system context for citizens' relationship to elections. It remains to be seen whether we should think of this as an issue of trade-offs between positive and negative effects, or whether we should be delving further into various combinations, ranges, dynamics, and interactions.

Notes

* Thanks to Shin-Goo Kang for his meticulous preparation of much of the data used in this paper and to Christopher Anderson and Russell Dalton for providing additional data from the CSES modules and other sources. The largest debt, of course, is owed to the CSES project.
1. These variables are described in the appendix to this volume.
2. Dalton's polarization formula is SQ Root of sum of ((partyiID-mean party ID)/5)SQ. See Dalton (2008*b*), as well as the appendix in Chapter 5, which also provides examples.
3. The manifesto approach uses coding of the party manifestos to estimate the Left–Right positions of the respective political parties. See Laver and Budge 1993; Budge et al. 2001; and Klingemann et al. 2006. The position of the median voter is estimated using a procedure devised by Kim and Fording (1998), which assumes voters support the most ideologically proximate party. For use in ideological congruence analysis see

McDonald, Mendes, and Budge 2004; McDonald and Budge 2005; Kim, Powell, and Fording 2010; Powell 2009.

4. The CSES countries are shown at the bottom of Table 9.2. The Manifesto countries in this data set overlap greatly with the "old" CSES democracies, but add Austria and Luxembourg and do not include Israel or the United States.

5. That is, the eight strong presidential systems are not included in Table 9.3 (Israel 1996, United States 1996 and 2004, Chile, Korea, Mexico, Peru, and Russia.) The semi-presidential systems, in which the prime minister is responsible to the legislature, are included.

6. Preelection coalitions may also play an important role, which I have not tried to explore in this chapter.

10

Electoral Supply, Median Voters, and Feelings of Representation in Democracies[*]

Christopher J. Anderson

Researchers have long thought that electoral systems affect what people think about the political system. While some scholars suggest that proportional (PR) electoral systems encourage popular discontent by breeding party system fragmentation and polarization, others argue that more proportional election rules elicit positive citizen responses because they produce more numerous and distinct partisan offerings that make people feel represented. Put in a nutshell: does the effect of electoral systems resemble the polarization and alienation of Weimar Germany or the positive diversity of modern day Scandinavia? As it turns out, we do not really know, in part because it is not entirely clear what aspects of electoral systems shapes voters' beliefs.

This chapter addresses the general question of how electoral rules shape citizen beliefs. I distinguish between the effects of electoral systems as a determinant of the electoral supply on one hand, and the effects of the electoral system as a determinant of policy representation on the other, on people's feelings of representation by elections, parties, and leaders. I analyze data collected by the Comparative Study of Electoral Systems (CSES) project and conclude that the electoral system shapes feelings of representation, in particular among voters in the political middle, by affecting both the nature of representational linkages (cf. Chapter 9) and the nature of choices. The findings suggest that polarized party systems increase the gap in feelings of representation between the median voter and voters located away from the median. At the same time, proportional electoral institutions, which provide for more congruence between citizens' views and government position, diminish differences in feelings toward elections and parties as mechanisms of representation between voters in the political middle and those further away from it. Thus, citizen attitudes about elections and agents of representation (parties, leaders) are shaped by the choices offered on Election Day and by whether voters expect their policy preferences to find representation in government.

This chapter proceeds as follows. I first describe different ways of measuring feelings of representation in contemporary democracies, with a focus on representation by parties, political leaders, and in elections generally. A second section discusses the ways in which electoral systems influence these attitudes by shaping the nature of party systems as well as the nature of representational linkages between voters' views and the positions of parliaments and governments. Third, I develop a set of hypotheses about the impact of electoral context on feelings of representation, which I subsequently test with a multi-level model and data from thirty-four democracies around the world. I conclude by offering a set of implications for the study of macro-political context and citizen behavior and attitudes.

Feelings of representation in contemporary democracies

Students of democracy typically view positive attitudes toward the political system on the part of the citizenry as an important indicator of a healthy democratic polity (Almond and Verba 1965; Booth and Seligson 2009). They commonly assume that disenchanted citizens are more likely to push for radical changes and that popular discontent can erode the legitimacy of democracy in the long run (Lipset 1959; Powell 1982).[1] Following David Easton's work (1965), attitudes toward the political system typically are conceptualized as a diffuse, long-term attachment to democracy. Researchers typically assess these attitudes by asking people about their preference for or against democracy, or for or against authoritarian rule (cf. Booth and Seligson 2009).

One problem with this approach is that support for democratic rule is almost uniformly high across the world today (Klingemann 1999). This makes it difficult to distinguish between more and less democratic political cultures that is, the extent to which people are truly committed to democratic institutions or are merely voicing the socially expected answer. To overcome this limitation, this chapter focuses on elections as a key instrument of representation. Based on surveys conducted as part of Module 2 of the CSES project, I examine responses to three survey questions. The CSES asked respondents about whether there is a political party or leader who represent their views well (also see Chapter 6). In addition, they were asked to assess to what extent elections represent voters' views generally.

These questions tap into two different dimensions of attitudes about representation. First, they measure attitudes about elections generally, and how well they perform at representing voters' interests in general. Second, these involve attitudes about whether there are specific actors (parties and leaders) who represent voters' individual views. As such, they are useful indicators for connecting the consequences of electoral institutions to what people think about representation. In Eastonian terms, they are more akin to measures of specific support in that they derive from citizens' evaluations of system outputs. And while they are positively correlated, these associations are far from perfect and indicate that these measures tap into different underlying attitudes.[2]

Table 10.1 shows the distributions of responses to the three questions across the thirty-four countries analyzed here (see chapter appendix for question wording). Majorities of the public–almost 60 percent on average–feel there is a political party or political leader who represents them. Moreover, roughly half feel that elections represent the will of the people. One way to read these numbers is to say that there are sizable segments of democratic electorates around the world who do not feel represented by parties, leaders, or elections. Feelings of representation by elections thus appear fairly low at first blush, given high levels of electoral participation (in the 70–90%) range in many of these countries. They suggest that a fair number of voters participate in elections but do not feel they represent people's views. Similarly, while partisans can be expected to be critical about government, especially one led by another party, they should support their own party and thus feel there is a party that represents them. While overall feelings of representation by parties and leaders are indeed systematically higher than faith in elections as instruments of democracy generally, the numbers indicate that a good number of people vote for a party that they do not feel represents them!

These overall averages mask significant cross-national variation. Feelings of being represented in elections range from lows of roughly 25–30 percent (Brazil 29.8%, the Czech Republic 28.4%, and Slovenia 27.7%) to highs of over 60 percent (Denmark 79.3% and the United States 71.2%). Similarly, the table shows sizable cross-country differences in citizens' assessments that their views are represented by political parties or political leaders, with Korea being particularly low on both scores (parties: 24.9%; leader: 22.2%). Similar patterns of low levels of feeling represented by parties or leaders also exist in the Philippines and Slovenia, with less than a third of the public expressing the view that a party or leader represents their views. In contrast, three-quarters or more of the public in several established democracies report feeling represented by parties and leaders. While some of these cross-national differences may reflect the politics of the day, it is clear that there are significant and sizable differences in the extent to which citizens across contemporary democracies feel represented.

Table 10.1 Feelings of representation

Country	Party	Leader	Elections
Albania	62.8	72.4	44.7
Australia	83.1	79.3	56.3
Bulgaria	46.0	43.6	52.3
Brazil	40.1	63.7	29.8
Canada	68.9	67.9	40.6
Chile	43.6	70.1	44.4
Czech Republic	77.9	55.7	28.4
Denmark	83.9	73.4	79.3
Finland	64.5	51.2	47.9
Germany	57.6	57.9	35.4
Hungary	73.2	81.1	51.8
Iceland	64.3	55.5	55.1
Ireland	78.1	77.8	64.5
Israel	68.2	56.9	46.9
Italy	42.6	40.9	46.2
Korea	24.9	22.2	–
Mexico	48.3	38.2	47.4
Netherlands	73.0	–	59.2
New Zealand	79.7	82.7	54.8
Norway	81.8	71.8	–
Peru	33.9	46.2	38.3
Philippines	28.7	30.5	58.3
Poland	40.1	39.2	48.6
Portugal	50.5	54.0	38.1
Romania	45.0	48.1	37.3
Russia	39.1	61.3	42.2
Slovenia	28.9	35.3	27.7
Spain	74.1	72.8	64.4
Sweden	77.7	63.7	58.4
Switzerland	86.6	79.6	59.1
Taiwan	37.2	46.1	51.1
United Kingdom	73.4	66.7	48.8
United States	74.1	77.4	71.2
Total	58.1	58.0	49.2

Source: Comparative Study of Electoral Systems, module II.

Electoral systems and feelings of representation: electoral supply and median voters

What, then, explains the variation in feelings of representation across individuals and countries? Given the various consequences of electoral institutions and electoral supply for citizens' voting behavior documented in several chapters in this volume (see, e.g., Chapters 6, 7, and 8), it should not be surprising that scholars point to electoral institutions as influencing what citizens think about the political system. I argue that electoral institutions have two sets of consequences that are relevant for understanding citizens' beliefs about the political system. First, as we noted in Chapter 1, institutions shape party systems and thus the nature of the electoral supply available to citizens. Second, they shape the representation of citizens' preferences in the policymaking process and in particular the odds that different segments of the electoral are represented differently (see Chapters 4 and 9).

Electoral systems and feelings of representation

Despite a long-standing interest in the connection between electoral systems and legitimacy beliefs, and strong intuitions that they shape legitimacy by determining the electoral supply, scholars offer seemingly contradictory explanations about how this works in practice. The classic position argues that, compared to single-member district systems, proportional electoral systems may diminish support for the political system. This view maintains that proportional electoral systems provide incentives and opportunities for extremist parties to gain an electoral foothold and mobilize opponents of democracy. These extremists then undermine democracy once the opportunity arises, as in the case of Weimar Germany (Hermens 1936). Similarly, in Sartori's view (1976), party systems characterized by "polarized pluralism"–as in post-WWII Italy are the least desirable. In such systems, extreme elites can attain power on the backs of relatively small slivers of disenchanted electorates and have few incentives to cooperate for the common good. This view presumes that the party system is an expression of the level of political consensus in society. Extreme voters–that is, voters who are located on the political fringes–do not like the way the existing system works, while those in the political middle take the opposite view. Thus, electoral institutions that allow ideologically extremist voters' positions to be represented in party systems leads to less cohesive democracy.[3]

These arguments are compelling, but they are not about electoral systems per se–that is, formal political institutions in the form of electoral laws. Instead, they are really about their consequences in the form of party system fragmentation and polarization and the extent to which fragmentation and polarization interact with citizens' ideological beliefs. As such, they reflect the confluence of elite decisions to appeal to the electorate in particular ways and the electorate's response to such appeals.

The purported popular appeal of proportional electoral systems is that they allow more diverse political positions to find expression, which may make people feel more represented and thus more attached to the political system. Starting from the idea that PR systems produce more parties (because of a lower effective threshold), and these parties have incentives to distinguish themselves along the ideological spectrum, this approach argues that PR and more distinct parties may lead voters to feel that their preferences can be represented. After all, with more parties, the odds increase that any one party more closely tracks one's own preferences. Moreover, the more distinct the choices are, the clearer it should be for voters to identify which of the parties best represents particular views. This may be especially crucial for voters with less centrist views. Voters who support minor parties (and major parties) see them gain electoral representation and thus may believe their interests are well represented via electoral channels. In contrast, the criticism of majoritarian systems is that the limited party choices they produce may alienate voters who feel they must choose between the lesser of two unappealing options.

This description is consistent with research, which suggests that electoral systems that produce a greater menu of choices may actually enhance citizen feelings about the existing political arrangements, including elections and parties. Several cross-national studies of advanced industrialized countries have found that citizens in more proportional electoral systems express higher levels of satisfaction with the functioning of the democratic system (Anderson 1998; Lijphart 1999; Norris 1999). This perspective, too, presumes that the performance of electoral systems shapes the reputation of processes of representation in citizens' eyes.

Miller and Listhaug (1990) explained this correlation by arguing that "flexible" party systems that represent small parties are better for legitimacy beliefs because they allow the discontented to voice their frustration within the existing democratic framework. Thus, citizens in systems with opportunities to express political discontent via extensive and differentiated party systems are more likely to find an option that meets their political needs and thus have more faith that they are not wasting their votes (Banducci and Karp 2009) and are more likely to have confidence in the system (see also Miller and Listhaug 1999).[4] Stepping back to the role of electoral systems, this approach views electoral systems as a contextual factor that shapes beliefs about representation by shaping the electoral supply, and they do so differently among voters with different preferences.

Policy representation and feelings of representation

Shaping the macro-political supply in the form of distinct party system configurations is not the only role electoral systems play in affecting the quality and quantity of representation experienced and ultimately judged by voters, however. Aside from helping to produce the choices on offer on Election Day, electoral systems also help shape the chain of policy representation. That is, electoral systems shape the translation of voter preferences into parliamentary preferences, which then translate up the representational chain to government preferences and ultimately public policy. Restricting the influence of electoral systems on how people view the political system to the effect of party systems potentially misses the important role they play in shaping processes of representation.

In recent years, a growing literature focuses on the effects of electoral institutions for representing voters' preferences. It finds that countries with more proportional electoral systems tend to produce governments that are systematically closer to the ideological median than systems with disproportional electoral systems like the single member district (SMD) system, though there is some debate about the stability and consistency of this effect (Powell 2000, 2009; McDonald and Budge 2005; see also Blais and Bodet 2006; Golder and Stramski 2010). As with the presumed effects of party systems on voters' beliefs, differentiating voters according to their preferences typically measured along an ideological dimension of left and right is key to this approach. In particular, the median voter is critical for understanding the effect that electoral systems have on policy representation and ultimately citizens' beliefs about institutions of representation. As McDonald, Mendes, and Budge (2004: 2) point out, the median voter indicates the preference of the majority voter:

Given that the median is that policy position crucial to the formation of a popular majority, it gives every voter the most they can hope for under the existing distribution of preferences as revealed by equal voting. The proper role of an election can be seen as the identification of this socially optimal position. To be truly democratic, the rules for aggregating votes into seats should empower the voter median by ensuring that it is also the policy position of the parliamentary median.

As such, the median voter has significant normative clout, and occupies an important empirical position. Given the closer congruence between voter and government positions in PR systems relative to SMD (and other less proportional systems), as documented by Powell (2000; also Chapter 9) and McDonald and Budge (2005; see also Chapter 4), median voters (and therefore typically the average voter) should feel more represented in countries with systems based on PR than in others. Moreover, polarized party systems that lack a centrist core should make it less likely that the middle voter will find a party or associated leader that represent her interests and more likely that voters located away from the political middle will feel this way. Stepping again back to the role of electoral systems, then, this approach views electoral systems as shaping beliefs about representation by shaping the nature of representation citizens experience in their political system, and this effect should differ depending on voters' ideological position in the political middle or away from it.[5]

Putting things together: electoral context, median voters, and feeling represented

As the above discussion suggests, there certainly is no shortage of competing theories and evidence about the connection between electoral laws, electoral options, processes of representation, and voters' views and behaviors. To bring some order to the thicket of competing claims requires a model that connects individual citizens and the electoral environment in which they make choices and express their beliefs. While connecting the electoral system with feelings of representation does not presuppose that voters know the intricacies of electoral rules, the logics of coalition formation, or the dynamics of party systems, it assumes that voters recognize the outcomes of electoral systems, such as the electoral supply or the nature of representation, that structure their electoral choices.

Starting from these assumptions, I argue that the electoral system shapes how people form opinions about electoral representation. To make this argument transparent requires a definition of electoral system and electoral supply. The electoral system refers to the characteristics of electoral laws that produce a more or less proportional translation of voters' political preferences into electoral outcomes, legislative representation, and government policy positions. The proportionality of electoral systems is a long-standing feature of the institutional environment studied by political scientists and does not require further explanation here. Everything else being equal, *voters in more proportional systems should be more likely to say they feel represented than voters in less proportional systems.*

The definition of electoral supply is slightly more complex. Building on the work by Klingemann and Wessels (2009) and Wessels and Schmitt (2008), I define the electoral supply as the extent to which elections provide voters with clear choices. These authors view the electoral supply as being largely a function of two dimensions: first, the differentiation of political supply; and second, the effectiveness with which voters' choices are translated into electoral outcomes. For this chapter, I focus on the differentiation of the political supply. Consistent with the arguments made by Wessels and his collaborators about the structure of the political supply, the term "meaningful choices" implies at least two properties of electoral offerings: first, the number of choices, and second, how distinct they are (see also Chapter 1). *Voters who have more meaningful options available to them should report more positive feelings of representation* than voters with less meaningful options.

This conceptualization of the effects of electoral and party system properties suggests that these macro-contextual conditions have a direct effect on voters' beliefs. In addition, when considering the impact that the electoral supply may have on voters' beliefs, one critical question is whether all voters should be equally sensitive to the nature of the (cross-nationally variable) context beliefs (again, see Chapter 1). In this study, I argue that they should not. In particular, I presume that the macro-electoral context affects the median voter differently from those further removed from the political center.

As I discussed earlier, while the median voter signifies the majority position in the electorate, this position often goes unrepresented in the party system and in government. And as is well known, convergence toward the center rarely happens even in pure two-party systems and it is highly unlikely in multiparty systems. Thus, given the general lack of ideological convergence toward the center in virtually all democratic political systems, *median voters should generally feel less represented than other voters*.

Moreover, the median voter's preferences also commonly lose out when it comes to where governments are located ideologically. Particularly in SMD systems but also in PR systems, the government's position can be quite distant from the median voter's own. As McDonald and Budge (2005) note, while the median voter's preferences are represented when considering the congruence of votergovernment positions over the long run of several decades (see also Powell 2000), *in*congruence between median voter and government position is particularly likely in the short run. As a result, this perspective, too, predicts that *median voters should express more negative feelings of representation*.

If this is the case, the question becomes whether this feeling of not being represented is more pronounced in some political contexts than in others. Following the logic of representation induced by electoral systems described above, the median voter should feel more represented, relative to other voters, in countries with PR electoral rules than in countries with less proportional rules. Moreover, relative to other voters, voters with more distinct ideological positions away from the center should feel particularly represented in countries where the electoral supply is more polarized and therefore, by definition, more dispersed.

Thus, instead of assuming that more or fewer parties or more or less polarization or more or less proportionality is equally good or bad for everyone, I posit that the characteristics of the macro-political context shape representation beliefs differently among voters in the middle and on the periphery of the ideological spectrum. In particular, a more abundant and differentiated electoral supply should allow those removed from the political middle a more distinctive opportunity to voice their preferences and feel represented. While the electoral supply may thus act as a safety valve for political extremists, it may also increase the gap in feelings of representation between median and other voters in countries with more polarized party systems. At the same time, median voters are compensated for the lack of suitable electoral choices through being represented in the policymaking process.

In the next section, I investigate these hypothesized direct and contingent effects of the macro-political context on feelings of representation.

Data and analysis

To see whether the macro-political context as conceptualized and measured here affects people's views of representation, the next step in the analysis examines their direct association with how citizens assess their representational environment. To do so, I merge information about the country-level electoral institutions and supply with the individual survey data. I then construct estimation models that include important individual-level and country-level control variables.

Sources of variation in feelings of representation

The first important question for the analysis is whether the data support the contention that representation perceptions are a function of both individual characteristics and the nature of the political context that varies across countries. To determine whether there is significant variation in these attitudes at the individual and country levels, I estimated multilevel regression models that decompose the variance in the dependent variables (cf. Steenbergen and Jones 2002).

Table 10.2 shows estimates of the variance components at the country level and the individual level. All variance components are statistically significant for

Table 10.2 Variance decomposition in feelings of representation

	Represented by party	Represented by leader	Represented in elections
Fixed effects			
Constant	.591 ***	.589***	2.448***
	(.033)	(.029)	(.032)
Variance components			
Country level	.190***	.163***	.179***
	(.024)	(.021)	(.023)
Individual level	.458***	.468***	.724***
	(.001)	(.002)	(.002)
-2Log likelihood	32456.85	32293.20	48867.09
Macro N	33	32	31
Micro N	50676	48762	44523

Notes: Entries are maximum likelihood estimates; standard errors in parentheses.
* $p < .05$; ** $p < .01$; *** $p < .001$.

Source: Comparative Study of Electoral Systems, Module II.

all three dependent variables, suggesting that there is significant variance in feelings of representation in elections, by parties, and by party leaders at both levels of analysis. In addition, country-level variance is proportionally smaller than individual-level variance for all three dependent variables. Specifically, individual-level variance constitutes 70.7% of the total variance in feeling represented by a party, 74.2% in feeling represented by a leader, and 80.2% in attitudes about the representative function of elections.[6] Given that these data are measured at the individual level, this is not entirely surprising (Steenbergen and Jones 2002: 231), but it does suggest that the sources of variation in these attitudes are to be found predominantly at the individual level. Put another way, there is less room for cross-country differences to explain these attitudes than for differences across individuals. Thus, I now turn to the question of whether the model I have specified can account for some of this variance.

Variation in electoral systems and supply

I rely on three key measures to tap cross-national differences in electoral institutions and supply. First, I classify countries by whether their electoral system is based on proportional representation rules (3), SMD rules (1), or whether it is a mix of the two (2). Second, I measure the effective number of electoral options (ENEP) and the distinctiveness of these options in terms of party system polarization as explained in the appendix of this volume.

We might assess whether the electoral system or the supply of electoral options are good candidates for explaining aggregate feelings of representation by seeing whether countries differ in the options they present voters. As the Introduction by Dalton and Anderson illustrates, there is wide variation on all of these dimensions across countries, with small and large party systems, polarized and convergent party systems, and proportional and disproportional electoral systems. Together, these dimensions of the electoral supply and electoral systems provide quite distinct macro-political conditions across countries and are not easily categorized as belonging to one single type. As argued above and importantly for the analyses reported below, this suggests the importance of distinguishing among different consequences of electoral systems and different dimensions of the electoral supply and the representational chain.[7]

Median voters

As Chapter 4 shows, in virtually every country investigated here, the ideological distribution of voters in contemporary democracies is clustered around the middle. Moreover, as related research (cf. Powell 2000) has shown, this distribution is normal, with a peak in the middle. Thus, most voters locate themselves in the political center and fewer locate themselves at the edges of the ideological spectrum.

At the individual level, I include a measure that categorizes respondents as belonging to the category of the median voter (see Appendix). I classified respondents as median voters with a survey question that asked people to locate themselves on the Left–Right scale. I then coded responses according to whether the respondent's self-positioning matched the median category of all respondents. Thus, if the respondent's reported Left–Right position matched the median category, I scored that individual as 1 (median); all others were scored 0 (see Appendix).[8] Across all countries considered here, 23.5 percent of respondents fall into this middle category. Put another way, 76.5 percent of respondents locate themselves away from their country's ideological middle.

To correctly specify the multivariate models, I controlled for a number of potentially important individual-level and country-level predictors of representation feelings. At the individual level, I included a standard set of demographic variables (age, gender, education, income, marital status), political ideology (Left–Right placement), minority status and electoral participation (cf. Anderson et al. 2005),[9] and electoral commitment (attempts to persuade others how to vote). Prior research found that older, married, male, and rich respondents who locate themselves on the political right are more likely to express support for the political system. As well, having voted, voting for the electoral winner, and being engaged in the electoral campaign differentiate more from less supportive citizens.

At the level of countries, I controlled for level of democracy (Freedom House) and the age of the party system. The level of democracy and the stability of the party system are particularly important control variables because they measure the freedom to exercise choices and the predictability of those choices from one election to the next. There is little point in talking about electoral supply or the representational consequences of electoral systems if voters cannot choose freely or learn about them over time because they change rapidly and unpredictably from one electoral contest to the next or because the political system does not allow for a free contest among competing political parties or candidates. At the same time, the stability of the choices, registered in the age of the party system, and the level of democracy, could also signify legitimacy and thus be endogenous to feelings of representation (see also Mainwaring 1999). Because of its importance but ambiguous causal connection to the dependent variables examined here, I include these variables as controls. Finally, I include a control variable for whether the election was a legislative or presidential election, with the expectation that voters in legislative elections will be more likely to say they feel represented by a party, and voters in presidential elections will be more likely to say they feel represented by a leader (see Chapter 6).

Direct effects of electoral institutions and supply on feelings of representation

To estimate the effect of macro-level variables on individual-level outcomes requires the estimation of multilevel models (cf. Steenbergen and Jones 2002). I estimate a series of random intercept models, using the xtlogit command available in STATA.[10] Table 10.3 reports the results of a set of multivariate, multilevel random intercept models estimating the direct effects of electoral institutions and supply on feelings of representation.

The results suggest that some aspects of electoral context indeed directly affect people's perceptions of being represented. Specifically, a more proportional electoral system produces more positive feelings of being personally represented by political parties and assessments that voters' views are well represented in elections generally. However, proportionality does not affect feelings of representation by a leader. Thus, the results show that, for the average citizen, greater proportionality in electoral systems is associated with enhanced feelings of representation.

In contrast, more numerous electoral options do not lead citizens to express more positive assessments of the degree of representation. In fact, quite the contrary: citizens in countries with a larger number of effective parties are systematically less likely to say that they feel represented parties or that people are represented in elections. As in the case of electoral system type, feelings of being represented by a leader are not affected by the electoral supply. The result for the effective number of parties is particularly interesting, given the positive association between proportional electoral systems and a larger party system long documented by electoral researchers going back to Duverger. Clearly, once we account for the effects of electoral system type generally, more numerous choices decrease the odds of feeling represented.

Finally, the results from the direct effects models show that levels of polarization are not a direct predictor of whether people report more positive or negative views of the political system. Among the only macro-level variables that reveal significant direct effects, the variable measuring the age of the country's party system shows that citizens in countries with more institutionalized party systems express more positive attitudes about being represented in elections, by parties, and leaders. Thus party system longevity enhances support for the political system, and perhaps vice versa.

In addition, several individual-level variables have significant effects on system support. This should not be surprising, given that the biggest portion of variation in the dependent variables stems from individual-level sources (cf. Table 10.2). Among them, most importantly, citizens in the median voter category are less likely to say that a party or leader represents their views, and they express significantly less faith in the representativeness of elections than other voters. Thus, consistent with

Table 10.3 Random effects models of feeling represented in democracies

	Represented by party	Represented by leader	Represented in elections
Electoral system (PR)	.443*	.228	.372*
	(.215)	(.217)	(.147)
ENEP	−.146	.101	.178**
	(.083)	(.085)	(.055)
Party system polarization	.089	.016	.014
	(.115)	(.111)	(.067)
Median voter	−.573***	−.459***	−.140***
	(.027)	(.027)	(.027)
Individual-level control variables			
Electoral participation	.824***	.691***	.611***
	(.040)	(.039)	(.040)
Political minority	−.032	−.101***	−.320***
	(.028)	(.028)	(.026)
Respondent ideology (Left–Right)	.002	.012*	.031***
	(.005)	(.005)	(.005)
Age	.116***	.139***	.068***
	(.013)	(.013)	(.012)
Female	−.067**	.009	.120***
	(.025)	(.024)	(.024)
Education	.025	.008	−.022
	(.017)	(.017)	(.016)
Income	.052***	.059***	−.004
	(.010)	(.010)	(.009)
Contacted	.158***	.160***	.051
	(.031)	(.031)	(.029)
Persuaded	.738***	.666***	.150***
	(.033)	(.032)	(.030)
Country-level control variables			
Level of democracy	−.070	−.100	−.025
	(.152)	(.155)	(.104)
Age of party system	.014***	.007*	.008**
	(.004)	(.004)	(.003)
Legislative election	.033	−.972	−.202
	(.498)	(.508)	(.337)
Constant	−1.869	.016	.575
	(.994)	(.995)	(.666)
Country-level variance component (SD)	.541***	.556***	.372***
	(.088)	(.086)	(.050)
ρ	.082	.086	.040
Macro N	33	32	31
Micro N	34429	32715	31131
-2 Log likelihood	19527.67	19440.13	20421.9

Notes: Random effects logistic models; standard errors in parentheses.
$p < .1$; * $p < .05$; ** $p < .01$; *** $p < .001$.

Source: Comparative Study of Electoral Systems, Module II.

expectations, there is a gap in feelings of representation between voters in the political middle and voters on the ideological periphery: median voters do not feel nearly as well represented as voters outside of the political middle.

The other individual-level variables exert results consistent with past research. People who were contacted during the election campaign, who persuaded others to go and vote and who voted themselves, and who located themselves on the right, expressed more positive attitudes about the processes and agents of electoral representation. The results also show that respondents whose parties ended up in the opposition are less likely to report they feel represented in elections or a leader. Age and gender have mixed effects: while older respondents report less faith in elections, they are more likely to feel represented by parties and leaders. The reverse is true for women: they feel that elections represent them, but parties do not. As expected, individuals with higher levels of income express significantly more positive attitudes about being represented by parties and leaders, but do not have more faith in elections than others. Unexpectedly, education does not have a statistically significant effect.

Together, these results suggest two preliminary conclusions: the electoral system and the effective number of political parties seem to influence feelings of representation independently, but the distinctiveness of choices does not. Moreover, there is a gap in views about representation, with citizens whose preferences place them in the political middle expressing systematically more negative views of elections and agents of representation than other voters. These results square with the literature on ideological congruence in that more proportional electoral systems facilitate representation of voter preferences but median voters tends to lose out in favor of left or right (cf. McDonald and Budge 2005; see also Chapter 9). But these results are inconsistent with received wisdom in that more numerous electoral choices do not appear to make it more likely for voters to feel represented once we control for electoral system type and the distinctiveness of these choices. Thus, everything else equal, more choices seem to muddle feelings of representation.

Contingent effects of electoral context on perceptions of representation

To establish whether the electoral context has contingent effects, I examine the interactive effects of the median voter category and electoral context on feeling represented based on models that are identical to those reported in Table 10.3, with the exception that they also include three interaction terms–median voters interacted with type of electoral system, polarization, and the effective number of electoral parties.

Table 10.4 shows that, as before, median voters are less likely to feel represented by parties or leaders. And as in Table 10.3, the results of these models

Table 10.4 Random effects models of median voters, electoral context, and feelings of representation in democracies

	Represented by party	Represented by leader	Represented in elections
Electoral system (PR)	.426*	.192	.391**
	(.216)	(.219)	(.148)
ENEP	−.148	−.102	−.185**
	(.083)	(.085)	(.056)
Party sytem polarization	.128	.023	−.003
	(.115)	(.112)	(.068)
Median voter	−.364**	−.389***	−.002
	(.109)	(.107)	(.099)
Median voter * electoral system	.055	.105*	−.052
	(.053)	(.052)	(.049)
Median voter * ENEP	.016	.018	.028
	(.021)	(.021)	(.021)
Median voter * polarization	−.133***	−.132***	−.044
	(.027)	(.027)	(.025)
Individual-level control variables			
Electoral participation	.821***	.688***	.609***
	(.040)	(.039)	(.040)
Respondent ideology (Left–Right)	.004	.014**	.032***
	(.005)	(.005)	(.005)
Age	.116***	.139***	−.067***
	(.013)	(.013)	(.012)
Female	−.066**	.011	.121***
	(.025)	(.025)	(.024)
Education	.023	.006	−.023
	(.017)	(.017)	(.016)
Income	.052***	.058***	−.003
	(.010)	(.010)	(.009)
Contacted	.160***	.161***	.052
	(.031)	(.031)	(.09)
Persuaded	.736	.663***	.150***
	(.033)	(.033)	(.030)
Country-level control variables			
Level of democracy	−.071	−.103	−.026
	(.153)	(.156)	(.104)
Age of party system	.014***	.007*	.008**
	(.004)	(.004)	(.003)

(continued)

Table 10.4 Continued

	Represented by party	Represented by leader	Represented in elections
Legislative election	.034	−.981	−.202
	(.499)	(.509)	(.338)
Constant	−1.952*	.007	−.627
	(.997)	(.999)	(.669)
Country-level variance	.542***	.558***	.373***
component (SD)	(.088)	(.086)	(.050)
ρ	.082	.087	.041
Macro N	33	32	31
Micro N	34429	32715	31131
-2 Log likelihood	19513.51	19426.31	20417.9

Notes: Random effects logistic models; standard errors in parentheses.
$p < .1$; * $p < .05$; ** $p < .01$; *** $p < .001$.

show that voters feel slightly more represented in countries with more proportional electoral systems and fewer political parties, and are more likely to say that a party represents them in countries with higher electoral system proportionality. As importantly for the purposes of this chapter, there are several contingent effects in these models of median voters, electoral context, and feelings of representation.

Specifically, Table 10.4 shows a positive interaction effect between proportional electoral systems at the macro level and median voter status at the individual level on feeling represented by a leader. Thus, in countries with more proportional electoral systems the gap in feeling represented by leaders between voters with different ideological positions is significantly diminished.[11] The substantively more important and statistically most consistent contingent effects appear between electoral context in the form of party system polarization on the one hand and median voter status on the other.

The results show that a more clearly differentiated electoral supply increases the odds that voters in the middle and voters at the edges of the ideological spectrum will differ in their assessment that either parties or leaders represent them and that elections provide representation. In contrast to the direct effects models reported in Table 10.3, these results support the contention that the electoral supply shapes the views of voters in different places on the ideological spectrum differently. They suggest that living in a country with more distinct (speak: polarized) choices serves to increase the gap in feelings of representation between individuals located in the political middle and those located at the ideological extremes. Another way to interpret this finding is to say that voters' feelings of being represented by parties, leaders, or the electoral process differ to a greater extent in countries that leave a hole in the middle with respect to party offerings. Taken together, these results clearly speak in favor of the interpretation that polarization may enhance feelings of representation generally and increase the gap in feelings of representation between median and other voters. Moreover, the results indicate that the direct effects for electoral system type and polarization, for example, reported in Table 10.3 constitute average effects that mask interesting individual-level heterogeneity in macro-contextual effects.

Discussion

Students of democratic politics have long recognized that elections play a critical role in shaping citizens' allegiance to the body politic (Banducci and Karp 2003). In particular, the literature on political involvement and legitimacy suggests that elections can enhance legitimacy through the participation of voters in the electoral process. On the positive side (normatively speaking), elections are not only a way for citizens to influence government, but also a way to express their attachment to the system. Participatory political theorists in fact view elections as a crucial element in raising people's consciousness and developing a democratic citizenry (Pateman 1970; Thompson 1970). In contrast, some argue that elections can tie citizens to the political system's status quo and enhance government control (Ginsberg 1982). Without making a judgment about the normative interpretation of the effect of elections on people's attitudes, we know from a number of empirical studies that people's feelings about government become more positive as a result of participating in elections (Clarke and Acock 1989). Simply put, participation breeds happiness with the political system, and happiness with the system, in turn, breeds participation (Finkel 1987).

Because elections and, by implication, political parties and the party systems they form are viewed by many political commentators as so central to the democratic process, a number of researchers have also examined the influence of the electoral process on system support in greater detail. Among the best-known attitudinal constructs and behaviors related to electoral processes that are assumed to affect system support have been partisanship and political involvement (Holmberg 2003; Dalton 2004). Thus, citizens with strong party ties are more likely to support their political systems than are weak partisans or nonidentifiers (Dennis 1966; Miller and Listhaug 1990; Paskeviciute 2006).

Theoretically and empirically, most of this scholarship on elections' role in shaping the connection of voters and their political systems focuses on the individual level. But there is growing evidence that macro-political structures and contexts intersect with individual-level characteristics and attitudes to shape system support (Anderson et al. 2005). This literature argues that, while elections may generate political support, they also have differentiated effects with an upside for some and a downside for others. Focusing on election winners and losers, a stream of scholarship has investigated the role institutions play in moderating the sense of loss or victory citizens feel. This research suggests that losers' incentives to deny the outcome and develop low levels of support for the political system are significantly affected by a country's political context. As a consequence, institutions have a role in blunting the rougher edge of losing (Anderson et al. 2005).

Oftentimes, however, such studies have taken a very broad measure of the macro-political by combining several institutional features to describe the type of democracy (Anderson and Guillory 1997; Criado and Herreros 2007). As I have tried to show in this chapter, it is important to separate the logics that make up these institutional configurations. To make this argument, I focus on the consequences of electoral institutions for what people think about politics.

Several chapters in this volume document the effects that electoral institutions and the electoral supply that accompany them have on how voters process information about and make choices in democratic elections. I build on these analyses by examining whether these macro-contextual conditions "matter" in the sense of also shaping people's sense of whether parties, leaders, and elections generally manage to represent citizens' views reasonably well. I also sought to put the beliefs of the median voter – a positively and normatively important group of citizens – under a microscope to see if their feelings of representation differ from the less centrist segments of the electorate.

These analyses suggest that more proportional electoral institutions and a more differentiated electoral supply have the most consistent impact on people's sense that their political views are represented. Speaking generally, more proportional electoral rules make it more likely that voters feel that there is a party that represents them and also that elections represent people's views. At the same time, a more numerous supply of options reduces the odds that voters express these views for the average voter, a more limited rather than a more expanded set of options thus enhance feelings of representations.

However, these effects differ among voters located in different positions on the ideological distribution. Thus, the electoral context shapes feelings of representation, but this effect differs, depending on whether voters are located in the political middle or away from it. Voters who locate themselves in the political middle – defined as the median ideological category – relative to their fellow citizens are less likely to say that parties, leaders, or elections represent their views. While this is the case generally, the gap in feelings of representation between median voters and others is smaller if they live in countries with proportional representation electoral rules. At the same time, controlling for the number of options voters can choose from, median voters and other voters are more likely to report differences in their sense of representation if they face a particularly polarized partisan supply. The flipside of the coin, of course, is that voters located away from the median generally feel more represented in countries with more disproportional electoral systems and countries with more ideologically distinct options.

At a minimum, these results suggest that a more differentiated and numerous electoral supply or more proportional electoral rules do not have unambiguously positive or negative consequences for citizens' sense that their preferences are represented by parties, leaders, or in elections generally. Instead, they highlight the possibility that electoral systems have varied consequences: formal electoral rules that encourage multipartism make median voters feel more represented (presumably because their views actually *are* represented in parliament or government), but multipartism and fragmented party systems themselves have a positive effect among voters outside of the ideological mainstream. Thus, voters whose ideology locates them away from the median may value distinct choices on Election Day, but they feel less represented in countries whose formal electoral system is associated with more numerous and distinct choices but which, at the same time, steers policy toward the political middle.

The broader implications of these findings are twofold. First, electoral systems can have manifold effects and they have to be specified as such: electoral systems condition the electoral supply, and the institutional devices that shape the quality and quantity of representation via producing systematically different kinds of governments. Moreover, these effects of electoral systems can have contradictory effects. While some aspects of proportional electoral systems facilitate representation and enhance voters' views of representation, others can diminish people's sense that their views are represented. Thus, even a single institutional characteristic like the electoral system has multiple consequences whose logic requires specification in models of citizen support.

Speaking more broadly, the chapter connects to literatures on representation and legitimacy that typically proceeded along parallel tracks. In particular, our findings show that the performance of electoral institutions shape citizens' views of whether democratic representation works. They do so, in particular, by focusing on important segments of the electorate–namely, median voters and voters with ideologically more distant positions. As such, the results speak to open questions in the growing literature on how electoral losers view the political system (cf. Anderson et al. 2005). For one, they show that policy losing is important; they suggest that electoral loss and relative ideological position have separable consequences. Moreover, they suggest that some findings in that literature – for example, that losers like consensual democracy (Anderson and Guillory 1997) – may be combining a set of structural and institutional factors – for example, party systems, polarization, and coalition government that require conceptual and empirical separation in order to adequately specify the ways in which electoral and policy losers react to the political context.

Taken together, our results show that the nature of the available choices and representational contexts (as proxied by electoral institutions) influence the attitudes of those citizens who already have incentives to take a dim view of the political system – median voters – such that ideologically dispersed partisan offerings further increase the gap between them and the rest of the electorate. Conversely, a distinctive electoral supply enhances feelings of representation among voters with less centrist views. At the same time, electoral rules that enhance the odds that the views of median voters are represented in government in the short term also make them feel more represented. Speaking generally, this means that countries' macro-level electoral contexts and individuals' ideological positions interactively shape citizen feelings of representation, complicating the story of how electoral contexts shape consent. But they also clearly suggest that polarization and multiparty systems do not necessarily delegitimize the state, as is commonly believed.

Appendix

CSES survey variables used

Variable	Question wording	Coding
Representation in elections	B3022: Thinking about how elections in [country] work in practice, how well do elections ensure that the views of voters are represented in [name of national parliament]?	4 = Very well, 3 = Quite well, 2 = Not very well, 1 = Not well at all.
Party representation	B3023: Would you say that any of the parties in [country] represents your views reasonably well?	1 = Yes, 0 = No.
Leader representation	B3025: Regardless of how you feel about the parties, would you say that any of the individual party leaders/ presidential candidates at the last election represents your views reasonably well?	1 = Yes, 0 = No.
Voted	B3004_1. Records whether respondent cast a ballot.	1 = Voted, 0 = Did not vote.
Left–Right self-placement	B3045: In politics people sometimes talk of left and right. Where would you place yourself on a scale from 0 to 10, where 0 means the left and 10 means the right?	0 = Left to 10 = Right
Median voter	Based on B3038. Records whether individual respondentÕs self-placement matches the electorateÕs median self-placement.	1 = Median voter, 0 = Others.
Contacted	B3003. During the last campaign did a candidate or anyone from a political party contact you to persuade you to vote for them?	1 = Yes; 0 = No.

Persuaded	B3001_1. Here is a list of things some people do during elections. Which if any did you do during the most recent election? ... talked to other people to persuade them to vote for a particular party or candidate?	1 = Yes, 0 = No.
Political minority	Based on B3005_1 and B3006_1. These variables report the presidential candidate or party affiliation of the presidential candidate (for presidential elections) and party (for legislative elections) for whom the respondent voted. If candidate or party choice matched with a post-election presidential loser or opposition party, respondents were coded as belonging to the political minority.	1 = Minority/opposition, 0 = All others.
Income	B2020. Household income quintile.	1 = Lowest quintile to 5 = Highest quintile.
Gender	B2002. Gender of respondent.	1 = Female, 0 = Male.
Education	B2003: Education of the respondent	1 = Lower (none, incomplete primary, complete primary, incomplete secondary), 2 = middle (complete secondary), 3 = upper (post-secondary vocational, incomplete university, complete undergrad university).
Age	B2001 Age	Coded in discrete years, 18+

Source: Comparative Study of Electoral Systems, Module II

Notes

* This is a substantially revised draft of a paper originally presented at the workshop on *Citizens, Context, and Choice: How Institutional Structures Shape Voter Behavior*, Cornell Institute for European Studies, Cornell University, Ithaca, NY, June 1920, 2009. I am grateful to the workshop participants for their constructive feedback, and especially to Russell Dalton and Michael McDonald for their helpful suggestions. Many thanks also to Steffen Blings for his help with the data.

1. Recently, scholars have suggested that dissatisfaction, when combined with a commitment to democratic values, should be viewed as less problematic and instead as a sign of developing critical citizenship (Norris 1999; Klingemann 1999; Dalton 2004).

2.

	Elections	Party
Party	0.254	
Leader	0.196	0.529

3. Beyond the paradigmatic cases of Weimar Germany and post-WWII Italy emphasized by Hermens and Sartori, Weil's study (1989) provides cross-national evidence that more polarized and more fragmented party systems are associated with lower levels of system support.

4. But, as Listhaug, Aardal, and Ellis (2009) note, only three countries were investigated in this study (Norway, Sweden, and the United States), and they speculate that this explanation may not work in Sweden after the party system there underwent significant changes in 1988–91.

5. Specifically, we know that systems with electoral laws based on PR are associated with an increased incidence of coalition government. If voters feel that their vote is relatively less consequential in such systems because it is ultimately elites rather than voter preferences who determine who actually forms the government, then PR systems should be associated with lessened feelings of representation (see also Aarts and Thomassen 2008). Because of this, Kedar (2005) argues, voters will vote strategically for the more extreme party because they are aware that their actual, preferred policy position will be watered down in coalition bargaining. Consistent with this, Listhaug and Wiberg (1995) argued that multiparty governments leads to a decline in confidence in political institutions (but see also Karp and Bowler 2001). This effect presumably applies to voters generally.

6. These calculations are based on the ratios of each variance component relative to the total variance in system support (cf. Bryk and Raudenbush 1992; Snijders and Bosker 1999).

7. The value of differentiating between the number of options and the nature of those options is also apparent when we compare the numbers in Chapter 1 to those reported by Klingemann and Wessels (2009: 2634) on the differentiation of the electoral supply, which is based at its core on the number of party and candidate offerings. The Klingemann and Wessels measure, for example, identifies Hungary as having a relatively lower differentiation of electoral supply. But our data reveal that this is true only with regard to the number of offerings, but not their distinctiveness. Similarly, they identify Spain as having a relatively high differentiation of electoral supply; as the numbers in the introduction show, this is primarily true only with regard to the distinctiveness of choices. This is meant to be illustrative since our measures and theirs are not strictly comparable.

8. I use the variable measuring the median voter, based on all respondents who indicated that they had voted in the election. However, the results do not change when the median category of all respondents is taken as the baseline. This is not surprising, as countries' median category does not change, depending on whether only voters or all respondents are taken into account. Moreover, the individual-level Pearson correlation between median voter and median respondent is .94. The results are also quite similar when the absolute distance from the median is used as a way to measure the "median-ness" of voters' preferences. Given the normative and positive role of the median voter category in existing research on representational congruence, I used the 0–1 median voter coding for the analyses.

9. Following the argument that participation enhances feelings of trust and external efficacy (and vice versa) (cf. Finkel 1987), I included a variable distinguishing voters and nonvoters to control for differences attributable to having participated in the election. I expect that those who participated in the election (coded 1) will have more positive attitudes toward the political system than those who did not (coded 0).

10. To make the models of feelings of electoral representation more directly comparable to those of party and leader representation (which are coded 0–1), I recoded the variable measuring feelings of electoral representation by combining the "very well" and "well" categories (coded 1), and the "not very well" and "not well at all" categories (coded 0). When I estimate models using the full four-point scale, the inferences are identical.

11. Collinearity is not a concern, as the Pearson correlation between the number of parties and polarization is .20, between polarization and electoral system type it is .44, and between the number of parties and electoral system type it is .54.

Conclusion

11

Nested Voters: Citizen Choices Embedded in Political Contexts

Christopher J. Anderson and Russell J. Dalton

Several years ago, a delegation from the Dutch government visited the University of California campuses at Irvine and San Diego to consult with electoral researchers on potential reforms to the country's electoral system. Under prompting by a minister from Democrats 66, they were considering changes in the electoral system to achieve a set of specific political goals. They wanted to increase turnout, to encourage citizens to feel closer ties to their representatives, to improve trust in government, to strengthen political parties, and achieve several other goals. They started with the assumption that the electoral system defines an incentive structure that can influence party and voter behavior. This immediately raised questions of which electoral arrangements might produce the desired effects. After returning to The Hague these ministry officials probably felt uncertain about the advice they received. On one hand, they had a better appreciation of the complex effects electoral systems can have, including results that were opposite to their initial expectations. On the other hand, they received conflicting advice on how electoral structures affect individual citizens because the empirical evidence scholars could provide was often limited or contradictory.[1]

This volume seeks to advance our understanding of how electoral rules (and other contextual factors) matter for voting behavior to answer the questions posed by the Dutch officials and others interested in democratic electoral politics. Several established democracies have reformed their electoral system or have considered doing so in recent years (Katz 2005; Carter and Farrell 2010). Israel, Italy, Japan, and New Zealand made basic changes in their electoral systems in the early 1990s. Major debates on changes to electoral rules have occurred in Belgium, Britain, Canada, The Netherlands, and several other established democracies. Ironically, some similar reforms were motivated by contrasting logics with different goals, which suggests the specific changes would not have the desired effect (Shugart and Wattenberg 2003). Third Wave democracies faced the challenge of building electoral systems de novo (Norris 1997). Constitutional conventions or parliamentary committees grappled with the complexities of electoral laws and constitutional structures that they believed would produce the electoral system and a party system that they desired.

Underlying these events is a belief that institutions and political context matters for what voters, parties, and governments do, even though significant reforms of electoral laws are relatively rare events. As political scientists, we assume the electoral institutions shape the incentive structure for citizens and elites. Some of these claims about institutional effects have been very strongly worded. Pippa Norris (2002: 261), for instance, states "we have demonstrated, as many others have long believed, that electoral systems represent some of the most powerful instruments available for institutional engineering with far-reaching consequences for party systems, the composition of legislatures, and democratic representation." Rein Taagepera (2007: ch. 17) similarly suggests that electoral institutions may provide a Rosetta Stone for understanding a wide range of electoral outcomes. Our research leads us to be less sanguine about such claims.

Over the years, several regularities of voter, candidate, and party behavior have been well established, although there is more that we do not know than what we can say with certainty (see, for example, the review of the turnout literature by Blais 2006). In aggregate terms, some institutional effects are clear-cut. Research consistently shows that proportional representation systems affect the number of political parties winning parliamentary representation and the equality of votes and seats (Taagepera and Shugart 1989). Proportional representation produces a larger number of parliamentary parties and stronger correspondence between the percentage of votes cast for a party and the percentage of seats won. In turn, the number of party choices has predictable consequences for the formation and stability of governments. At the same time, the impact of the electoral system and other institutional structures on individual electoral behavior is more speculative.

This volume focuses on developing a deeper and potentially more complex understanding of the consequences of the institutional structure and political context: how a country's macro-political context influences voters' thinking and electoral behavior. If democracy is to be representative, do certain institutional structures facilitate or hinder representation? If democracy requires accountability, do certain structures increase or decrease accountability? And what are the mechanisms by which contextual factors affect individual electoral behavior? In short, does a nation's institutional structure significantly influence how democracy works by affecting electoral behavior?

This chapter summarizes our collective findings on how the political context affects electoral behavior. We also discuss how these effects are potentially interrelated; for instance, how the impact of party system polarization improves the clarity of party choice, but may simultaneously diminish the overall representativeness of elected governments. Finally, we consider the larger implications of our findings for electoral politics and the functioning of the democratic process.

How context matters

As a preface to our discussion of contextual effects, recall that the multilevel analyses in this volume combine measures of individual voters' attitudes and behaviors collected in many countries with data measuring important aspects of the institutional and macro-contextual environments that vary cross-nationally. How these two connect – that is, how macro contexts affect the beliefs and behaviors of individuals – raises important theoretical questions. Specifically, any theory of contextual effects really is a theory of two theories: first, a theory of (electoral and other political) institutions and how they work (Anderson 2007a, 2009). These theories have long been the territory of political science research on formal and informal institutions, and they have been subjected to systematic examination at the aggregate, cross-national level by electoral scholars focused on the institutional conditions for democratic representation (for instance, Taagepera and Shugart 1989; Lijphart 1994; Powell 2000; McDonald and Budge 2005). Second, a theory of context and individuals requires a theory of why individual voters behave as they do. By that we mean a theory of the psychological effects of institutions – what aspects of institutions are relevant to voters and how they make decisions in the political arena. For context to be relevant to voters and shape their decisions, it has to affect the content or process of electoral choice, as voters perceive it. For instance, voters in proportional systems generally recognize they effectively have more party choices and casting a vote will directly affect a party's share of parliamentary seats.

Before moving on to contextual effects and how they work, we must first emphasize that many of the basic predictors of individual behavior work in the same direction even across the wide range of democracies in the CSES. For instance, education is related to turnout, and a person's Left–Right attitude is related to voting choices across nearly all the nations in our analyses, regardless of a country's institutional design and contextual conditions. Seldom does context fully negate or reverse the general causal processes linking individual characteristics and attitudes with voter choices that researchers have previously documented in single-nation electoral studies. Instead, contextual factors seem to modify these general (individual level) processes of electoral choice, rather than producing different processes altogether.

Judging the impact of context is a complex research question. Previously, much of the electoral systems literature examined the *direct effects of context* through aggregate level analyses. This was most clearly seen in research on turnout, where a host of institutional and political factors are related to national turnout levels (Norris 2002; Brockington 2004; Blais 2006). However, when we shift our focus to the study of individual political behavior with the help of a multilevel research design, the causal processes become more complex. For instance, the direct effect of an institutional variable might appear significant in aggregate cross-national analyses if it produces a few percentage point change in turnout levels. But when we study individual level behavior, many other factors have a greater impact on individual behavior.

Miki Kittilson and Christopher Anderson most directly demonstrate the prime importance of individual-level processes by showing that interpersonal variance in turnout is five times greater than country-level variance; Timothy Hellwig and Anderson display similar findings in Chapter 7 and 10. The basic multilevel model of turnout reported by Kittilson and Anderson also shows that turnout varies significantly as a function of education, income, age, and political attitudes, but there are no statistically significant direct context effects for the six contextual variables they analyze. Similarly, Andre Blais and Thomas Gschwend present several models in which none of their context variables directly affects levels of strategic defection, and Hellwig finds that most contextual variables are unrelated to incumbent vote choice. Perhaps the most striking evidence comes from G. Bingham Powell (Chapter 9), where he demonstrates that the representation gap in contemporary democracies is not directly affected by the PR/majoritarian structure of the electoral system – one of the core assumptions of electoral studies research. Thus, it is useful to put the magnitude of contextual- versus individual-level effects in perspective: most of the variation in outcomes – that is, in individuals' responses – is due to differences across individuals, rather than the countries they live in. Thus, relatively speaking, there is less room for contextual effects to explain voter behavior than for individual effects.

In terms of predicting individual political behavior, contextual factors often appear more important in producing indirect and contingent effects (see Chapter 1). The *indirect effects* of context can occur by shaping people's political beliefs and values, which then alter electoral behavior. For instance, Duverger's psychological effect of majoritarian electoral systems worked by changing citizen orientations, which, in turn, decreased their likelihood to vote for smaller parties in such systems (Blais and Carty 1991; Clark and Golder 2006). In this vein, Kittilson and Anderson demonstrate that the polarization of party systems affects public images of the importance of elections, which then affects levels of turnout. Jeffrey Karp and Susan Banducci show that the strength of party preferences and party contacting mediate the substantial impact of context on campaign activity. Hellwig similarly demonstrates that several contextual variables – the concentration of political responsibility, the length of democratic responsibility, and constitutional regime form – directly affect political knowledge, which in turn is important in predicting levels of strategic defection. Such indirect effects provide a causal explanation of how direct context effects may appear in aggregate analyses by shaping individual attitudes.

The *contingent effects* of context appear when characteristics of the electoral system or party system interact with the individual-level correlates of electoral behavior. The chapters in this volume reference substantial previous literature that claims the political context interacts with individuals' attitudes to affect their electoral behavior. And this is what we find: contingent effects appear to be the most common contextual effects in this volume. In the case of political participation, for example, Kittilson and Anderson found the perceived importance of the election had a much stronger impact on turnout in systems where the political parties were highly polarized. Karp and Banducci find that party system polarization has both direct negative effects on levels of campaign activity as well as contingent effects as it interacts with party attachments and party contacting to shape campaign activity.

Many predictors of voting choice also show strong contingent effects. Russell Dalton finds a strong correlation between Left–Right attitudes and the vote with substantial cross-national variation in this relationship. He explores many different attributes of the electoral system, party system, and institutional context to explain these cross-national differences. Most clearly, the diversity of parties' Left–Right positions has a very strong effect on voting patterns. In party systems with dispersed choices – where parties are highly polarized on the Left–Right scale – Left–Right voting is twice as strong as in the least polarized systems. Hellwig (Chapter 7) similarly shows that performance evaluations matter more for vote choice when policy responsibility is concentrated and when the party system is highly polarized. For instance, the impact of performance evaluations increases nearly fivefold over the range of the party system polarization index. Blais and Gschwend demonstrate that the strength of party attachments in predicting strategic defection is contingent on the disproportionality of the electoral system.

At the aggregate level, too, we find contingent effects. Powell examines the effects of institutional features, especially the party system, on the ideological congruence between the median citizen and the government. He finds that the polarization of the party system has particularly large effects on ideological (in) congruence. In addition to this direct effect, he shows that party system polarization effects are larger in systems with SMD election rules and smaller in presidential systems. Similarly, Anderson reports that voters' attitudes are shaped by contextual factors, but that these affect voters in the ideological middle differently from voters who place themselves on the outer edges of the Left–Right spectrum.

Contingent effects can also occur through the interaction of two individual-level variables across different contexts. For example, Dalton shows that when party systems are highly polarized, the relationship for Left–Right voting is relatively constant across levels of political knowledge. But in less polarized party systems where party positions are less distinct, the strength of Left–Right voting significantly increases as the voter's level of political knowledge increases.

Yuliya Tverdova's multilevel analysis of party-based and candidate-based voting yields more limited evidence of contextual effects. Going beyond other multilevel analyses in this volume, she develops an innovative analysis of vote choice as a function of individual level, party level, and national level factors, yielding only modest contextual effects. This may offer an insight of a different form. Because she examines effects for voters of individual parties nested within national contexts, the contextual effects that work collectively on party systems might not translate to specific parties. For instance, the simple bivariate relationships for party-based and candidate voting vary substantially across nations, and is related to some of the standard contextual variables in this study (see discussion below for Table 11.1). But these same contextual variables do not systematically produce contingent effects when she disaggregates the analysis to individual parties. In other words, to identify the impact of context on electoral behavior may require that we analyze choices across parties, because it is through these interparty comparisons that their collective context may become apparent.

This multifaceted analysis of contextual effects suggests that the direct effects that are most easily observed in aggregate statistical analyses are only a small part of contextual influences. What is more, they do not provide tests of the causal mechanisms that we often assume undergird these effects. As a result, past aggregate analyses of direct effects in all likelihood have produced a biased and limited assessment of the importance of context. This is because the indirect and contingent effects of context appear to be more important in explaining individual level behavior than do direct contextual effects. Thus, going back to how we can view the impact of macro contexts on citizen behavior, the findings collected in this volume speak in favor of seeing the effects of institutional structures as secondary, in the sense that institutions have the consequences electoral researchers have long recognized. The relationship between context and individual behavior is more complex and indirect than implied from aggregate cross-national analyses where individual-level heterogeneity often cancels out. In this way, we can think of institutional effects as the origin in the chain of causality that underlies our story: institutions have consequences, and it is these consequences that citizens observe and react to, at least in the short term, not the institutions themselves.

Going forward, we suspect that indirect and contingent effects will prove even more common as further research examines their impact on individual behavior. However, these effects can only be examined by merging contextual- and individual-level analyses across many nations as we have done in this volume. And lacking such cross-national comparisons, the importance of context is invisible in single-national electoral studies – even though such forces are inevitably shaping citizen choices. Bringing them into relief, however, is critical if we are to make progress toward substituting variable names for country names in comparative electoral analyses.

Which aspects of context matter

If context does matter, then the question shifts to what aspects of context are most important. Our analyses suggest, not surprisingly, that there is not a single answer to this question. We should first recognize that representative democracy involves multiple values and there is not a single institutional arrangement that can maximize outcomes on all value dimensions (Powell 1982; Katz 1997). Similarly, the rationale for the second module of CSES was to examine the tension between accountability and representation in electoral choice (Wessels and Schmitt 2008). Some aspects of context might maximize political participation, while others might affect the accountability of electoral choices, party organization and behavior, or the representativeness of elections. In addition, each aspect of the electoral system or party system can have multiple and sometimes contradictory effects. A nation that benefits from its institutional arrangement along one dimension may suffer in another area because of the same institutions. Consequently, without a clearer sense of the actual impact of context, a government might enact a reform to maximize one democratic value and experience unanticipated consequences in another area.

At the same time, there are broad patterns in our findings that warrant additional discussion. Most of the chapters in this volume examined contextual variables that could be grouped within three categories (see Chapter 1). The first is the *amount of choice*. This is the most extensively researched area for this part of electoral studies, focusing on the number of party choices. Its roots lie in Duverger's (1954) and Douglas Rae's early studies (1971) of the impact of PR/ majoritarian electoral systems. More recent research has refined the measures of electoral system characteristics, and their impact on the effective number of parties that compete in elections (e.g., Taagepera and Shugart 1989; Lijphart 1994; Farrell 2001; Taagepera 2007).[2]

This research presumed that formal electoral rules not only predict the number of significant parties competing in elections but also more basically define the incentive structure that influences party and voter behavior. For instance, Pippa Norris's study (2002) of electoral choice examined how PR/majoritarian electoral systems are related to social cleavage voting, levels of partisanship, images of government, and other factors. Arend Lijphart's (1999) and G. Bingham Powell's studies (1987) of democracy focused on the cluster of variables related to the PR/majoritarian electoral system, such as district magnitude and the effective number of parties. To a degree, the choice of a PR/majoritarian electoral system was the holy grail of electoral studies and presumably defined the most important aspect of the electoral context.

We expanded the contextual comparisons to include a second category that we labeled the *clarity of party choices*. Underlying the literature on the number of party choices in an election is a deeper logic about the diversity of these choices (Sartori 1976; Dalton 2008*b*). Diverse choices presumably stimulate turnout, increase the opportunities for representation, and affect electoral accountability. We measure the clarity of party choice as the dispersion of political parties along the Left–Right scale (see Chapters 4 and 5). While the amount of choice might be a surrogate for the diversity of these choices, the findings reported in this volume show that diversity itself produces many of the putative effects of electoral systems. Similarly, several recent empirical studies had suggested that the clarity of party choices has a much more direct and substantial effect on citizen electoral behavior than the simple number of party choices (Thomassen 2005; Dalton 2008*b*). This variable is also important because it reflects a characteristic of the party system – as opposed to the electoral system – as an influence on voters. There are theoretical and empirical grounds to expect that the nature of party choices, party strategies, and election activities have a more immediate and proximate impact on voter behavior than the formal system of electoral rules.

Finally, we examined a third category of the *institutionalization of the party system*. We expected that new democracies would have more fluid party alignments, and voters would not yet be fully integrated into democratic electoral politics. Similarly, when political or cultural factors produce instability in a party system so that the party alignment is very fluid, this might attenuate the kinds of individual-level relationships seen in long-standing democracies. Thus several chapters examined whether electoral behavior was affected by the level of democracy in a nation, the history of democracy, or the age of the party system.

The empirical findings of this volume are diverse and multifaceted – but we want to summarize the general empirical patterns with some evidence drawn from the contributors' chapters. We first assembled measures of the three contextual variables for the CSES nations examined in this volume (see volume appendix). A PR/majoritarian electoral system, district magnitude, and the effective number of electoral parties represent the nature of the electoral system. These are all central variables in the PR/majoritarian model of electoral systems. For the clarity of choice we used the public's perception of the Left–Right polarization of the party system. Then to measure democratization we used a simple dichotomy of established or new democracy, the World Bank's index of voice and accountability, and the years of continuous democracy for the nation.

To illustrate the potential effects of these different contextual variables, we selected different aspects of electoral behavior from the chapters in this volume. We measured citizen participation by turnout in the election and engagement in the campaign.[3] To examine contextual effects on electoral behavior we included the strength of Left–Right voting from Chapter 4 and a measure of party-based voting derived from Chapter 5.[4] To consider the representativeness of elections we included the gap between the median voter's Left–Right position and the Left–Right position of the elected government from Powell (Chapter 9).

This evidence of contextual effects is incomplete, and does not include all the areas in this volume. Some examples are testing for direct effects of context, such as in the percentage voting in elections or active in campaigns. Other variables are looking at contingent effects of predictors on voting choice, such as Left–Right voting or party-based voting. Ideally we should also include other indicators of individual political behavior, but these often involve complex contingent and indirect effects and so are not easily summarized as by a single statistical value (e.g., see Hellwig). And even variables such as voting and campaign activity are examined without controlling for other factors that might influence participation, such as compulsory voting or the length of campaigns. So we use this empirical evidence to illustrate the general discussion of contextual effects that follows, recognizing that the contextual effects described in this volume are often more complex and multilayered.

This subset of contextual and behavioral variables was factor analyzed to determine the interrelationships among the variables for the thirty-six legislative elections in the CSES survey (Table 11.1).[5] We extracted three dimensions to summarize these variables. The first dimension is defined by the development of democracy in a nation. The contextual content of the second dimension reflects the clarity of choice. The third dimension reflects the amount of choice in the political context. These three dimensions defined by contextual variables is evidence that the three dimensions of context we identified in Chapter 1 are empirically distinct.

The first dimension of democratization has very high loadings for the years of continuous democracy, whether the nation is an established or new democracy, and the World Bank rating of democratic voice and accountability. Other measures of democratization – such as the Freedom House statistic or the age of the party system – would also load on this dimension if included in the analysis. This is a well-defined dimension as shown by its ranking as the first dimension extracted from the data. However, these contextual variables are only weakly related to the five examples of citizen electoral behavior included in the analysis. Only election turnout is substantially related to democratization (.554).

The second dimension represents the clarity of choice – defined by the single contextual variable of party system polarization. This sampling of findings indicates that the clarity of choice is strongly related to several different aspects of electoral behavior. The clarity of choice is positively related to the strength of

Table 11.1 Dimensions of context and behavioral effects

Variable	Democratization	Clarity of choice	Amount of choice
Established/new democracy	.932	.135	−.089
Years continuous democracy	.941	−.025	.032
WB Voice and accountability	.812	.342	−.120
PR/majoritarian electoral system	−.088	.489	.655
District magnitude	−.116	.178	.493
Effective number of electoral parties	.152	−.066	.912
Party system polarization	.028	.842	.151
Election turnout	.554	−.030	.461
Campaign involvement	.062	−.520	−.311
Party representation and vote	.202	.698	−.106
Left–Right attitude and vote	.193	.856	.127
Voter–government LR agreement	−.041	−.447	−.063
Eigenvalue	2.85	2.81	1.89
Variance Explained	23.7	23.4	15.8

Note: Table presents results from varimax rotated factor analysis, with pairwise deletion for the module II nations.
Source: CSES, module II, N = 36 nations.

Left–Right voting (.856) as well as party-based voting (.698). Simultaneously, clarity of choice has some significant negative effects. Campaign activity tends to be lower in highly polarized systems (see Karp and Banducci) and voter – government agreement is weaker in highly polarized systems (see Chapter 9).

Contextual variables measuring the amount of choice – a PR electoral system, district magnitude, and the effective number of parties – define the third dimension. This dimension is modestly related to election turnout (.461), but is virtually unrelated to Left–Right voting, party-based voting, or voter–government agreement. The chapters in this volume often found that the amount of choice variables had statistically significant contingent or indirect effects, and in the direction predicted by previous theory and empirical work. But the effects are typically quite modest as depicted in this summary factor analysis.

One of this volume's most striking empirical findings is the importance of the clarity of choice across different aspects of electoral behavior, especially in comparison to the contextual variables measuring the amount of choice. Prior electoral studies have typically stressed the importance of electoral system traits linked to the amount of choice (the PR/majoritarian framework). However, we generally find broader and stronger effects for the clarity of choice over the amount of choice for different aspects of individual electoral behavior.

The individual chapters underscore the importance of the clarity of choice in the party system as an influence on electoral behavior. Kittilson and Anderson show that party system polarization has significant direct effects on turnout and contingent effects through interactions with political efficacy, but the number of parties lacks significant effects. Karp and Banducci find strong indirect and contingent effects for party system polarization on campaign activity. Dalton finds that polarization very strongly affects the level of Left–Right voting, while nearly all of the standard electoral system traits and the effective number of parties are not significant. In Hellwig's analyses of performance voting, party system polarization is the only context variable that has direct effects on incumbent voting, as well as having several contingent effects with other individual-level predictors. Anderson finds that polarized partisan choices increase the gap in feelings of representation between voters who locate themselves in the political middle and those on the edges; at the same time, proportional electoral systems diminish such differences.

To an extent, the emergence of party system polarization as an important contextual variable should not be surprising. Much of the theoretical literature on the importance of party choice implicitly or explicitly discussed the clarity of choices rather than simply the amount of choice.[6] However, previous empirical analyses generally lacked an objective measure of the clarity of choice and therefore used the number of parties as a surrogate – presuming these two were strongly related. Chapter 1 demonstrated that these two dimensions are unrelated in the set of CSES nations investigated in this volume ($r = .15$). It may be that the effective number of parties is relevant for parties for defining their electoral strategies, coalition formation, government stability, and other systemic outcomes. However, our results suggest that party system polarization is an important missing element in understanding how the political context shapes electoral behavior. Previous studies that examined only the PR/majoritarian elements of electoral systems have probably misspecified the contextual processes affecting electoral choice.

Context and democratic politics

This volume has focused on the interrelationships between contextual structures and citizen electoral behavior. Empirically studying individual voters as embedded in and interacting with the institutional and structural contexts in which they live and act is relatively new in the comparative study of political behavior (Anderson 2007a, 2009). But significant research streams aimed at both the methodology of investigating such multilevel relationships as well as the substance of particular sets of questions have developed over the past decade.

As the contributions to this volume attest, scholars' growing ease of connecting micro and macro levels of analysis holds significant promise for integrating the study of behavioral politics with other areas of political science scholarship by linking institutions and behavior or by developing and testing more complex models of the interaction of party behavior with the study of citizen politics. In addition, this area of inquiry holds much promise for integrating the study of established democracies with research on emerging and transitioning democracies, as well as the institutionalization of multilevel polities such as the European Union or interactions among international politics, subnational politics, and citizen behavior.

As a side point, we should also note the methodological diversity of statistical analyses applied across the chapters to address the statistical assumptions of multilevel analyses.[7] In several instances, the authors compared alternative techniques, generally yielding equivalent results. This is still a methodological field in transition, as seen by this diversity of methodologies, in part because of the unique demands that cross-national, survey-based data structures impose. For the kinds of research projects undertaken as part of this volume, the number of individual-level cases is typically large, but the number of higher-level (country-level) variables more modest. Over the next few years, we expect rapid progress in identifying the tradeoffs between various estimation methods and the robustness of multilevel analyses to violations of statistical assumptions.

On a theoretical level, these multilevel research endeavors carry with them distinct and frequently unstated assumptions about the political world that are worth keeping in mind. Importantly, students of institutions commonly assume that formal institutions are the most proximate predictors of behavior. Yet, our findings suggest that the formal institutional structure of the electoral system or constitutional structures generally matters less than the structure of the party system.

This central finding holds several implications for how we think about the connection between formal political institutions and citizen behavior. First, the staying power of individual-level predictors of behavior relative to institutional context documented in most chapters may be taken to imply that citizen attitudes and values predominate regardless of the institutional structure and that the quest for institutional explanations of behavior (and the quest to change behavior by changing formal institutions) will see limited success. But assuming for the moment that contextual and institutional factors have an important place and warrant further study, our findings imply a clear demarcation for understanding institutional effects. Formal institutions matter insofar as they structure the electoral supply and the incentives for political actors. Thus, a proportional/majoritarian electoral system or the district magnitude of the electoral system affect the number of parties, and this has implications for patterns of coalition formation. However, the characteristics of the party system and the parties themselves generally frame voter choice and electoral behavior in the most proximate sense. Our findings thus prompt us to ask whether we should worry less about formal rules and more about the informal and therefore dynamic characteristics of party systems.

Our findings also can be seen as challenges to the narrower approaches to behavior taken by rational choice theorists who expect that institutions define incentive structures, and incentive structures influence behavior. One possibility, of course, is that our findings may simply be evidence that these specific institutions we investigate in this volume do not produce sufficient incentives to influence citizen behavior and that other institutions or aspects of context (e.g., polarization) are more important.

Furthermore, our findings tend to argue against the logic of political change through institutional reform that is common in much of the electoral studies literature. Ironically, many of the aspects of electoral systems that are amenable to institutional reform – such as PR/majoritarian system, district magnitude, electoral thresholds, and even the effective number of electoral parties – are often secondary influences on citizen political behavior. Although these variables generally have effects consistent with the prior literature, their impact is often overshadowed by the characteristics of party competition (party system polarization). Moreover, the diversity of party choice appears to be less institutionally structured, and thus less easily manipulated by changing electoral rules. In other words, the factors that actually can be changed by institutional designers matter less than what cannot be changed through institutional engineering because it is an outcome produced by the dynamic interactions of political parties (parties and candidates) and voters. And while there is a large and rich body of literature examining the formal institutions of the electoral system and predicting the number of parties competing in elections and winning seats in parliament, we yet lack systematic and convincing explanations of how party systems themselves change and evolve internally, such as measured by party system polarization. Almost certainly, this should shine the light on the incentives political elites have under different institutional configurations to structure the electoral supply – be it through the formation of political parties or the strategic choice of particular policy offerings.

At least we now know it is not simply the number of parties competing in an election or other basic traits of the electoral system that affect voters' choices. Instead, the options available to voters seem to reflect strategic or ideological decisions by party leaders. For instance, British Labour's substantial move to the center in 1997 reflected Tony Blair's desire to chart a new course for the party and garner centrist votes; the same logic guided Gerhard Schröder's movement of the SPD in 1998. Certainly U.S. presidential elections illustrate such swings as the primary process produces candidates of different political leanings across subsequent elections. Many candidates (and some parties) have apparently adopted ideological positions for reasons separate than electoral advantage.

In some cases, polarization seems to be an enduring characteristic of a party system, perhaps generated by intense ideological divisions in the past that become engrained in a culture of political competition. Or, the electoral success and institutionalization of one extremist party may create a dynamic that affects the entire party system. For instance, we have cited Spain as a case with a relatively small number of effective electoral parties but high levels of polarization. Having identified the importance of party system polarization – and the inability of the simple number of parties to capture these forces – further research might productively explore the short and long-term sources of polarization.

Another common and typically implicit assumption in scholarship presumes that political structures are exogenous and stable as predictors of electoral behavior. While these assumptions may be safe under many conditions, on occasion they may not hold. In fact, one of the perhaps more interesting yet undeveloped research areas in this subfield of political science is the rigorous analysis of the conditions under which these assumptions are safe or should be challenged. This would also affect how we model the impact of context on behavior in longitudinal analyses.

While political science is mostly a quasi-experimental science, there are occasional situations that allow scholars of institutions to take advantage of "natural experiments" to investigate their claims. Some scholars have used such natural changes to examine the impact of electoral system pre/post a major institutional reform. For example, research has examined how New Zealand's voters reacted to the changes in electoral rules in that country (Banducci, Donovan, and Karp 1999; Karp and Bowler 2001), and in particular how different kinds of voters were affected differently by alternative electoral system designs. Major electoral reforms were also introduced in Israel, Italy, and Japan, as well as several other developing democracies (Shugart and Wattenberg 2003). Other researchers have examined the impact of institutional change on voter behavior in an experimental setting (Bowler and Donovan 2004). In addition, there are probably many instances where voters themselves seek to effect such change in institutions. The fluidity or stability of structures – and concomitantly the exogeneity and endogeneity of context – is particularly likely to differ in established versus new democracies, with the presumption of greater endogeneity or at least potential for it in newer democracies.

However, the lesson from several recent major electoral reforms that provided opportunities to examine voter and party behavior under different sets of rules – in Israel, Italy, Japan, and New Zealand – underscores the general conclusions of this volume. These four cases have yielded very mixed results as far as the predictions of political scientists and the expectations of institutional reformers are concerned. Israel and Italy soon returned to their previous electoral systems in frustration with the consequences of the reform. Dissatisfaction with the New Zealand experience has lead to a new referendum on electoral reform planned for 2012. The change in the Japanese electoral system seems likely to endure, but even in this case the reform did not produce the intended results. Reviewing this experience, David Farrell (2010) concludes "The fact that large-scale electoral reform in established democracies is rare, and hasn't actually worked in the few instances where it has been tried, should give pause for thought."

Because research to date has focused mainly on voters' electoral choices and decisions to participate in elections, this first generation of scholarship needs to establish which institutions matter, how they matter, and what kinds of behavior they matter for. One can easily imagine a proliferation of studies that examine the interactive effects of institutional features and individual-level factors, but absent some more general theories about the interactions of structures and voting, such efforts are unlikely to yield cumulative understandings of either institutions or behavior. Our results suggest that it is especially fruitful to focus on the consequences of the electoral supply – a consequence of formal institutions – in the form of the number and distinctiveness of electoral choices citizens perceive and select from.

Another critical question is how much institutions matter across different political domains (beyond electoral behavior), and how much they matter relative to individual-level factors. To establish that institutions influence voter behavior and how they do so is one thing – to establish that they make a significant difference and how much of a difference they make is quite another but critical matter. Our results indicate that institutions and macro-contextual conditions often shape the ways in which individual-level factors like ideology relate to voter choices. At the same time, context cannot compete with individual-level variables in a race to predict the vote. Instead, the analyses reveal that context and individual differences jointly paint a fuller and more vibrant picture of how voters come to make their decisions.

At the end of the day, what is particularly noteworthy about cross-level investigations of behavioral politics is that they hold the promise of producing a more nuanced and contextualized understanding of political life. They can connect hitherto unconnected streams of scholarship in the areas of institutions, political economy, policy, and behavior. They can provide a better and more complex empirical and theoretical understanding of the how's and why's of citizen politics. And this, ideally, can be used to strengthen the democratic process.

Notes

1. In the end, the government did not pursue major electoral reform for several reasons. Some proposed changes would have required a constitutional revision, which was not seen as politically possible. They also realized that some of the suggested reforms might actually be counterproductive. D66 also tempered its reformist zeal. And, we suspect, when confronted with the alternatives they felt more positive about the Dutch proportional representation system.
2. This research examined the impact of district magnitude, electoral thresholds, and other formal aspects of the electoral system on the effective number of parties

competing in elections with extensions to the logic that parties should follow in these different electoral settings.

3. Voter turnout is measured as the percentage of registered who voted in the election, using data drawn from the Institute for Democracy and Electoral Systems website (www.idea.int/vt/). Campaign participation is the average of activity in the campaign and trying to persuade others how to vote, which is presented in Table 3.1.

4. The Left–Right voting correlations are from Table 5.1. The party-based voting measure using the feelings of being represented by a party from Chapter 5, and calculates a simple bivariate relationship between this variable and legislative vote choice (Cramer's V correlation).

5. We conducted a factor analysis with varimax rotation, extracting three dimensions (the fourth dimension barely passed the threshold of an eigenvalue greater than 1.0). We used pairwise deletion of missing data.

6. For instance, Downs (1957: 127) discusses the importance of diversity for ideological voting: "voters in multiparty systems, however, are given a wide range of ideological choice, with parties emphasizing rather than soft-pedaling their doctrinal differences. Hence regarding ideologies as a decisive factor in one's voting decision is usually more rational in a multiparty system than in a two-party system." Similarly, Sartori's discussion (1976: 131–45, 173–92) of party system emphasizes the centripetal/centrifugal distribution of parties as more important than the simple number of parties.

7. Some chapters used the HLM program. Several chapters used STATA to estimate models, and at least one chapter used a generalized least squares model available in SPSS. Another chapter used a clustered error adjustment to compensate for the multilevel structure of the data.

APPENDIX

MACRO-LEVEL DATA[*]

Matias Bargsted, Steffen Blings, Christopher J. Anderson,
and Russell J. Dalton

The data used throughout the volume consists of an expanded and updated version of the dataset prepared by Matias Bargsted for the Comparative Study of Electoral Systems (CSES) project. We began with Bargsted's version of the macro data (2007) for the CSES module I and II nations. We then subsetted these data to include the module II variables used in this volume, updated some entries, and added a few variables. This appendix displays information for thirty-eight nations; Kyrgyzstan and Hong Kong are not included in our analyses but are in the initial CSES release.

Introduction

This appendix presents thirty variables that are used in the various chapters of this volume. Additional macro variables are available through the CSES release of the macro file.[1] The file includes a wide range of topics such as electoral systems, party system characteristics, and socioeconomic information.

The collection of these data started with the preparation of the materials for the CSES Module III Planning Committee. After identifying several public sources of macro-level data that could complement the information delivered by CSES country members, a version of this dataset was distributed through the CSES web site in 2007. The research project for this volume began with this dataset, and added several nations that were late additions to the second CSES module. In the course of research, the contributors to this volume also identified additional variables for this data collection.

Some general comments about the data are appropriate. We have tried to minimize the missing data problem by incorporating information from multiple sources, but in some cases no reliable information is available. Two polities, Taiwan and the Philippines, have a significant amount of missing data because they are often missing from standard country-level data sources. We deleted two non-democracies from the file because they are not included in this volume (Hong Kong and Kyrgyzstan). We also edited and updated some variables from the original CSES macro file. These macro data were distributed to all participants in this project so that the same measures could be used across chapters.

The following pages list the included variables with the sources from where we obtained the data. A table at the end presents the values for each of the module II nations in this project.

Variables

Country

Name of the country.

Year

Year of the election in the CSES study.

Legelec

If election was legislative coded "1," otherwise coded as 0.

Exelec

If election was executive coded "1," otherwise coded as 0.

Executive

Executive authority of country:

(0) Presidential system: if both the Head of State and Head of Government are the same person

(1) Semi-presidential system: if the Head of State is directly elected, but the Head of Government is not

(2) Parliamentary system: if the Head of State and Head of Government are not directly elected.

For details about this coding rule, see CSES Module 1 and Module 2 Macro Booklet, contributed by Ana Espírito-Santo, Diogo Moreira, André Freire, Marina Costa Lobo, and Pedro Magalhães; available at cses.org/download/contributions/contributions.htm

E_POWER

This is an additive index of the powers of the Head of Government. It codes whether the Head of Government has the authority to (a) select cabinet officers, (b) dismiss cabinet officers, (c) make policy by setting the legislative agenda, and (d) dissolve the legislature and call for votes of confidence. The scale runs from (0) a weak head of government, (i.e., none of these items), to (4) a strong head of government (all four items).

Source: www.cses.org

Formula

Whether the country uses (1) a majoritarian formula, (2) a mixed formula, or (3) a proportional formula to choose parliamentarian representatives (lower chamber if bicameral).

Sources: ACE Project; Golder (2005); and Inter-Parliamentary Union.

Magnitude

This is the weighted mean district magnitude of the Lower House. This variable uses the weighted average of the number of representatives elected by each constituency size. If this information was not available, we used the number of seats divided by the number of constituencies. See Keefer (2005) for full details about coding procedures.

Source: ACE Project and Database of Political Institutions.

Federal

Is the nation a federal system? (0 = not a federal system; 1 = federal system).

Federations means "compound polities, combining strong constituent units and strong general government, each possessing powers delegated to it by the people through a constitution and each empowered to deal directly with the citizens in the exercise of the legislative, administrative and taxing powers, and each directly elected by the citizens" (Watts 1999). Although Spain does not incorporate this label in the constitution, it is predominantly a federation and is coded as a federal system.

Compulse

Does country have compulsory voting? (1 = yes; 0 = no)

Source: IDEA International – Voter Turnout.

Enep

Effective Number of Electoral Parties calculated by the Laakso and Taagepera (1979) formula:

$$ENEP = \frac{1}{\sum v_i^2}$$

where v_i is the percent of votes obtained by the ith party.[2]

Source: Data from multiple sources were employed to estimate this index.

ENPP

Effective Number of Parliamentary Parties calculated by the Laakso and Taagepera (1979) formula:

$$ENEP = \frac{1}{\sum p_i^2}$$

where p_i is the percent of seats obtained by the ith party.[2]

Source: Data from multiple sources were employed to estimate this index.

Disprop

The Gallagher Index of Disproportionality measures the difference between the percentage of votes received and the percentage of seats a party obtains after legislature elections (Gallagher 1991). The formula is:

$$DISPROP = \left[\frac{1}{2}\sum(Vote_i\% - Seat_i\%)^2\right]^{1/2}$$

where $Votes_i\%$ is the percent of the popular vote and $Seat_i\%$ is the percent of the seats the ith party obtains.[2]

Source: Data from multiple sources were employed to estimate this index.

PTY_CAND

This measures whether the structure of the ballot emphasizes candidate-centered voting, such as in the Irish single transferable vote system (a 10 on the index), or party-centered voting such as closed party-list ballots (a 1.4 on the index).

Source: Farrell and McAllister (2006).

POLARIZE

This index measures the dispersion of parties along the Left/Right scale (Dalton 2008*b*). It is based on the Left/Right location of parties as determined by the publics in each nation, weighted by the vote share for each party. For Belgium, we used party positions from Benoit and Laver (2006). The Polarization Index is measured as:

PI = SQRT{Σ(party vote share$_i$)*([party L/R score$_i$ – party system average L/R score]/5)^2} (i represents individual parties).

Source: Calculated from party vote shares in the CSES macro file and party Left–Right scores from the electorate in each nation.

Freedom

Freedom House Scores at the year of the election study. This score is the average between the civic liberties and political rights indicators. The highest level of freedom is 1 and the lowest is 7.

Source: Freedom House.

Polity

This variable is equal to the democracy minus the autocracy score classification of POLITY IV at the year of the election study. The results range from +10 (strongly democratic) to -10 (strongly autocratic).
Source: Polity IV Project.

WB_V&A

The World Bank's Voice and Accountability Index measures "various aspects of the political process, civil liberties, and political rights, measuring the extent to which citizens of a country are able to participate in the selection of governments." We use the percentile rank for each nation.
Source: World Bank Governance Indicators (www.worldbank.org/wbi/governance).

Pressfree

This variable measures the degree of press freedom in the nation. It combines scores for the legal environment, the political environment, and the economic environment that affect press freedom. The results range from 0 (highest level) to 100 (lowest level).
Source: Freedomhouse.

Yearsdem

This index is equal to the number of years since 1955 a country has scored at +6 or above on Polity IV's democracy scale.
Source: http://www.systemicpeace.org/polity/polity4.htm

Partyage

Average age of political parties in a country. This weights the parties by their vote share in the CSES election. For new democracies, party age is calculated to begin with the start of democracy, even if some form of the party existed previously.
Source: Database of Political Institutions; Dalton and Weldon (2007).

HDI

The Human Development Index (HDI) measures the average achievements in a country in three basic dimensions of human development: a long and healthy life, knowledge, and a decent standard of living. If the HDI was not available for the year of the survey, the nearest HDI statistic was used.
Source: United Nations Development Program.

Growth

GDP growth (annual %) at the year of the election study.
   Source: World Bank Indicators.

GDP_PPP

GDP per capita, PPP (constant 2000 international dollars) at the year of the election study.
   Source: World Bank Indicators.

NGP_T1

The number of governing parties immediately before the election. *Note*: For some governments in which members of parties other than the Prime Minister's/President's party held a cabinet portfolio, we did not code this as representing the membership of the respective other party in the government (e.g., Norman Mineta, a Democrat, in George W. Bush's cabinet).
   Source: Data from multiple sources were employed to estimate this variable.

NGP_T2

The number of governing parties immediately after the election. *Note*: For some governments in which members of parties other than the Prime Minister's/President's party held a cabinet portfolio, we did not code this as representing the membership of the respective other party in the government (e.g., Norman Mineta, a Democrat, in George W. Bush's cabinet).
   Source: Data from multiple sources were employed to estimate this variable.

ENGP_T1

The effective number of governing parties immediately before the election is calculated by:

$$ENGP = \frac{1}{\sum s_i^2}$$

where s_i is the number of seats in the lower house obtained by the ith party divided by the total number of seats obtained by all governing parties.
   Source: For governing parties, see NGP_T1. For seats in parliament, see ENEP.

ENGP_T2

The effective number of governing parties immediately after the election is calculated by:

$$ENGP = \frac{1}{\sum s_i^2}$$

where s_i is the number of seats in the Lower House obtained by the ith party divided by the total number of seats obtained by all governing parties.

Source: For governing parties, see NGP_T2. For seats in parliament, see ENEP.

CON_RESP

This index measures the concentration of government responsibility prior to the election. It is a variant of the Duch and Stevenson indicator (2008) based on a comparison of the actual distribution of cabinet portfolios among parties with the hypothetical case where portfolios are distributed evenly across all parties represented in the legislature.

$$Concentration\ of\ Responsibility = (1 - \phi)\sqrt{\sum\nolimits_{j=1}(\lambda_{jk}^c - \delta_k)^2} + \phi\sqrt{\sum\nolimits_{j=1}(\lambda_{jk}^c - \delta_k)^2}$$

where λ^c in the first term is the actual share of cabinet portfolios held by party j just before the election in country k *and* λ^s is the actual share of seats held by the party in the lower (only) legislative chamber. The other term, δ, is the share of portfolios/seats held by each party if the responsibility were spread evenly over all n parties with seats in the legislature (such that $\delta = 1/n$). The two terms are combined using a mixing parameter ϕ, which is equal to 0 for majority governments and for minority governments. This means that for cases where the government held a majority of seats prior to the election, Concentration of Responsibility is based only on cabinet portfolios, and the measure is discounted by seat allocations in cases of minority governments.

GOV_LR

The ideological position of the government directly following the election, based on the Left/Right location of parties with cabinet portfolios as determined by the publics in each nation, weighted by number of cabinet portfolios for each party:

GOV_LR = Σ(party cabinet portfolio share$_i$)*(party L/R score$_i$)

(i represents individual parties).

Sources: The CSES data for the Left/Right placement; for the governing parties, see NGP_T2 above.

Govstable

The duration of the three governments prior to the CSES election (in months).

Source: Governments, 1950–95 dataset by Michael D. McDonald and Silvia M. Mendes, updated with data from the Political Data Yearbooks of the European Journal of Political Research.

STABLE_PRCT

The duration of the last three governments as a proportion of three full electoral terms.
  Source: See GOVSTABLE above.

country	year	legelec	exeelec	executive	E_Power	formula	magnitude	federal
Albania	2005	1	0	2		2	11.10	0
Australia	2004	1	0	2	4	1	0.90	1
Belgium	2003	1	0	2		3	7.50	1
Brazil	2002	1	1	0	1	3	19.00	1
Bulgaria	2001	1	1	1	1	3	7.70	0
Canada	2004	1	0	2	4	1	1.00	1
Chile	2005	0	1	0		3	2.00	0
Czech Republic	2002	1	0	2	2	3	25.00	0
Denmark	2001	1	0	2	0	3	10.50	0
Finland	2003	1	0	2	1	3	13.33	0
France	2002	1	1	1	4	1	1.00	0
Germany	2002	1	0	2	1	2	11.20	1
Hungary	2002	1	0	2	4	2	1.96	0
Iceland	2003	1	0	2	0	3	7.90	0
Ireland	2002	1	0	2	1	3	4.00	0
Israel	2003	1	0	2	1	3	120.00	0
Italy	2006	1	0	2		3	23.70	0
Japan	2004	1	0	2	1	2	1.54	0
Korea, South	2004	1	0	0	1	2	8.60	0
Mexico	2003	1	0	0	1	2	16.60	1
Netherlands	2002	1	0	2	0	3	150.00	0
New Zealand	2002	1	0	2	2	2	24.00	0
Norway	2001	1	0	2	2	3	10.00	0
Peru	2006	1	1	0		3	4.80	0
Philippines	2004	1	1	0	0	3	1.00	0
Poland	2001	1	0	1	0	3	16.70	0
Portugal	2002	1	0	1	1	3	10.50	0
Portugal	2005	1	0	1	1	3	10.50	0
Romania	2004	1	1	1		3	7.80	0
Russia	2004	0	1	0		2	113.00	1
Slovenia	2004	1	0	1		2	11.00	0
Spain	2004	1	0	2	1	3	6.90	1
Sweden	2002	1	0	2	0	3	11.60	0
Switzerland	2003	1	0	2	2	3	9.10	1
Taiwan	2001	1	0	1	3	2	11.50	0
Taiwan	2004	1	1	1	3	2	11.50	0
United Kingdom	2005	1	0	2	4	1	1.00	0
United States	2004	1	1	0	1	1	1.00	1

country	compulse	enep	enpp	disprop	pty_cand	Polarize	freedom	polity	WB_V&A
Albania	0	2.77	2.25	11.68	3.6	4.47	3.0	9	48.6
Australia	1	3.13	2.44	8.52	8.6	1.96	1.0	10	94.2
Belgium	1	8.86	7.03	5.59	2.9	4.53	1.0	10	96.2
Brazil	1	8.37	8.41	0.08	2.9	2.00	2.5	8	57.2
Bulgaria	0	3.92	2.92	7.52	1.4	4.37	2.0	9	60.1
Canada	0	3.77	3.03	10.06	4.3	2.06	1.0	10	96.6
Chile	1	6.05	5.56	6.63	2.9	4.95	1.0	9	88.9
Czech Republic	0	4.81	3.67	5.97	2.9	5.43	1.5	10	76.4
Denmark	0	4.70	4.48	1.61	7.1	3.57	1.0	10	96.6
Finland	0	5.92	4.93	3.74	7.1	2.85	1.0	10	99
France	1	5.07	2.24	21.97	5.7	3.29	1.0	9	83.2
Germany	0	3.87	3.38	4.31	3.6	2.70	1.0	10	94.7
Hungary	0	2.80	2.21	7.30	5.7	5.85	1.5	10	88.5
Iceland	0	3.93	3.71	2.20	1.4	4.08	1.0	10	98.6
Ireland	0	3.95	3.30	6.77	10	2.20	1.0	10	90.9
Israel	0	6.97	6.17	3.68	1.4	3.87	2.0	10	64.4
Italy	1	7.73	7.70	2.26	1.4	3.89	1.0	10	85.1
Japan	0	3.82	2.88	13.25	3.6	2.77	1.5	10	76.9
Korea, South	0	3.36	2.36	12.07	3.6	3.55	1.5	8	69.2
Mexico	1	3.41	2.99	6.74	3.6	2.10	2.0	8	55.3
Netherlands	0	6.02	5.79	1.00	2.9	3.64	1.0	10	97.6
New Zealand	0	4.10	3.76	4.15	3.6	3.35	1.0	10	100
Norway	0	6.15	5.35	4.07	1.4	3.75	1.0	10	96.6
Peru	1	6.36	3.72	14.16	2.9	1.71	2.5	9	49
Philippines	1	3.19	4.94		3.6	0.46	2.5	8	50
Poland	0	4.50	3.60	6.33	3.6	4.92	1.5	9	84.6
Portugal	0	3.15	2.58	5.33	2.9	3.44	1.0	10	90.9
Portugal	0	3.31	2.56	5.74	1.4	3.77	1.0	10	91.8
Romania	0	3.80	3.32	4.14	1.4	2.43	2.5	9	58.7
Russia	0	5.15	3.38	13.01	1.4	3.11	5.5	7	33.2
Slovenia	0	5.92	4.89	5.58	2.9	3.15	1.0	10	87.5
Spain	0	3.04	2.50	5.39	1.4	4.33	1.0	10	89.9
Sweden	0	4.51	4.23	1.64	2.9	4.07	1.0	10	98.1
Switzerland	0	5.46	4.99	2.26	7.1	4.01	1.0	10	95.2
Taiwan	0	3.56	3.47	4.20	3.6	1.14	1.5	9	76
Taiwan	0	3.37	3.27	2.55	3.6	0.59	1.5	10	77.4
United Kingdom	0	3.59	2.45	16.77	4.3	2.36	1.0	10	93.8
United States	0	2.18	2.02	3.27	5.7	2.43	1.0	10	89.4

Citizens, Context, and Choice

country	pressfree	yearsdem	party_age	HDI	growth	gdp_ppp	ngp_t1	ngp_t2
Albania	51	8	10.3	0.801	5.90	4729	2	6
Australia	14	49	86.0	0.959	3.00	27872	2	2
Belgium	9	48	56.3	0.948	1.11	27709	5	4
Brazil	32	17	18.3	0.789	1.90	7480	4	5
Bulgaria	29	11	12.0	0.802	4.10	6333	1	3
Canada	15	49	77.0	0.963	2.90	28809	1	1
Chile	24	16	13.0	0.871	5.56	10700	3	3
Czech Republic	25	9	12.0	0.883	1.49	16556	1	3
Denmark	9	46	94.8	0.936	1.56	28706	2	2
Finland	10	48	81.0	0.945	1.88	26551	4	3
France	17	47	47.0	0.945	1.18	26613	4	1
Germany	15	47	53.0	0.935	0.18	25546	2	2
Hungary	23	12	12.8	0.864	3.50	14159	3	2
Iceland	8	48	55.0	0.959	4.02	29197	2	2
Ireland	16	47	54.0	0.949	6.92	35653	2	2
Israel	27	48	11.3	0.923	1.29	21853		4
Italy	35	51	12.0	0.945	1.87	25381	6	7
Japan	18	49	20.3	0.951	2.70	27338	3	3
Korea, South	29	16	9.0	0.917	8.49	16204	1	1
Mexico	38	6	26.0	0.827	1.41	8798	1	1
Netherlands	15	47	45.0	0.952	0.24	29550	3	3
New Zealand	8	47	56.8	0.393	4.41	20657	2	2
Norway	9	46	95.0	0.960	2.73	34828	1	3
Peru	39	26	6.0	0.788	7.56	5373	1	1
Philippines	34	17	23.5	0.739	6.15	4218		
Poland	18	12	9.5	0.852	1.02	10611	1	3
Portugal	15	26	28.5	0.879	0.40	18398	1	2
Portugal	14	29	31.5	0.899	0.91	18158	2	1
Romania	47	14	14.0	0.811	8.30	7721	1	3
Russia	67	4	7.0	0.802	7.21	9128	1	1
Slovenia	19	13	14.0	0.911	4.57	19251	3	4
Spain	19	26	29.0	0.942	3.10	23453	1	1
Sweden	8	47	47.3	0.957	2.10	26468	1	1
Switzerland	10	48	99.8	0.950	−0.40	30656	4	4
Taiwan	21	9	61.0		−2.20		2	3
Taiwan	23	12	43.7		6.20		3	3
United Kingdom	18	50	120.0	0.944	1.90	29571	1	1
United States	13	49	152.5	0.949	4.40	36665	1	1

country	engp_t1	engp_t2	con_resp	gov_lr	govstable	stable_prct
Albania	1.11	1.88	0.88	7.63	67	47
Australia	1.37	1.32	0.60	6.96	103	95
Belgium	4.72	4.00	0.31	4.41	134	93
Brazil	3.84	3.30	0.36	4.07	118	82
Bulgaria	1.00	2.08	0.89	5.91	78	54
Canada	1.00	1.00	0.89	5.11	84	47
Chile			0.29	4.20	144	100
Czech Republic	1.00	1.87	0.54	3.98	114	79
Denmark	1.22	1.53	0.54	7.18	86	60
Finland	3.16	2.28	0.38	5.53	98	68
France	1.49	1.00	0.63	6.61	85	47
Germany	1.31	1.43	0.72	3.38	141	98
Hungary	1.56	1.22	0.64	2.14	101	70
Iceland	1.80	1.84	0.55	7.17	143	99
Ireland	1.10	1.20		6.41	102	57
Israel		2.42	0.33		13	9
Italy			0.51	3.33	72	40
Japan	1.32	1.32	0.80	7.30	39	27
Korea, South	1.00	1.00	0.82	3.72	144	100
Mexico	1.00	1.00	0.82	6.32	216	100
Netherlands	2.57	2.79	0.48	6.87	141	98
New Zealand	1.39	1.08	0.59	3.71	57	53
Norway	1.00	1.99	0.62	6.79	60	42
Peru	1.00	1.00		5.23	120	67
Philippines			0.86	–	–	–
Poland	1.00	1.58	0.50	1.85	68	47
Portugal	1.00	1.27	0.89	7.39	105	73
Portugal	1.27	1.00	0.53	4.68	92	64
Romania	1.00	1.75	0.60	6.24	73	51
Russia	1.00	1.00		6.90	–	–
Slovenia	1.86	2.43	0.65	6.65	46	32
Spain	1.00	1.00	0.95	3.30	108	75
Sweden	1.00	1.00	0.59	3.52	96	67
Switzerland	3.93	3.74	0.43	5.68	36	25
Taiwan	1.18	1.97	0.59	4.87	54	50
Taiwan	1.97	1.76		4.87	57	53
United Kingdom	1.00	1.00	0.94	4.70	157	87
United States	1.00	1.00	0.71	6.61	144	100

Data Sources

Adam Carr's web site (psephos.adam-carr.net/)

CIA Factbook (www.cia.gov/cia/publications/factbook/index.html)

Database of Political Institutions (DPI): Data are available at: (go.worldbank.org/2EAGGLRZ40)

Election Guide (www.electionguide.org/)

Election World (www.electionworld.org)

ACE Electoral Knowledge Network (www.aceproject.org/)

Freedom House, *Freedom in the World Comparative Rankings* (www.Freedomhouse.org)

IDEA International – Electoral System Design (www.idea.int/esd/index.cfm)

IDEA International – Voter Turnout (www.idea.int/vt/index.cfm)

Inter-Parliamentary Union (www.ipu.org/english/home.htm)

McDonald, Michael, Silvia Mendes. *Parties in Parliaments and Governments: Codebook 2002.* Unpublished manuscript, SUNY Binghamton.

Polity IV Project (www.cidcm.umd.edu/inscr/polity/)

Project on Political Transformation and the Electoral Process in Post-Communist Europe, University of Essex (www.essex.ac.uk/elections/)

United National Development Program (www.undp.org)

Wikipedia Elections (en.wikipedia.org/wiki/List_of_election_results)

World Bank Indicators. Data are available at: (go.worldbank.org/RVW6YTLQH0)

Notes

* Bargsted's acknowledgment: Many people have given invaluable help to collect all the information available in this dataset. Matt Golder, whose dataset for Module I countries provided one of the most important sources for these data; Dave Howell, whom I thank for giving me great advice; and CSES staff members, Angela Pok and Bojan Todosijevic, for much help. Obviously, they are not responsible for any error or omission in the present data file.

1. www.cses.org

2. There are three special cases: (*a*) Chile's 1999 score was calculated considering congressional elections from 1997, (*b*) Russia's 2000 score was calculated considering congressional election from 1999, (*c*) Russia's 2004 score was calculated considering congressional election from 2003. In all three cases, the election corresponding to the election study was only presidential, so to avoid losing data, the index was estimated with information from the previous legislative election.

Bibliography

Aardal, Brendt and P. van Wijnen (2005). Issue voting. In Jacques Thomassen, ed., *The European Voter: A Comparative Study of Modern Democracies*. Oxford: Oxford University Press.

Aarts, Kees and Bernard Wessels (2005). Electoral turnout. In Jacques Thomassen, ed., *The European Voter: A Comparative Study of Modern Democracies*. Oxford: Oxford University Press.

—— and Jacques Thomassen (2008). Satisfaction with democracy: Do institutions matter? *Electoral Studies* 27: 5–18.

—— André Blais, and Hermann Schmitt, eds. (2010). *Political Leaders and Democratic Elections*. Oxford: Oxford University Press.

—— André Blais, and Hermann Schmitt, (ed.) (forthcoming). *Political Leaders and Democratic Elections*. Oxford: Oxford University Press.

Abramson, Paul, John Aldrich, and David Rohde (2005). *Change and Continuity in the 2004 Elections*. Washington, DC: CQ Press.

—— —— Phil Paolino, and David Rohde (1992). "Sophisticated" voting in the 1988 presidential primaries. *American Political Science Review* 88: 55–69.

—— —— André Blais et al. (2010). Comparing strategic voting under FPTP and PR systems. *Comparative Political Studies* 43: 61–90.

—— —— —— et al. (forthcoming). Comparing strategic voting under FPTP and PR systems. *Comparative Political Studies* 43: 61–90.

Achen, Christopher (1992). Social psychology, demographic variables, and linear regression: Breaking the iron triangle in voting research. *Political Behavior* 14: 195–211.

—— (2005). Two-step hierarchical estimation: Beyond regression analysis. *Political Analysis* 13: 447–56.

Adams, James (2001). A theory of spatial competition with biased voters: Party policies viewed temporally and comparatively. *British Journal of Political Science* 31: 121–58.

—— Samuel Merrill III, and Bernard Grofman (2005). *A Unified Theory of Party Competition*. New York: Cambridge University Press.

Albright, Jeremy (2007). Estimating multilvel models using SPSS, Stata, and SAS (www.indiana.edu/statmath/stat/all/hlm/hlm.pdf).

Aldrich, John, André Blais, Indridi Indridason, and Renan Levine (2005). Coalition considerations and the vote. In Asher Arian and Michal Shamir, eds., *The Elections in Israel–2003*. New Brunswick: Transaction Press.

Almond, Gabriel and Sidney Verba (1965). *The Civic Culture: Political Attitudes and Democracy in Five Nations*. New York: Little, Brown and Company.

Alvarez, Michael, Frederick Boehmke, and Jonathan Nagler (2006). Strategic voting in British elections. *Electoral Studies* 25: 1–19.

Ames, Barry, Andy Baker, and Lucio Renno (2009). Split-ticket voting as the rule: Voters and permanent divided government in Brazil. *Electoral Studies* 28: 8–20.

Anderson, Cameron (2006). Economic voting and multilevel governance: A comparative individual-level analysis. *American Journal of Political Science* 50: 449–63.

Anderson, Christopher J. (1995a). *Blaming the Government: Citizens and the Economy in Five European Democracies*. Armonk, NY: M.E.Sharpe.

—— (1995b). Party systems and the dynamics of government support: Britain and Germany, 1960–1990. *European Journal of Political Research* 27: 93–118.

—— (1998). Party systems and satisfaction with democracy in the new Europe. *Political Studies* 46: 572–88.

—— (2000). Economic voting and political context: A comparative perspective. *Electoral Studies* 19: 151–70.

—— (2007a). The interaction of structures and voter behavior. In Russell Dalton and Hans-Dieter Klingemann, eds., *Oxford Handbook of Political Behavior*. New York: Oxford University Press.

—— (2007b). The end of economic voting? Contingency dilemmas and the limits of democratic accountability. *Annual Review of Political Science* 10: 271–96.

—— (2009). Nested citizens: Macropolitics and microbehavior in comparative politics. In Mark Lichbach and Alan Zuckerman, eds., *Comparative Politics: Rationality, Culture, and Structure*. New York: Cambridge University Press.

—— and Christine Guillory (1997). Political institutions and satisfaction with democracy: A cross-national analysis of consensus and majoritarian systems. *American Political Science Review* 91: 66–81.

—— and Carsten Zelle, eds. (1998). *Stability and Change in German Elections: How Electorates Merge, Converge, or Collide*. Westport, CT: Praeger.

—— and Frank Brettschneider (2003). The likable winner v. the competent loser: Candidate images and the German election of 2002. *German Politics and Society* 21(1): 95–118.

—— and Yuliya Tverdova (2003). Corruption, political allegiances, and attitudes toward government in contemporary democracies. *American Journal of Political Science* 47: 91–109.

Andersen, Robert and Geoffrey Evans (2003). Who Blairs wins? Leadership and voting in the 2001 election. *Journal of Elections, Public Opinion and Parties* 13: 229–47.

Arceneaux, Kevin and David Nickerson (2009). Modeling certainty with clustered data: A comparison of methods. *Political Analysis* 17: 177–90.

Arian, Asher and Michal Shamir (2001). Candidates, parties and blocs: Israel in the 1990s. *Party Politics* 7: 689–710.

Arrow, Kenneth (1951). *Social Choice and Individual Values*. New York: Wiley.

Bafumi, Joseph and Robert Shapiro (2009). A new partisan voter. *Journal of Politics* 71: 1–24.

Banducci, Susan and Jeffrey Karp (2003). How elections change the way citizens view the political system: Campaigns, media effects, and electoral outcomes in comparative perspective. *British Journal of Political Science* 33: 443–67.

Balch, George I. (1974). Multiple indicators in survey research: The concept of "sense of political efficacy". *Political Methodology* 1(1): 1–43.

—— and Jeffrey Karp (2009). Electoral systems, efficacy, and voter turnout. In Hans-Dieter Klingemann, ed., *The Comparative Study of Electoral Systems*. New York: Oxford University Press.

Bargsted, Matias (2007). *Codebook Complementary Macro Level Data for CSES Module 1 and 2 Countries* (July 2007 edition) (www.cses.org).

—— and Orit Kedar (2009). Coalition-targeted Dugergerian voting: How expectations affect voter choice under proportional representation. *American Journal of Political Science* 53: 307–23.

Barnes, Samuel, M. Kent Jennings, Ronald Inglehart, and Barbara Farah (1988). Party identification and party closeness in comparative perspective. *Political Behavior* 10: 215–31.

Bartels, Larry (2000). Partisanship and voting behavior, 1952–1996. *American Journal of Political Science* 44: 35–50.

—— (2002). The impact of candidate traits in American presidential elections. In Anthony King, ed., *Leaders' Personalities and the Outcomes of Democratic Elections*. Oxford: Oxford University Press.

Bartle, John (2003). Partisanship, performance and personality: Competing and complementary characterizations of the 2001 British general election. *Party Politics* 9: 317–45.

—— and Ivor Crewe (2002). The impact of party leaders in Britain: Strong assumptions, weak evidence. In Anthony King, ed., *Leaders' Personalities and the Outcomes of Democratic Elections*. Oxford: Oxford University Press.

Bean, Clive (1993). The electoral influence of party leader images in Australia and New Zealand. *Comparative Political Studies* 26: 111–32.

—— (2003). "Leadership and Voting: The Connection at the State Level." *Australian Journal of Political Science* 38: 465–78.

—— and Anthony Mughan (1989). Leadership effects in parliamentary elections in Australia and Britain, *American Political Science Review* 83: 1165–79.

Beck, Paul (2002). Encouraging political defection: The role of personal discussion networks in partisan desertions to the opposition party and Perot votes in 1992. *Political Behavior* 24: 309–37.

—— et al. (2004). The social calculus of voting: Interpersonal, media and organizational influences on presidential choices. *American Political Science Review* 96: 57–73.

Beck, Thorsten, George Clarke, Alberto Groff, Philip Keefer, and Patrick Walsh (2001). New tools in comparative political economy: The database of political institutions. *World Bank Economic Review* 15: 165–76.

Béland, Daniel (2007). Insecurity and politics: A framework, *Canadian Journal of Sociology* 32: 317–40.

Bélanger, P., Ken Carty, Monroe Eagles (2003). The geography of Canadian parties' electoral campaigns: Leaders' tours and constituency election results. *Political Geography* 22: 439–55.

Benoit, Kenneth and Michael Laver (2006). *Party Policy in Modern Democracies*. New York: Routledge.

Biezen, Ingrid van (2003). *Political Parties in New Democracies*. London: Palgrave.

Black, Duncan (1948). On the rationale of group decision making. *Journal of Political Economy* 56: 23–34.

Black, Duncan (1958). *The Theory of Committees and Elections*. Cambridge: Cambridge University Press.

Black, Jerome (1978). The multicandidate calculus of voting: Application to Canadian federal elections. *American Journal of Political Science* 22: 639–55.

Blais, André (2000). *To Vote Or Not To Vote? The Merits and Limits of Rational Choice Theory*. Pittsburgh, PA: University of Pittsburgh Press.

—— (2002). Why is there so little strategic voting in Canadian plurality rule elections? *Political Studies* 50: 445–54.

—— (2004). Y a-t-il un vote stratégique en France? In Bruno Cautres and Nonna Mayer, eds., *Le nouveau désordre electoral*. Paris: Fondation nationale des sciences politiques.

—— (2006). What affects turnout? *Annual Review of Political Science* 9: 111–25.

—— and R. K. Carty (1991). The psychological impact of electoral laws: Measuring Duverger's elusive factor. *British Journal of Political Science* 21: 79–93.

—— and Richard Nadeau (1996). Measuring strategic voting: A two-step procedure. *Electoral Studies* 15: 39–52.

—— and Agnieszka Dobrzynska (1998). Turnout in electoral democracies. *European Journal of Political Research* 33: 239–61.

—— and Marc André Bodet (2006). Does proportional representation foster closer congruence between citizens and policy makers? *Comparative Political Studies* 39: 1243–62.

—— and François Gélineau (2007). Winning, losing, and satisfaction with democracy. *Political Studies* 55: 425–41.

—— Peter Loewen, and Marc André Bodet (2004). Strategic voting. In J. Vowles, P. Aimer, S. Banducci, J. Karp, and R. Miller, eds., *Voters' Veto: The 2002 Election and the Consolidation of Minority Government*. Auckland: Auckland University Press.

—— Eugénie Dostie-Goulet, and Marc André Bodet (2009). Voting strategically in Canada and Britain. In Bernard Grofman, André Blais, and Shaun Bowler, eds., *Duverger's Law of Party Competition in Canada, India, the United Kingdom and the United States*. New York: Springer.

—— John Aldrich, Indridi Indridason, and Renan Levine (2006). Do voters care about government coalitions? *Party Politics* 12: 691–705.

—— Richard Nadeau, Elisabeth Gidengil, and Neil Nevitte (2001). Measuring strategic voting in multiparty plurality elections. *Electoral Studies* 20: 343–52.

—— E. Gidengil, R. Nadeau, and N. Nevitte (2002). *Anatomy of a Liberal Victory: Making Sense of the Vote in the 2000 Canadian Election*. Peterborough: Broadview Press.

—— —— Agnieszka Dobrzynska, Neil Nevitte, and Richard Nadeau (2003). Does the local candidate matter? *Canadian Journal of Political Science* 36: 657–64.

—— Mathieu Turgeon, Elisabeth Gidengil, Neil Nevitte, and Richard Nadeau (2004). Which matters most? Comparing the impact of issues and the economy in American, British, and Canadian elections. *British Journal of Political Science* 34: 555–64.

Blondel, Jean and Maurizio Cotta, eds. (2001). *The Nature of Party Government: A Comparative European Perspective*. London: Palgrave Macmillan.

Booth, John and Mitchell Seligson (2009). *The Legitimacy Puzzle in Latin America: Political Support and Democracy in Eight Nations*. New York: Cambridge University Press.

Bowler, Shaun, David Lanoue, and Paul Savoie (1994). Electoral systems, party competition, and strength of partisan attachment: Evidence from three countries. *Journal of Politics* 56: 991–1007.

Brader, Ted and Joshua Tucker (2008). Pathways to partisanship: Evidence from Russia. *Post-Soviet Affairs* 24: 263–300.

Brady, Henry (1985). The perils of survey research: Interpersonally incomparable responses. *Political Methodology* 11: 269–90.

Brockington, David (2004). The paradox of proportional representation: The effect of party systems and coalitions on individuals' electoral participation. *Political Studies* 52: 469–90.

—— (2009). Its about the benefits: Choice environments, ideological proximity and individual participation in 28 countries. *Party Politics* 15(4): 435–54.

Brown, Steven, Ronald Lambert, Barry Kay, and James Curtis (1988). In the eye of the beholder: Leader images in Canada. *Canadian Journal of Political Science* 21: 729–55.

—— Cees van der Eijk, and Mark Franklin (2007). *The Economy and the Vote: Economic Conditions and Elections in Fifteen Countries*. New York: Cambridge University Press.

Bryk, Anthony and Stephen W. Raudenbusch (1992). *Hierarchical Linear Models*. Newbury Park, CA: Sage Publications.

Budge, Ian, Ivor Crewe, and Dennis Farlie (1976). *Party Identification and Beyond*. London and New York: Wiley.

—— Hans-Dieter Klingemann, Andrea Volkens, J. Bara, and E. Tanenbaum (2001). *Mapping Policy Preferences*. New York: Oxford University Press.

Burden, Barry (2005). Minor parties and strategic voting in recent U.S. presidential elections. *Electoral Studies* 24: 603–18.

Cain, Bruce (1978). Strategic voting in Britain. *American Journal of Political Science* 22: 639–55.

—— John Ferejohn, and Morris Fiorina (1987). *The Personal Vote: Constituency Service and Electoral Independence*. Cambridge, MA: Harvard University Press.

Campbell, Angus, Gerald Gurin, and Warren E. Miller (1954). *The Voter Decides*. Evanston, IL: Row, Peterson.

—— Philip Converse, Warren Miller, and Donald Stokes (1960). *The American Voter*. New York: Wiley.

—— —— —— —— (1966). *Elections and the Political Order*. New York: Wiley.

Campus, Donatella (2002). Leaders, dreams and journeys: Italy's new political communication. *Journal of Modern Italian Studies* 7: 171–91.

Caplan, Bryan (2007). *The Myth of the Rational Voter: Why Democracies Choose Bad Policies*. Princeton, NJ: Princeton University Press.

Carey, John and Matthew Shugart (1995). Incentives to cultivate a personal vote. *Electoral Studies* 14: 417–39.

Carter, Elisabeth and David Farrell (2010). Electoral systems and electoral management. In Larry LeDuc, Richard Niemi, and Pippa Norris, eds., *Comparing Democracies 3*. London: Sage.

Caul, Miki and Mark Gray (2000). From platform declarations to policy outcomes. In Russell Dalton and Martin Wattenberg, eds., *Parties Without Partisans*. Oxford: Oxford University Press.

Clark, William and Matt Golder (2006). Rehabilitating Duverger's theory: Testing the mechanical and strategic modifying effects of electoral laws. *Comparative Political Studies* 39: 679–708.

Clarke, Harold and Alan Acock (1989). National elections and political attitudes: The case of political efficacy. *British Journal of Political Science* 19: 551–62.

—— Nitish Dutt, and Allan Kornberg (1993). The political economy of attitudes toward polity and society in Western European countries. *Journal of Politics* 55: 998–1021.

Clarke, Harold et al. (2008). *Performance Politics: The British Voter*. New York: Cambridge University Press.

Colomer, Joseph (2001). *Political Institutions*. New York: Oxford University Press.

Colton, Timothy (2002). The leadership factor in the Russian presidential election of 1996. In Anthony King, ed., *Leaders' Personalities and the Outcomes of Democratic Elections*. Oxford: Oxford University Press.

Conrad, Courtenay Ryals and Sona Golder (2010). Measuring government duration and stability in central Eastern European democracies. *European Journal of Political Research* 49: 119–50.

Converse, Philip (1964). The nature of belief systems in mass publics. In David Apter, ed., *Ideology and Discontent*. New York: Free Press.

—— (2000). Assessing the capacity of mass electorates. *Annual Review of Political Science* 3: 331–53.

Cox, Gary (1990). Centripetal and centrifugal incentives under alternative voting institutions. *American Journal of Political Science* 34: 903–35.

—— (1997). *Making Votes Count: Strategic Coordination in the World's Electoral Systems*. Cambridge: Cambridge University Press.

—— (1999). Electoral rules and the calculus of mobilization. *Legislative Studies Quarterly* 24(3): 387–420.

—— and Matthew Soberg Shugart (1996). Strategic voting under proportional representation. *Journal of Law, Economics, and Organization* 12: 299–324.

Craig, Stephen, Michael Martinez, Jason Gainous, and James Kane (2006). Winners, losers, and election context: Voter responses to the 2000 presidential election. *Political Research Quarterly* 59: 579–92.

Criado, Henar and Francisco Herreros (2007). Political support: Taking into account the institutional context. *Comparative Political Studies* 40: 1511–32.

Curtice, John and André Blais (2001). Follow my leader? A cross-national analysis of leadership effects in parliamentary democracies. Paper presented at the American Political Science Association annual meeting, August 30–September 2, San Francisco.

—— and Sarinder Hunjan (2006). The impact of leadership evaluations on voting behaviours: Do the rules matter? Centre for Research into Elections and Social Trends (CREST) working paper No. 110.

Dahl, Robert (1989). *Democracy and Its Critics*. New Haven, CT: Yale University Press.

—— (1998). *On Democracy*. New Haven, CT: Yale University Press.

—— (2002). *How Democratic is the American Constitution?* New Haven, CT: Yale University Press.

Dalton, Russell (2004). *Democratic Challenges, Democratic Choices. The Erosion of Political Support in Advanced Industrial Democracies*. New York: Oxford University Press.

—— (2006). Social modernization and the end of ideology debate: Patterns of ideological polarization. *Japanese Journal of Political Science* 7: 1–22.

274

Dalton, Russell (2008*a*). *Citizen Politics: Public Opinion and Political Parties in Advanced Industrial Democracies*. Washington, DC: CQ Press.

—— (2008*b*). The quantity and quality of party systems. *Comparative Political Studies* 41: 899–920.

—— (2009). Ideology, partisanship and democratic development. In Larry Leduc, Richard Niemi, and Pippa Norris, eds., *Comparing Democracies III*. Newbury Park, CA: Sage Publications.

—— and Martin Wattenberg, eds. (2000). *Parties Without Partisan: Political Change in Advanced Industrial Democracies*. Oxford: Oxford University Press.

—— and Steven Weldon (2007). Partisanship and party system institutionalization. *Party Politics* 13: 179–96.

—— Scott Flanagan, and Paul Beck, eds. (1984). *Electoral Change in Advanced Industrial Democratices*. Princeton, NJ: Princeton University Press.

—— David Farrell, and Ian McAllister (forthcoming 2011). *Political Parties and Democratic Linkage*. Oxford: Oxford University Press.

Dawes, Christopher and James Fowler (2009). Partisanship, voting, and the dopamine D2 receptor gene. *Journal of Politics* 71: 1157–71.

Delli Carpini, Michael and Scott Keeter (1996). *What Americans Know About Politics and Why It Matters*. New Haven, CT: Yale University Press.

Dennis, Jack (1966). Support for the party system by the mass public. *American Political Science Review* 60: 600–15.

Dinas, Elias (2005). Was it Karamanlis who won it or Papandreou who lost it? The impact of leaders' image in the 2004 Greek election. The 2nd Hellenic Observatory PhD Symposium on Modern Greece: "Current Social Science Research on Greece." London School of Economics.

Downs, Anthony (1957). *An Economic Theory of Democracy*. New York: Harper.

Duch, Raymond and Harvey Palmer (2002). Strategic voting in post-communist democracy? *British Journal of Political Science* 32: 63–91.

—— and Randolph Stevenson (2008). *The Economic Vote: How Political and Economic Institutions Condition Election Results*. Cambridge: Cambridge University Press.

Duverger, Maurice (1951). *Les Partis Politiques*. Paris: Armand Colin.

—— (1954). *Political Parties: Their Organization and Activity in the ModernState* (North B, North R., trans.). New York: John Wiley.

Easton, David (1965). *A Systems Analysis of Political Life*. New York: John Wiley and Sons.

Eijk, Cees van der and Mark Franklin (1996). *Choosing Europe? The European Electorate and National Politics in the Face of Union*. Ann Arbor, MI: University of Michigan Press.

—— Mark Franklin, and Michael Marsh (1996). What voters teach us about Europe-wide elections: What Europe-wide elections teach us about voters. *Electoral Studies* 15: 149–66.

—— Hermann Schmitt, and J. Binder (2005). Left-Right orientations and party choice. In Jacques Thomassen, ed., *The European Voter: A Comparative Study of Modern Democracies*. Oxford: Oxford University Press.

Elff, Martin (2008). Social divisions, political sophistication, and political equality in comparative perspective. Paper delivered at the annual meetings of the American Political Science Association.

Ensley, Michael (2007). Candidate divergence, idology and vote choice in the U.S. Senate elections. *American Politics Research* 35: 103–22.

Erikson, Robert, Michael MacKuen, and James Stimson (2001). *The Macro Polity.* New York: Cambridge University Press.

Evans, Geoffrey and Robert Andersen (2005). The impact of party leaders: How Blair lost Labour votes, *Parliamentary Affairs* 58: 818–36.

—— —— (2006). The political conditioning of economic perceptions. *Journal of Politics* 68: 194–207.

Ezrow, Lawrence (2007). The variance matters: How party systems represent the preferences of voters. *Journal of Politics* 69: 182–92.

Farrell, David (2001). *Electoral Systems: A Comparative Introduction.* London: Palgrave MacMillan.

—— (2010). Reforming the electoral system is not going to be enough. *Irish Times* February 1.

—— and Ian McAllister (2006). *The Australian Electoral System: Origins, Variations and Consequences.* Sydney: University of New South Wales Press.

Fearon, James (1999). Electoral accountability and the control of politicians: Selecting good types versus sanctioning poor performance. In Adam Przeworski, Bernard Manin, and Susan Stokes, eds., *Democracy, Accountability, and Representation.* New York: Cambridge University Press.

Finkel, Steven (1987). The effects of participation on political efficacy and political support. *Journal of Politics* 49: 441–64.

—— Edward Muller, and Mitchell Seligson (1989). Economic crisis, incumbent performance and regime support: A comparison of longitudinal data from West Germany and Costa Rica. *British Journal of Political Science* 19: 329–51.

Fiorina, Morris (1981). *Retrospective Voting in American National Elections.* New Haven, CT: Yale University Press.

Fowler, James and Oleg Smirnov (2007). *Mandates, Parties, and Voters: How Elections Shape the Future.* Philadelphia, PA: Temple University Press.

Franklin, Mark (2002). The dynamics of electoral participation. In Laurence LeDuc, Richard Niemi, and Pippa Norris, eds., *Comparing Democracies 2: New Challenges in the Study of Elections and Voting.* London: Sage.

—— (2004). *Voter Turnout and the Dynamics of Electoral Competition in Established Democracies Since 1945.* Cambridge: Cambridge University Press.

—— Tom Mackie, and Henry Valen, eds. (1992). *Electoral Change.* New York: Cambridge University Press.

Fuchs, Dieter and Hans-Dieter Klingemann (1989). The Left–Right schema. In M. Kent Jennings and Jan van Deth, eds., *Continuities in Political Action.* Berlin: de Gruyter.

—— Giovanna Guidorossi, and Palle Svensson (1995). Support for the democratic system. In Hans-Dieter Klingemann and Dieter Fuchs, eds., *Citizens and the State.* New York: Oxford University Press.

Gabel, Matthew and John Huber (2000). Putting parties in their place. *American Journal of Political Science* 44: 94–103.

Gallagher, Michael (1991). Proportionality, disproportionality, and electoral systems. *Electoral Studies* 10: 33–51.

Gallego, Aina (2007). Inequality in political participation: Contemporary patterns in European countries. Center for the Study of Democracy, paper 07-01 (http://reposi-tories.cdlib.org/csd).

Gelman, Andrew, and Jennifer Hill (2007). *Data Analysis Using Regression and Multilevel/ Hierarchical Models*. Cambridge: Cambridge University Press.

Geys, Benny (2006). Explaining voter turnout: A review of aggregate-level research. *Electoral Studies* 25: 637–63.

Gibbard, Allan (1973). Manipulation of voting schemes: A general result. *Econometrica* 41: 587–601.

Ginsberg, Benjamin (1982). *The Consequences of Consent: Elections, Citizen Control, and Popular Acquiescence*. New York: Random House.

—— and Robert Weissberg (1978). Elections and the mobilization of popular support. *American Journal of Political Science* 22: 31–55.

Glass, David (1985). Evaluating presidential candidates: Who focuses on their personal attributes? *Public Opinion Quarterly* 49: 517–34.

Golder, Matthew (2005). Democratic electoral systems around the world, 1946–2000. *Electoral Studies* 24: 103–21.

—— and Jacek Stramski (2010). Ideological congruence and electoral institutions. *American Journal of Political Science* 54: 90–106.

Golder, Sona (2006). *The Logic of Pre-Electoral Coalition Formation*. Columbus, OH: The Ohio State University Press.

Gomez, Brad and J. Matthew Wilson (2001). Political sophistication and economic voting in the American electorate: A theory of heterogeneous attribution. *American Journal of Political Science* 45: 899–914.

Gordon, Stacy and Gary Segura (1997). Cross-national variation in the political sophisti-cation of individuals: Capability or choice? *Journal of Politics* 59: 126–47.

Graetz, Brian and Ian McAllister (1987). Party leaders and election outcomes in Britain, 1974–1983. *Comparative Political Studies* 19: 484–507.

Gray, Mark and Miki Caul (2000). Declining voter turnout in advanced industrial democ-racies, 1950 to 1997: The effects of declining group mobilization. *Comparative Political Studies* 33: 1091–122.

Green, Donald, Bradley Palmquist, and Erik Schikler (2002). *Partisan Hearts and Minds: Political Parties and the Social Identities of Voters*. New Haven, CT: Yale University Press.

Grofman, Bernard (2004). Downs and two-party convergence. *Annual Review of Political Science* 7: 25–46.

—— André Blais, and Shaun Bowler (2009). Introduction: Evidence for Duverger's Law from four countries. In Bernard Grofman, André Blais, and Shaun Bowler, eds., *Duver-ger's Law of Plurality Voting: The Logic of Party Competition in Canada, India, the United Kingdom and the United States*. New York: Springer.

—— Arend Lijphart, et al. (1986). *Electoral Laws and Their Political Consequences*. New York: Agathon Press.

Gross, Donald and Lee Sigelman (1984). Comparing party systems: A multidimensional approach. *Comparative Politics* 16: 463–79.

Gschwend, Thomas (2004). *Strategic Voting in Mixed Electoral Systems*. Reutlingen: SFG-Elsevier.

Gschwend, Thomas (2007*a*). Ticket-splitting and strategic voting under mixed electoral rules: Evidence from Germany. *European Journal of Political Research* 46: 1–23.

—— (2007*b*). Institutional incentives for strategic voting and party system change in Portugal. *Portuguese Journal of Social Science* 6: 15–31.

—— (2009). District magnitude and the comparative study of strategic voting. In Hans-Dieter Klingemann, ed., *The Comparative Study of Electoral Systems*. Oxford: Oxford University Press.

—— and Dirk Leuffen (2005). Divided we stand – unified we govern? The issue of cohabitation in the French elections of 2002. *British Journal of Political Science* 35: 691–712.

Gunther, Richard, Hans-Jürgen Puhle, and José Ramón Montero, eds. (2007). *Democracy, Intermediation, and Voting on Four Continents*. Oxford: Oxford University Press.

Hardin, Russell (2009). *How Do You Know? The Economics of Ordinary Knowledge*. Princeton, NJ: Princeton University Press.

Harmel, Robert and John Robertson (1986). Government stability and regime support: A cross-national analysis. *Journal of Politics* 48: 1029–40.

Hellwig, Timothy (2008). Explaining the salience of left-right ideological in postindustrial democracies. *European Journal of Political Research* 47: 687–709.

—— (2010). Elections and the economy. In Larry LeDuc, Richard Niemi, and Pippa Norris, eds., *Comparing Democracies 3*. Thousand Oaks, CA: Sage.

—— and David Samuels (2008). Electoral accountability and the variety of democratic regimes. *British Journal of Political Science* 38: 65–90.

Henderson, Ailsa (2008). Satisfaction with democracy: The impact of winning and losing in Westminster systems. *Journal of Elections, Public Opinion & Parties* 18(1): 3–26.

Hermens, F. A. (1936). Proportional representation and the breakdown of German democracy. *Social Research* 3: 411–33.

Hetherington, Marc (1998). The political relevance of political trust. *American Political Science Review* 92: 791–807.

—— (2001). Resurgent mass partisanship: The role of elite polarization. *American Political Science Review* 95: 619–31.

Holmberg, Sören (2003). Are political parties necessary? *Electoral Studies* 22: 287–99.

Huber, John and Ronald Inglehart (1995). Expert interpretations of party space and party locations in 42 societies. *Party Politics* 1: 73–111.

—— and G. Bingham Powell (1994). Congruence between citizens and policymakers in two visions of liberal democracy. *World Politics* 46: 291–326.

—— Georgia Kernell, and Eduardo Leoni (2005). Institutional context, cognitive resources, and party attachments across democracies. *Political Analysis* 13: 365–86.

Huckfeldt, Robert (1986). *Politics in Context: Assimilation and Conflict in Urban Neighborhoods*. New York: Agathon Press.

—— (2009). Citizenship in democratic politics: Density dependence and the micro–macro divide. In Mark Irving Lichbach and Alan S. Zuckerman, eds., *Comparative Politics: Rationality, Culture, and Structure*. New York: Cambridge University Press.

—— and John Sprague (1987). Networks in context: The social flow of political information *American Political Science Review* 81: 1197–216.

—— —— (1992). Political parties and electoral mobilization: Political structure, social structure, and the party canvass. *American Political Science Review* 86: 70–86.

Inglehart, Ronald (1990). *Culture Shift in Advanced Industrial Society.* Princeton, NJ: Princeton University Press.

—— and H. Klingemann (1976). Party identification, ideological preference and the Left–Right dimension among Western mass publics. In Ian Budge, David Crewe, and John Farlie, ed., *Party Identification and Beyond.* London: Wiley.

Iyengar, Sheena and Mark Lepper (2000). When choice is demotivating: Can one desire too much of a good thing? *Journal of Personality and Social Psychology* 79: 995–1006.

Jackman, Robert (1987). Political institutions and voter turnout in industrial democracies. *American Political Science Review* 81: 405–23.

—— and Ross Miller (1995). Voter turnout in the industrial democracies during the 1980s. *Comparative Political Studies* 27: 467–92.

Janda, Kenneth (1993). Comparative political parties: Research and theory. In Ada Finifter, ed., *Political Science: The State of the Discipline II.* Washington, DC: American Political Science Association.

Johnston, Richard (2002). Prime ministerial contenders in Canada. In Anthony King, ed., *Leaders' Personalities and the Outcomes of Democratic Elections.* Oxford: Oxford University Press.

Jouvenel, Bertrand de (1961). A seminar exercise: The chairman's problem. *American Political Science Review* 55: 368–72.

Jusko, Karen Long and W. Phillips Shively (2005). Applying a two-step strategy to the analysis of cross-national public opinion data. *Political Analysis* 13: 327–44.

Karp, Jeffrey and Shaun Bowler (2001). Coalition politics and satisfaction with democracy: Explaining New Zealand's reaction to proportional representation. *European Journal of Political Research* 40: 57–79.

—— and Susan Banducci (2007). Party mobilization and political participation in new and old democracies. *Party Politics* 13: 217–34.

—— —— (2008). Political efficacy and participation in twenty-seven democracies: How electoral systems shape political behavior. *British Journal of Political Science* 38: 311–34.

—— Shaun Bowler, and Susan A. Banducci (2003). Electoral systems, party mobilization, and turnout: Evidence from the European parliamentary elections. *British Elections and Parties Review*, Vol. 13. London: Frank Cass Publishers, 210–28.

—— —— and Shaun Bowler (2008). Getting out the vote: Party mobilization in a comparative perspective. *British Journal of Political Science* 38: 91–112.

—— Jack Vowles, Susan Banducci, and Todd Donovan (2002). Strategic voting, party activity and candidate effects: Testing explanations for split voting in New Zealand's new mixed system. *Electoral Studies* 12: 1–22.

Karvonen, Lauri (2007). The personalization of politics: What does research tell us so far, and what further research is in order? Paper presented at the European Consortium of Political Research conference, September 6–8, Pisa.

Katosh, John and Michael Traugott (1982). Costs and values in the calculus of voting. *American Journal of Political Science* 26: 361–76.

Katz, Richard (1995). *Democracy and Elections.* New York: Oxford University Press.

—— (2005). So many (or so few) electoral reforms? In Michael Gallagher and Paul Mitchell, eds., *Politics of Electoral Systems.* Oxford: Oxford University Press.

Katz, Richard and Bernhard Wessels, eds. (1999). *The European Parliament, National Parliaments, and European Integration*. Oxford: Oxford University Press.

Kayser, Mark Andreas and Christopher Wlezien (forthcoming). Performance pressure: Patterns of partisanship and the economic vote. *European Journal of Political Research*.

Kedar, Orit (2005). When moderate voters prefer extreme parties: Policy balancing in parliamentary elections. *American Political Science Review* 99: 185–99.

—— and W. Philips Shively (2005). Introduction to the Special Issue. *Political Analysis* 13: 297–300.

Keefer, Philip (2005). DPI2004 Database of Political Institutions: Changes and Variable Definitions. *World Bank* (http://siteresources.worldbank.org/INTRES/Resources/DPI2004_variable-definitions.pdf).

Kernell, Samuel (1977). Presidential popularity and negative voting: An alternative explanation of the midterm congressional decline of the president's party. *American Political Science Review* 71: 44–66.

Key, V. O. (1966). *The Responsible Electorate*. New York: Vintage.

Kim, HeeMin and Richard C. Fording (1998). Voter ideology in Western democracies. *European Journal of Political Research* 33: 73–97.

—— —— (2002). Government partisanship in Western democracies, 1945–1998. *European Journal of Political Research* 41: 187–206.

—— —— (2003). Voter ideology in Western democracies: An update. *European Journal of Political Research*.

—— and Michael McDonald (2009). On observing the variety of party policy offerings in national Left–Right policy space. Paper presented at the annual meetings of the Midwest Political Science Association, Chicago, IL.

—— G. Bingham Powell, and Richard Fording (2010). Party systems and substantive representation. *Comparative Politics* 43.

King, Anthony (2002*a*). Do leaders' personalities really matter? In Anthony King, ed., *Leaders' Personalities and the Outcomes of Democratic Elections*. Oxford: Oxford University Press.

—— (2002*b*). Conclusions and implications. In Anthony King, ed., *Leaders' Personalities and the Outcomes of Democratic Elections*. Oxford: Oxford University Press.

Klingemann, Hans-Dieter (1999). Mapping political support in the 1990s: A global analysis. In Pippa Norris, ed., *Critical Citizens: Global Support for Democratic Governance*. New York: Oxford University Press.

—— (2005). Political parties and party systems. In Jacques Thomassen, ed., *The European Voter: A Comparative Study of Modern Democracies*. Oxford: Oxford University Press.

—— ed. (2009). *The Comparative Study of Electoral Sytems*. Oxford: Oxford University Press.

—— and Bernard Wessels (2009). How voters cope with the complexity of their environment. In H. Klingemann, ed., *The Comparative Study of Electoral Systems*. Oxford: Oxford University Press.

—— Andrea Volkens, J. Bara, Ian Budge, and Michael McDonald (2006). *Mapping Policy Preferences II*. New York: Oxford University Press.

Knutsen, Oddborn (1998). Expert judgments of the Left–Right location of political parties: A comparative longitudinal study. *West European Politics* 21: 63–94.

—— (1999). Left–Right party polarization among the mass publics. In H. Narud and T. Aalberg, eds., *Challenges to Representative Democracy*. Bergen: Fagbokforlaget.

Kostadinova, Tatiana (2003). Voter turnout dynamics in post-Communist Europe. *European Journal of Political Research* 42: 741–59.

Kreuzer, Marcus (2001). *Institutions and Innovation: Voters, Parties, and Interest Groups in the Consolidation of Democracy, France and Germany, 1870–1939.* Ann Arbor, MI: University of Michigan Press.

Kroh, Martin (2003). *Parties, Politicians, and Policies: Orientations of Vote Choice across Voters and Contexts.* Amsterdam: Universiteit van Amsterdam (Academisch Proefschrift).

—— (2009). The ease of ideological voting: Voter sophistication and party system complexity. In Hans-Dieter Klingemann, ed., *The Comparative Study of Electoral Systems.* Oxford: Oxford University Press.

Kuklinski, James and Buddy Peyton (2007). Belief systems and political decision making. In Russell Dalton and Hans-Dieter Klingemann, eds., *The Oxford Handbook of Political Behavior.* Oxford: Oxford University Press.

Laakso, Markku and Rein Taagepera (1979). Effective number of parties: A measure with application to West Europe. *Comparative Political Studies* 12: 3–27.

Lachat, Romain (2008). The impact of party polarization on ideological voting. *Electoral Studies* 27: 687–98.

Ladd, Jonathan and Gabriel Lenz (2008). Reassessing the role of anxiety in vote choice, *Political Psychology* 29: 275–96.

Lago, Ignacio (2008). Rational expectations or heuristics? *Party Politics* 14: 31–49.

Lane, Jan-Erik and Svante Ersson (1991). *Politics and Society in Western Europe.* 2nd edn. London: Sage.

Lane, Robert (1959). *Political Life.* Glencoe, IL: Free Press.

Langer, Ana Inés (2007). A historical exploration of the personalisation of politics in the print media: The British Prime Ministers (1945–1999). *Parliamentary Affairs* 60: 371–87.

Lau, Richard (2003). Models of decision-making. In David Sears, Leonie Huddy, and Robert Jervis, eds., *The Oxford Handbook of Political Psychology.* Oxford: Oxford University Press.

Laver, Michael and Ian Budge, eds. (1993). *Party Policy and Coalition Government in Western Europe.* London: Macmillan.

—— and Norman Schofield (1990). *Multiparty Government: The Politics of Coalition in Europe.* Oxford: Oxford University Press.

Leighley, Jan (1995). Attitudes, opportunities and incentives: A review essay on political participation. *Political Research Quarterly* 48(1): 181–209.

—— (1996). Group membership and the mobilization of political participation. *Journal of Politics* 58: 447–63.

Lewis-Beck, Michael (1988). *Economics and Elections.* Ann Arbor, MI: University of Michigan Press.

—— and Mary Stegmaier (2000). Economic determinants of electoral outcomes. *Annual Review of Political Science* 3: 183–219.

—— —— (2006). Economic models of voting. In Russell Dalton and Hans-Dieter Klingemann, eds., *Oxford Handbook of Political Behavior.* Oxford: Oxford University Press.

—— Richard Nadeau, and Angelo Elias (2008). Economics, party, and the vote: Causality issues and panel data. *American Journal of Political Science* 52: 84–95.

—— William Jacoby, Helmut Norpoth, and Herbert Weisberg (2008). *The American Voter Revisited.* Ann Arbor, MI: University of Michigan Press.

Liddle, William and Saiful Mujani (2007). Leadership, party, and religion: Explaining voting behavior in Indonesia. *Comparative Political Studies* 40: 832–57.

Lijphart, Arend (1984). *Democracies: Patterns of Majoritarian and Consensus Government in Twenty-One Countries*. New Haven, CT: Yale University Press.

—— (1994). *Electoral Systems and Party Systems: A Study of Twenty-Seven Democracies, 1945–1990*. Oxford: Oxford University Press.

—— (1999). *Patterns of Democracy: Government Forms and Performance in Thirty Six Countries*. New Haven, CT: Yale University Press.

Lipset, Seymour Martin (1959). *Political Man: The Social Bases of Politics*. Garden City, NY: Doubleday.

Listhaug, Ola and Matti Wiberg (1995). Confidence in political and private institutions. In Hans-Dieter Klingemann and Dieter Fuchs, eds., *Citizens and the State*. New York: Oxford University Press.

—— Bernt Aardal, and Ingunn Opheim Ellis (2009). Institutional variation and political support: An analysis of CSES data from 29 countries. In Hans-Dieter Klingemann, ed., *The Comparative Study of Electoral Systems*. New York: Oxford University Press.

Little, Anthony, Robert Burriss, Benedict Jones, and Robert Craig (2007). Facial appearance affects voting decision. *Evolution and Human Behavior* 28: 18–27.

Lobo, Marina Costa (2006). Short-term voting determinants in a young democracy: Leader effects in Portugal in the 2002 legislative elections. *Electoral Studies* 25: 270–86.

—— (2008). Parties and leader effects: Impact of leaders in the vote for different types of parties. *Party Politics* 14: 281–98.

Loewen, Peter and André Blais (2006). Testing publius' federalism: Losers consent, winners lament? Paper prepared for conference on the Comparative Study of Electoral Systems, Seville, Spain, March 23.

Mainwaring, Scott (1998). Party systems in the Third Wave. *Journal of Democracy* 9: 67–81.

—— (1999). *Rethinking Party Systems in the Third Wave of Democratization: The Case of Brazil*. Palo Alto, CA: Stanford University Press.

—— and Edurne Zoco (2007). Political sequences and the stabilization of interparty competition. *Party Politics* 13: 155–78.

Mair, Peter (2007). Left-Right orientations. In Russell Dalton and Hans-Dieter Klingemann, eds., *Oxford Handbook of Political Behavior*. Oxford: Oxford University Press.

—— and Ingrid van Biezen (2001). Party membership in twenty European democracies, 1980–2000. *Party Politics* 7: 5–21.

Marsh, Michael, Richard Sinnott, John Garry, and Fiachra Kennedy (2008). *The Irish Voter: The Nature of Electoral Competition in the Repubic of Ireland*. Manchester: Manchester University Press.

Martin, Lanny and Randolph Stevenson (2001). Government formation in parliamentary democracies. *American Journal of Political Science* 45: 33–50.

Massicotte, Louis and André Blais (1999). Mixed electoral systems: A conceptual and empirical survey *Electoral Studies* 18: 341–66.

McAllister, Ian (1996). Leaders. In Lawrence LeDuc, Richard Niemi, and Pippa Norris, eds., *Comparing Democracies: Elections and Voting in Global Perspective*. Thousand Oaks, CA: Sage Publications.

McAllister, Ian (1999). The economic performance of governments. In Pippa Norris, ed., *Critical Citizens: Global Support for Democratic Governance*. New York: Oxford University Press.

—— (2007). The personalization of politics. In Russell Dalton and Hans-Dieter Klingemann, eds., *Oxford Handbook of Political Behavior*. Oxford: Oxford University Press.

McCarty, Nolan, Keith Poole, and Howard Rosental (2006). *Polarized America: The Dance of Ideology and Unequal Riches*. Cambridge, MA: MIT Press.

McDonald, Michael D. and Silvia Mendes (2002). *Parties in Parliaments and Governments. 1950–1995: Dataset Codebook*. Binghamton: Department of Political Science. Binghamton University.

—— and Ian Budge (2005). *Elections, Parties, Democracy: Conferring the Median Mandate*. New York: Oxford University Press.

—— Silvia Mendes, and Ian Budge (2004). What are elections for? Conferring the median mandate. *British Journal of Political Science* 34: 1–26.

Meffert, Michael and Thomas Gschwend (2009). Strategic coalition voting: Evidence from austria. Working paper (http://www.sowi.uni-mannheim.de/gschwend/pdf/papers/Meffert Gschwend_StrategicCoalitionVoting_EvidenceAustria.pdf).

Merolla, Jennifer and Elizabeth Zechmeister (2006). Holding out for a hero: An experimental study of crisis, leadership, and vote choice. Paper presented at the Midwest Political Science Association conference, Chicago, IL.

—— and Laura Stephenson (2007). Strategic voting in Canada: A cross time analysis *Electoral Studies* 26: 235–46.

Miller, Arthur and Ola Listhaug (1990). Political parties and confidence in government: A comparison of Norway, Sweden and the United States. *British Journal of Political Science* 29: 357–86.

—— —— (1999). Political performance and institutional trust. In Pippa Norris, ed., *Critical Citizens: Global Support for Democratic Governance*. New York: Oxford University Press.

Miller, Warren and J. Merrill Shanks (1996). *The New American Voter*. Cambridge, MA: Harvard University Press.

Mondak, Jeffrey (1993). Public opinion and heuristic processing of source cues. *Political Behavior* 15: 167–92.

Mughan, Anthony (2000). *Media and the Presidentialization of Parliamentary Elections*. Basingstoke: Palgrave.

Müller, Wolfgang, and Kaare Strøm (2000). Conclusion: Coalition governance in Western Europe. In Wolfgang Müller and Kaare Strøm, eds., *Coalition Governments in Western Europe*. Oxford: Oxford University Press.

Nelson, Philip and Kenneth Greene (2002). *Signaling Goodness: Social Rules and Public Choice*. Ann Arbor, MI: University of Michigan Press.

Nevitte, Neil, André Blais, Elizabeth Gidengil, and Richard Nadeau (2009). Socioeconomic status and nonvoting: A cross-national comparative analysis. In Hans-Dieter Klingemann, ed., *The Comparative Study of Electoral Systems*. New York: Oxford University Press.

Nie, Norman, Sidney Verba, and John Petrocik (1979). *The Changing American Voter*. Cambridge, MA: Harvard University Press.

Niemi, Richard (1969). Majority decision-making with partial unidimensionality. *American Political Science Review* 63: 488–97.

Nishizawa, Yoshitaka (2009). Economic voting: Do institutions affect the way voters evaluate incumbents? In Hans-Dieter Klingemann, ed., *The Comparative Study of Electoral Systems*. Oxford: Oxford University Press.

Noelle-Neumann, Elisabeth (1993). *The Spiral of Silence: Public Opinion—Our Social Skin*. Chicago: University of Chicago Press.

—— and Renate Köcher (2002). *Allensbacher Jahrbuch der Demoskopie 1998–2002*. Munich: K.G. Saur.

Norpoth, Helmut, Michael S. Lewis-Beck, and Jean-Dominique Lafay, eds. (1991). *Economics and Politics: The Calculus of Support*. Ann Arbor, MI: University of Michigan Press.

Norris, Pippa (1997). Choosing electoral systems: Proportional, majoritarian and mixed systems. International Political Science Review 18: 297–312.

—— (1999). Institutional explanations for political support. In Pippa Norris, ed., *Critical Citizens: Global Support for Democratic Governance*. New York: Oxford University Press.

—— (2002). *Democratic Phoenix: Reinventing Political Activism*. Cambridge: Cambridge University Press.

—— (2004). *Electoral Engineering: Voting Rules and Political Behavior*. New York: Cambridge University Press.

Ohr, Dieter and Henrik Oscarsson (2003). Leader traits, leader omage and vote choice. Paper presented at the European Consortium for Political Research meeting, Marburg.

Oskarson, Maria (2005). Social structure and party choice. In Jacques Thomassen, ed., *The European Voter: A Comparative Study of Modern Democracies*. Oxford: Oxford University Press.

Page, Benjamin and Robert Shapiro (1992). *The Rational Public: Fifty Years of Trends in Americans' Policy Preferences*. Chicago, IL: University of Chicago Press.

Paldam, Martin (1991). How robust is the vote function? A study of seventeen nations over four decades. In H. Norpoth, M.S. Lewis-Beck, and J-D. Lafay, eds., *Economics and Politics: The Calculus of Support*. Ann Arbor, MI: University of Michigan Press.

Paskeviciute, Aida (2006). Elections, policy representation, and system legitimacy in contemporary democracies. Paper prepared for presentation at the annual meeting of the American Political Science Association 2007, Philadelphia, PA.

Pateman, Carol (1970). *Participation and Democratic Theory*. New York: Cambridge University Press.

Pattie, Charles, Patrick Seyd, and Paul Whiteley (2003). Citizenship and civic engagement: Attitudes and behaviour in Britain. *Political Studies* 51: 443–68.

Peltzman, Sam (1990). How efficient is the voting market? *Journal of Law and Economics* 33: 27–63.

Pennings, Paul (1998). The triad of party system change: Votes, office and policy. In P. Pennings and J. Lane, eds., *Comparing Party System Change*. London: Routledge.

Perea, E. A. (2002). Individual characteristics, institutional incentives and electoral abstention in Western Europe. *European Journal of Political Research* 41: 643–73.

Pérez-Linan, Aníbal (2001). Neoinstitutional accounts of voter turnout: Moving beyond industrial democracies. *Electoral Studies* 20: 281–97.

Plutzer, Eric (2002). Becoming a habitual voter: Inertia, resources, and growth in young adulthood. *American Political Science Review* 96: 41–56.

Poguntke, Thomas and Paul Webb, eds. (2005). *The Presidentialization of Modern Democracies*. Oxford: Oxford University Press.

Powell, G. Bingham (1980). Voter turnout in thirty democracies. In Richard Rose, ed., *Electoral Participation: A Comparative Analysis*. London: Sage.

—— (1982). *Contemporary Democracies: Participation, Stability and Violence*. Cambridge, MA: Harvard University Press.

—— (1986). American turnout in comparative perspective. *American Political Science Review* 80: 17–43.

—— (2000). *Elections as Instruments of Democracy: Majoritarian and Proportional Visions*. New Haven, CT: Yale University Press.

—— (2006). Election laws and representative government. *British Journal of Political Science* 36: 291–315.

—— (2008). Party system change, election rules and ideological congruence. Chicago, IL: Midwest Political Science Association.

—— (2009). The ideological congruence controversy: The impact of alternative measures, data and time periods on the effects of election rules. *Comparative Political Studies* 42: 1475–97.

—— and Guy Whitten (1993). A cross-national analysis of economic voting: Taking account of the political context. *American Journal of Political Science* 37: 391–414.

—— and G. Vanberg (2000). Election laws, disproportionality and the Left–Right dimension. *British Journal of Political Science* 30: 383–411.

Putnam, Robert (1993). *Making Democracy Work: Civic Traditions in Modern Italy*. Princeton, NJ: Princeton University Press.

Raudenbush, Stephen and Anthony Bryk (2002). *Hierarchical Linear Models: Applications and Data Analysis Methods*, 2nd edn. Thousand Oaks, CA: Sage.

Rae, Douglas (1971). *Political Consequences of Electoral Laws*. New Haven, CT: Yale University Press.

Rahat, Gideon and Tamir Sheafer (2007). The personalization(s) of politics: Israel, 1949–2003. *Political Communication* 24: 65–80.

Riker, William (1980). Implications from the disequilibrium of majority rule for the study of institutions. *American Political Science Review* 74: 432–46.

—— (1982). The two-party system and Duverger's Law: An essay in the history of political science. *American Political Science Review* 76: 753–68.

—— and Peter Ordeshook (1968). A theory of the calculus of voting. *American Political Science Review* 62: 25–42.

Rivers, Douglass (1988). Heterogeneity in models of electoral choice. *American Journal of Political Science* 32(3): 737–57.

Roberts, Kenneth and Erik Wibbels (1999). Party systems and electoral volatility in Latin America: A test of economic, institutional, and structural explanations. *American Political Science Review* 93: 575–90.

Rohrschneider, Robert and Stephen Whitefield (2009). Understanding divisions in party systems: Issue position and issue salience in 13 post-communist democracies. *Comparative Political Studies* 33(6–7): 845–79.

Rose, Richard and Neil Munro (2003). *Elections and Parties in New European Democracies*. Washington, DC: Congressional Quarterly Press.

Rosenstone, Steven and John Mark Hansen (1993). *Mobilization, Participation, and Democracy in America*. New York: MacMillan.

Rovny, Jan and Erika Edwards (2009). Stuggle over dimensionality: Party competition in Europe. Manuscript, University of North Carolina.

Bibliography

Samuels, David (1999). Incentives to cultivate a party vote in candidate-centric electoral systems: Evidence from Brazil. *Comparative Political Studies* 32: 487–518.

Sartori, Giovanni (1976). *Parties and Party Systems: A Framework for Analysis.* Cambridge: Cambridge University Press.

Satterthwaite, Mark (1975). Strategy-proofness and Arrow's conditions: Existence and correspondence theorems for voting procedures and social welfare functions. *Journal of Economic Theory* 10: 1–7.

Schattschneider, Elmer Eric (1942). *Party Government.* New York: Rinehart.

Schmitt, Hermann (1983). Party government in public opinion: A European cross-national comparison. *European Journal of Political Research* 11: 353–76.

—— and Dieter Ohr (2000). Are party leaders becoming more important in German elections? Leader effects on the vote in Germany, 1961–1988. Paper presented at the American Political Science Association Annual Meeting, Washington DC.

Seligson, Mitchell (2002). The impact of corruption on regime legitimacy: A comparative study of four Latin American countries. *Journal of Politics* 64: 408–33.

Shapiro, Robert and Yaeli Bloch-Elkon (2008). Do the facts speak for themselves? Partisan disagreement as a challenge to democratic competence. *Critical Review: A Journal of Politics and Society* 20: 115–39.

Shepsle, Kenneth (1977). Institutional arrangements and equilibrium in multi-dimensional voting models. *American Journal of Political Science* 23: 27–59.

—— and Barry Weingast (1981). Structure-induced equilibrium and legislative choice. *Public Choice* 37: 503–19.

Shugart, Matthew 2001. Electoral "efficiency" and the move to mixed-member systems, *Electoral Studies* 20: 173–93.

—— and John Carey (1992). *Presidents and Assemblies.* New York: Cambridge University Press.

—— and Martin Wattenberg (2003). *Mixed-Member Electoral Systems:The Best of Both Worlds?* Oxford: Oxford University Press.

Sigelman, Lee, and Syng Nam Yough (1978). Left-right polarization in national party systems: A cross-national analysis. *Comparative Political Studies* 11: 355–79.

Singer, Mathew (forthcoming, 2011). Who says "it's the economy"? Cross-national and cross-individual variation in the salience of economic performance. *Comparative Political Studies* 44.

Sniderman, Paul, Richard Brody, and Philip Tetlock (1991). *Reasoning and Choice: Explorations in Political Psychology.* New York: Cambridge University Press.

Snijders, Tom and Roel Bosker (1999). *Multilevel Analysis: An Introduction to Basic and Advanced Multilevel Modelling.* Thousand Oaks, CA: Sage Publications.

Somin, Ilya (1998). Voter ignorance and the democratic ideal. *Critical Review: A Journal of Politics and Society* 12: 413–35.

—— (2006). Knowledge about ignorance: New directions in the study of political information. *Critical Review: A Journal of Politics and Society* 18: 255–78.

Soroka, Stuart and Christopher Wlezien (2004). Opinion representation and policy feedback: Canada in comparative perspective. *Canadian Journal of Political Sceince* 37(3): 531–60.

—— —— (2005). Opinion–policy dynamics: Public preferences and public expenditure in the UK. *British Journal of Political Science* 35: 665–89.

Steenbergen, Marco and Bradford Jones (2002). Modeling multilevel data structures. *American Journal of Political Science* 46: 218–37.

Stevenson, Randy (2009). Executive selection and political knowledge. Paper presented at the Annual Meetings of the Midwest Political Science Association, Chicago, IL.

Strøm, Kaare (1990). *Minority Government and Majoritary Rule*. New York: Cambridge University Press.

Taagepera, Rein (2007). *Predicting Party Sizes: The Logic of Simple Electoral Systems*. Oxford: Oxford University Press.

—— and Matthew Shugart (1989). *Seats and Votes: The Effects and Determinants of Electoral Systems*. New Haven, CT: Yale University Press.

Tavits, Margit (2009). Direct presidential elections and turnout in parliamentary contests. *Political Research Quarterly* 62(1): 42–54.

Thomassen, Jacques, ed. (2005). *The European Voter: A Comparative Study of Modern Democracies*. Oxford: Oxford University Press.

Thompson, Dennis (1970). *The Democratic Citizen*. New York: Cambridge University Press.

Tillman, Erik (2008). Economic judgments, party choice, and voter abstention in cross-national perspective. *Comparative Political Studies* 41: 1290–309.

Tóka, Gabor (1995). Political support in East–Central Europe. In Hans-Dieter Klingemann and Dieter Fuchs, eds., *Citizens and the State*. New York: Oxford University Press.

Ulbig, Stacey and Carolyn Funk (1999). Conflict avoidance and political participation. *Political Behavior* 21: 265–82.

van der Brug, Wouter and Cees van der Eijk, eds. (2007). *European Elections and Domestic Politics. Lessons from the Past and Scenarios for the Future*. Notre Dame, IN: University of Notre Dame Press.

van Wijnen, Peter: *see* Wijnen, Pieter van (2001).

Verba, Sidney (2003). Would the dream of political equality turn out to be a nightmare? *Perspectives on Politics* 1: 663–79.

—— and Norman Nie (1972). *Participation in America: Political Democracy and Social Equality*. New York: Harper & Row.

—— —— and Jae-On Kim (1978). *Participation and Political Equality*. Chicago, IL: University of Chicago Press.

—— Kay Lehman Schlozman, and Henry Brady (1995). *Voice and Equality: Civic Voluntarism in American Politics*. Cambridge, MA: Harvard University.

Warwick, Paul (1994). *Government Survival in Parliamentary Democracies*. New York: Cambridge University Press.

Wattenberg, Martin (2006). *Is Voting for Young People?* New York: Longman.

Watts, Ronald (1999). *Comparing Federal Systems*. Institute of Intergovernmental Relations, Queen's University, Kingston, Ontario, Canada.

Weatherford, M. Stephen (1984). Economic "stagflation" and public support for the political system. *British Journal of Political Science* 14: 187–205.

—— (1987). How does government performance influence political support? *Political Behavior* 9: 5–28.

Weil, Frederick (1989). The sources and structure of legitimation in Western democracies: A consolidated model tested with time-series data in six countries since World War II. *American Sociological Review* 54: 682–706.

Bibliography

Wessels, Bernhard (2009). Parteien und Kanzlerkandidaten bei den Bundestagwahlen 2002 und 2005. In Oscar Gabriel, Bernhard Wessels, and Juergen Falter, eds., *Wahlen und Waehler: Analyzsen aus Anlass der Bundestagswahl 2005*. Wiesbaden, Germany: Verlag fuer Sozialwissenschaften.

—— and Hermann Schmitt (2008). Meaningful choices, political supply, and institutional effectiveness. *Electoral Studies* 27: 19–30.

Whiteley, Paul (1995). Rational choice and political participation – Evaluating the debate. *Political Research Quarterly* 48: 211–33.

Whitten, Guy and Harvey Palmer (1999). Cross-national analyses of economic voting. *Electoral Studies* 18: 49–67.

Wlezien, Christopher (2004). Patterns of representation: Dynamics of public preferences and policy. *Journal of Politics* 66: 1–24.

—— (2005). On the salience of political issues: The problem with "most important problem." *Electoral Studies* 24: 555–79.

Wijnen, Pieter van (2001). *Policy Voting in Advanced Industrial Democracies: The Case of the Netherlands1971–1998*. University of Twente: The Netherlands.

Wodendorp, Joap, Hans Keman, and Ian Budge (2000). *Party Government in 48 Democracies (1945–1998): Composition, Duration, Personnel*. Dordrecht: Kluwer.

Wolfinger, Raymond and Steven Rosenstone (1980). *Who Votes?* New Haven, CT: Yale University Press.

Zaller, John (1992). *The Nature and Origins of Mass Opinion*. New York: Cambridge University Press.

—— (2004). Floating voters in U.S. presidential elections, 1948–2000. In William Saris and Paul Sniderman, eds., *Studies in Public Opinion: Attitudes, Nonattitudes, Measurement Error, and Change*. Princeton, NJ: Princeton University Press.

Index